The Lincoln Trail in Pennsylvania

The Lincoln Trail in Pennsylvania

A History and Guide

Bradley R. Hoch

with a Foreword by Gabor S. Boritt

To Anna Jane,
    Best wishes to a friend and fellow
researcher and writer. I admire your
work.
                                    Brad Hoch
A Keystone Book Gettysburg, PA.
                        December 4, 2001

The Pennsylvania State University Press · University Park, Pennsylvania

A Keystone Book is so designated to distinguish it from the typical scholarly monograph that a university press publishes. It is a book intended to serve the citizens of Pennsylvania by educating them and others, in an entertaining way, about aspects of the history, culture, society, and environment of the state as part of the Middle Atlantic region.

Library of Congress Cataloging-in-Publication Data

Hoch, Bradley R., 1948–

    The Lincoln trail in Pennsylvania / Bradley R. Hoch ; with an introduction by Gabor S. Boritt.

      p.   cm.

    "A Keystone book."

    Includes bibliographical references (p.   ) and index.

    ISBN 0-271-02119-5 (alk. paper)

      1. Lincoln, Abraham, 1809–1865—Homes and haunts—Pennsylvania. 2. Pennsylvania—History—19th century—Anecdotes. 3. Pennsylvania—History, Local. 4. Historic sites—Pennsylvania. 5. Presidents—United States—Biography. I. Title.

    E457.64.H64 2001

    973.7'092—dc21

                                                     00-67019

Frontispiece: *Lincoln at Gettysburg.* Mural by Violet Oakley, circa 1920. Senate Chamber of the Pennsylvania State Capitol, Harrisburg, Pennsylvania. Photograph by Brian Hunt. Courtesy of the Pennsylvania Capitol Preservation Committee.

I long ago lost a hound, a bay horse, and a turtledove, and am still on their trail. Many are the travelers I have spoken concerning them, describing their tracks and what calls they answered to. I have met one or two who had heard the hound, and the tramp of the horse, and even seen the dove disappear behind a cloud, and they seemed as anxious to recover them as if they had lost them themselves.

—Henry David Thoreau, *Walden*

THIS BOOK IS DEDICATED TO ALL THOSE WHO ARE ON THE TRAIL.

Contents

Illustrations

Lincoln in Pennsylvania

Known Travels Within the State

June 1848	Philadelphia—Whig National Convention
September 1848	To New England—campaign trip
October 1848	To Springfield—lake steamer voyage
February 1860	To New York City—Cooper Institute
February 1861	Inaugural Train
June 1862	To and from West Point
November 1863	Gettysburg
June 1864	Philadelphia—Great Central Sanitary Fair
April 1865	Funeral Train

Probable Travels Within the State

November 1847	To Washington, D.C.—Congress
December 1848	To Washington, D.C.—Congress
March 1849	To Springfield—return from Congress
June 1849	To and from Washington, D.C.—job hunting
July 1857	To and from Niagara Falls
March 1860	To Springfield—from New York City

Foreword

by Gabor S. Boritt

The Republican National Convention in Philadelphia nominated as its presidential candidate in 1856 one of the most romantic figures of the time, John C. Frémont, explorer, politician, "the Pathfinder of the West." The party was brand-new and the enthusiasm and the energy of the delegates appeared boundless. To the surprise of many, when it came to the vice presidency, a Pennsylvania representative put forth the name of Abraham Lincoln of Illinois. "The prince of good fellows," the crowd was told. "As pure a patriot as ever lived," came the second from his home state.

When news reached Lincoln, he showed his usual humble self: "I reckon that ain't me; there's another great man in Massachusetts named Lincoln, and I reckon it's him." But it *was* the Lincoln that the country would soon come to know. Although he lost the nomination, he received 110 votes on the first informal ballot, the second highest among the candidates and one-fifth of the total. The Philadelphia convention provided the first indication that he was on the road to being a national figure.

The Republicans lost the election, but for a new-born political party they put on a very strong showing. Had they carried Pennsylvania and either Illinois or Indiana, the party would have captured the White House. The Keystone State loomed large for the Republican future. So did the Sucker State, as Lincoln's home state was then known. Indeed, at the 1860 convention in Chicago, the candidate from Illinois came out on top, and the support of the Pennsylvania delegation played a crucial part in Lincoln's nomination.

When a group of delegates traveled to his home in Springfield to notify him in person about the nomination, Lincoln broke the awkwardness of the formal occasion by singling out a Pennsylvanian, the looming William D. Kelly, and asking him his height. "Six feet three," came the reply.

Lincoln laughed: "I beat you. I am six feet four without my high heeled boots."

Kelly: "Pennsylvania bows to Illinois. I am glad that we have found a candidate for the Presidency who we can look up to."

In the election of that year, too, the Keystone State played its part, helping to ensure that Lincoln would have a chance for greatness. But long before the crucial year of 1860—the last year of peace before the Civil War—Lincoln had important ties to the state. Some of his ancestors had lived there. The opinions of the state's people, their support, and that of their leaders truly mattered to his life and work. He repeatedly traveled to Pennsylvania and through Pennsylvania, and though the world knows of the visit to Gettysburg, other, less-known occasions carried great weight, too.

Bradley Hoch tells this story very well. He follows in Lincoln's footsteps, travels to every nook and cranny of Pennsylvania, to places famous and places barely known, discovers much new interesting information, and takes the delighted reader along with him. What a ride for the Lincoln buff—and also for the serious student of history. Experts always carried a sense of the significance of Pennsylvania's Lincoln connections, but all will be surprised by the breadth of the terrain Hoch visits. We travel along, sometimes amused, sometimes bemused, happy, sad, questioning, enlightened, and at the end of the road we are better people.

Gabor Boritt
Farm by the Ford
Gettysburg
February 2001

Preface

What is *The Lincoln Trail in Pennsylvania*? It is the story of Abraham Lincoln and Pennsylvania, the chronicle of where Lincoln went, what he saw, what he did, and what he said in the state. The Trail passes by Lincoln's Pennsylvania ancestors; moves on to his travels, public appearances, and speeches; and finally it reaches his funeral train. This book tells a story for the reader, but it also outlines a tangible trail that may be followed. One may go where Lincoln went, and, limited by the passage of time and the changes that time brings, one may see what Lincoln saw. The Lincoln Trail is both figurative and literal.

I came to the story perhaps by predestination. Two of my great-grandfathers fought as volunteers in Pennsylvania regiments during the Civil War. Peter L. Hoch was mustered in at Harrisburg on August 10, 1862, as a private in Company D, 130th Regiment, Pennsylvania Volunteers. He fought at Antietam, Fredericksburg, and Chancellorsville. My mother's grandfather Josiah Piper was a private in Company I, 198th Regiment, Pennsylvania Volunteers. The 198th was the sixth regiment enrolled by the Union League of Philadelphia. He was mustered in at Philadelphia on September 2, 1864. He fought at Petersburg, Five Forks, and was at Appomattox. The effect that Lincoln had on my great-grandfathers, in a very personal sense, and on the people of Pennsylvania as a whole is an important subject. The same is true of Lincoln's policies, but these are outside the scope of this book. *The Lincoln Trail in Pennsylvania* is not primarily an interpretive work: it is a guide for those who would travel the state figuratively or literally, eager to recover the memory of a great man.

Writing this book was pure joy. To some, each new concept is a treasured possession. So it is with me. Somewhat to my surprise, every day's work brought a new thought or a new understanding. Many of my recently found treasures, I am sure, are new only to me. For example, historians and attorneys have always known of the unreliability of eyewitness accounts. Yet the sheer number of differences in eyewitness accounts amazed me. I learned, I hope, to evaluate who said what and how many years after the fact. I also was astounded by discrepancies in stated time. How could so many people look at the same event and yet vary so widely in reporting at what time the event took place? I learned that there was no standard time until 1883 when the railroads, desperate to coordinate train schedules, adopted a national plan. Before the 1880s, timepieces were set to a town clock or, as in Gettysburg, to the pocket watch of a local professor. Time could vary widely from watch to watch and from town to town. Once I understood such secrets they were mine forever, and I added them to my store of wondrous things.

I learned other things too. Abraham Lincoln was a different man from the one I had imagined many years ago. That Lincoln was born in a log cabin and came off the western prairies to save the nation and its people. This created a certain image in my mind, which changed with the writing of this book. My boyhood understanding was incomplete. Lincoln was very much a product of his time and was so very complex. He was born in a log cabin, but he did not live there throughout his life. Examine the photographs of the hotels in which Lincoln the president stayed. Those hotels were some of the finest in America. Lincoln was also a man very much interested in using the technology of his day. He traveled extensively by railroad. He traveled the rivers and Great Lakes of America at a time when steamboats were not entirely safe. He utilized the telegraph to get the most up-to-date war news possible, and he sought out new inventions, especially if they might prove helpful in winning the war. He was much more modern and more human than I had thought.

Reading a book is usually a solitary endeavor. Writing a book takes a lot of friends. Thanks go to my wife Kay for her critical eye and diligent proofreading, to my children Adam, Emily, and Jon for their kindness and support, to Dr. Charles Glatfelter and the Adams County Historical Society, to Warren Wirebach and the Historical Society of Dauphin County, to Mike Sherbon and the Pennsylvania State Archives, to Nancy and Dr. Roger Stemen and the Lancaster County Historical Society, to Joseph Benford and the Free Library of Philadelphia, to Dr. Mike Birkner and the Eisenhower Society, to Barbara Gill and the Historical Society of Berks County, to Steven J. Wright and the Civil War Library and Museum in Philadelphia, to the Historical Society of Pennsylvania, to Paul Kudda and the National Railway Historical Society, to Ron Bryant and the Kentucky Historical Society, to the Historical Society of Western Pennsylvania, to Dr. Norman Forness, to the State Library of Pennsylvania, to the Carnegie Library of Pittsburgh, to the Gettysburg College Library, to research assistants Deborah Baran and Joan Reichart, and finally, to the members, officers, and board of directors of the Lincoln Fellowship of Pennsylvania.

One of the most intelligent, learned, and talented individuals that I know is Gabor Boritt, director of the Civil War Institute and Fluhrer Professor of Civil War Studies at Gettysburg College. I single him out for my greatest thanks. By luck Gabor is my good friend who lives just down the tree-lined road from my house. The road runs along the quiet, beautiful Marsh Creek. I live at the site of Pickett's Division wagon park and field hospital. Gabor lives at the historic Crawford Farm. We are neighbors. Without his friendship, his encouragement, and his help, *The Lincoln Trail in Pennsylvania* would not have been born. Thank you, Gabor!

The Lincoln Trail in Pennsylvania

Abraham Lincoln speaks at the flag-raising ceremony at Independence Hall, Philadelphia, February 22, 1861. The only photographs of Lincoln during his Inaugural Train tour were taken from a window across Chestnut Street as he stood at the front of the wooden speakers' platform. Photograph by F. DeB. Richards. Courtesy of the Print and Picture Collection, the Free Library of Philadelphia.

I

"An Omen of What Is to Come"

Washington's Birthday 1861

I have often inquired of myself, what great principle or idea it was that kept this Confederacy so long together. It was not the mere matter of the separation of the colonies from the mother land; but something in that Declaration giving liberty, not alone to the people of this country, but hope to the world for all future time.

—Abraham Lincoln, speech at Independence Hall, Philadelphia, February 22, 1861

But, if this country cannot be saved without giving up that principle—I was about to say I would rather be assassinated on this spot than to surrender it.

—Abraham Lincoln, speech at Independence Hall, Philadelphia, February 22, 1861

I have already gone through one exceedingly interesting scene this morning in the ceremonies [flag-raising ceremony] at Philadelphia. . . . I could not help hoping that there was in the entire success of that beautiful ceremony, at least something of an omen of what is to come.

—Abraham Lincoln, speech before the combined General Assembly of Pennsylvania, Harrisburg, February 22, 1861

On Thursday evening, February 21, 1861, Allan Pinkerton and Frederick W. Seward were trying desperately to get to Abraham Lincoln. Both men carried secret intelligence about an assassination attempt planned for February 23 in Baltimore. Neither man knew if he could reach Lincoln in time, or if the president-elect would believe the extraordinary information. Neither agent knew about the other.

Months earlier, Philadelphian Samuel M. Felton, president of the Philadelphia, Wilmington, and Baltimore Railroad, suspected that Maryland's Confederate sympathizers might sabotage his rail line between Philadelphia and Baltimore. Several bridges and the rail ferry across the Susquehanna River at Perryville were especially vulnerable. Felton hired Chicago detective Allan Pinkerton and his agents, and they quietly infiltrated secessionist groups in and around Baltimore, the largest Southern city in the nation (population slightly more than 212,000). Searching for information about plots to destroy railroad bridges and ferry, the detectives inadvertently uncovered a plan to kill Abraham Lincoln in Baltimore.

In the November 1860 presidential election, Maryland had voted with nine future Confederate states and had given her eight electoral votes to Southern Democrat John C. Breckinridge. Baltimore had a reputation for political violence, and the city fathers did not support Abraham Lincoln. In fact, it was the only major city on the Inaugural Train's route not to extend an official invitation to the president-elect. In a letter dated February 15, 1861, Baltimore Republican William G. Snethen warned Lincoln that it would be unwise "to attempt any organized display" in Baltimore, but local Republicans "in their individual capacity" would meet Lincoln en route and accompany him through the city.

Baltimore Police Chief George P. Kane was a Southern sympathizer and future resident of the Confederacy. Local conspirators counted on him to provide only a token police escort for Lincoln. Knowing security would be intentionally lax, the would-be

In 1868 Allan Pinkerton published the forty-two-page monograph History and Evidence of the Passage of Abraham Lincoln from Harrisburg, Pa., to Washington, D.C., on the 22d, and 23d of February 1861 *and included this* 1860 *photograph of himself. Courtesy of the author.*

ALLAN PINKERTON
1860

assassins planned to shoot or knife Lincoln as he transferred from the Northern Central Railroad Station at Calvert Street to the Baltimore and Ohio Railroad Station at Camden Street. Lincoln would be vulnerable as he came through the narrow vestibule of Calvert Street Station and again during the one and one-quarter mile open carriage ride to Camden Street Station. Pinkerton sent agents to hand deliver this information to fellow Chicagoan Norman B. Judd, Lincoln's good friend who was traveling with the president-elect. Judd decided not to tell Lincoln of the assassination plot until after he had spoken face-to-face with Pinkerton in Philadelphia.

After Lincoln's election to the presidency in November 1860, the nation began to unravel. Six Southern states—South Carolina, Georgia, Florida, Alabama, Mississippi, and Louisiana—seceded from the Union; and in a seventh, Texas, a secession convention had voted to leave the Union pending popular ratification—an almost sure thing. Tensions ran high, and Lincoln received death threats. As these events continued to unfold, Lincoln and his advisers planned a grand rail tour to precede the inauguration. Following custom, Lincoln had not personally campaigned in the presidential

The Continental Hotel, on the southeast corner of Ninth and Chestnut Streets, Philadelphia, hosted Abraham Lincoln on February 21, 1861, and on June 16, 1864. The president born in a log cabin stayed in the finest of American hotels. Engraving, circa 1870. Courtesy of the Print and Picture Collection, the Free Library of Philadelphia.

election, and this would be the first opportunity for most citizens to see the president-elect. For Lincoln, it would enable him to see the people, to take measure of their sentiment, and to plum the depths of their support for him and his administration. It would be an exhausting and stressful thirteen days.

Lincoln departed Springfield, Illinois, on February 11, 1861, the day before his fifty-second birthday. He traveled with his forty-two-year-old wife Mary Todd Lincoln and their sons, seventeen-year-old Robert, ten-year-old Willie, and seven-year-old Tad. Also traveling on the train were Lincoln's personal secretaries John G. Nicolay and John M. Hay, bodyguard Ward Hill Lamon, brother-in-law and personal physician Dr. William S. Wallace, longtime friend and unofficial campaign manager Judge David Davis, Chicago attorney and political supporter Norman B. Judd, and First United States Cavalry Colonel Edwin V. Sumner, a future commander of the Second Corps, Army of the Potomac. The Inaugural Train visited the Northern cities of Indianapolis, Columbus, Pittsburgh, Cleveland, Buffalo, Albany, and New York.

The train arrived at Philadelphia's Kensington Station on the afternoon of February 21, 1861. The Minute Men of '76 welcomed the president-elect with a thirty-four-gun salute, one for each of the thirty-four states. Nearly 100,000 people lined the streets as Lincoln traveled by open carriage from the railroad station to the Continental Hotel. Shortly after 5 P.M. Allan Pinkerton and Samuel Felton were conferring in La Pierre House Hotel at Broad and Sansom Streets when they heard the music from Lincoln's procession as it came down Walnut Street. The Chicago detective ran outside in time to see agent George H. Burns break through the police escort and deliver a message to Norman Judd, who was riding in the carriage with Lincoln. The message asked Judd to meet in Pinkerton's room at the St. Louis Hotel at 7:30 that night. As soon as Burns came away from the carriage with a yes from Judd, Pinkerton met him on the sidewalk and told him that 7:30 was now too late. Burns broke through police lines again. Once again Judd said yes—this time to meeting as soon as possible.

Lincoln himself was scheduled for another long evening. After he arrived at the Continental Hotel's Ninth Street door, he immediately went inside. A short time later Mayor Alexander Henry appeared on the hotel's balcony, followed by Lincoln. The mayor extended the city's welcome, and the president-elect addressed the crowd below. Later he met privately with Pennsylvania political leaders, a gathering arranged by Judge James Milliken, a proponent of Pennsylvania iron interests and confidant of Senator Simon Cameron. The Curtin Republican faction, Lincoln was told, had withdrawn its objection to the proposed nomination of Cameron as secretary of war. The impasse had been resolved, and Lincoln was relieved.

Lincoln also received guests at a private reception given in his honor at the Continental. Along the way he declined an invitation to visit Wilmington, Delaware. "I feel highly flattered . . . but circumstances forbid." After the reception it was time to greet the general public. The president-elect stood on an inside balcony overlooking the hotel lobby. It was separated from, but very close to, the main staircase that ascended from the lobby to the second floor. He bowed as people filed up the stairs

Frederick W. Seward, son of William H. Seward, brought secret information from Washington, D.C., to Philadelphia on the evening of February 21, 1861. He later became assistant secretary of state under his father. Matthew Brady Studios, circa 1861–65. Photograph NWDNS 111 B 3879 "Frederick A.[sic] Seward"; National Archives at College Park, College Park, Maryland.

within a few feet of where he stood. Social etiquette required a polite bow. In Lincoln's era, a handshake was generally disdained.

While Lincoln's toilsome evening continued, Norman Judd, Allan Pinkerton, and Samuel Felton met at the St. Louis Hotel. Beginning at 6:45 P.M. Pinkerton and Felton outlined everything that had been uncovered in Baltimore. In their opinion it was vital that Lincoln change his plans, pass through Baltimore secretly, and go on to Washington that very night. After the meeting ended at 9 P.M., Pinkerton accompanied Judd back to the Continental Hotel. On the way, Pinkerton tried to run an errand at the Girard House Hotel, which took him into the mass of people filling Chestnut Street between the two hotels. Not only could Pinkerton not get into the Girard House, but it took him thirty minutes to extract himself from the crowd. When at last free, he went to the Continental Hotel's Sansom Street entrance, joined the slow-moving line going up the staircase past Lincoln, got on the other side of the police lines, and went to Judd's room. Judd and E. S. Sanford, president of the American Telegraph Company, were already there.

At 10:25 P.M. Judd was able to bring Lincoln to the room, where he introduced Pinkerton as a trustworthy man. The detective told all he knew. There were Southern sympathizers in Maryland and paramilitary groups along the rail lines from Philadelphia to Baltimore and from Harrisburg to Baltimore, and in Baltimore itself. He told Lincoln of the assassination plan and recommended that Lincoln secretly leave Philadelphia that evening, the twenty-first. Lincoln refused. He had promised to raise a flag the next day in Washington's Birthday ceremonies at Independence Hall and to address the Pennsylvania General Assembly in Harrisburg. He had given his word, and he was determined to keep it. He did, however, agree to a secret trip from Harrisburg to Washington, through Philadelphia and Baltimore, on the evening of the twenty-second after his commitments were completed. Judd asked Pinkerton if it could be done, and Pinkerton replied yes. Lincoln said that his wife would have to know, and that she would probably insist that Ward Hill Lamon go too—to protect him. Lincoln left Judd's room about 11 P.M.

Unknown to Lincoln, Frederick Seward had arrived in Philadelphia earlier that evening and was now awaiting the president-elect in his room. New York City police detectives, working undercover in Baltimore at the request of men inside the government, had also uncovered a plot to assassinate Lincoln. Seward carried secret letters to Lincoln from his father Senator William H. Seward, from Winfield Scott, general-in-chief of the United States Army, and from a trusted army colonel. The colonel wrote that a New York detective, "has himself heard men declare that if Mr. Lincoln was to be assassinated they would like to be the men." The letter advised, "All risk might be easily avoided by a change in the traveling arrangements which would bring Mr. Lincoln & a portion of his party through Baltimore by a night train without previous notice."

When Seward arrived at the Continental Hotel at 10 P.M., he found Robert Lincoln. The president-elect's eldest son approached Ward Hill Lamon, who took the young Seward to Lincoln's bedroom. In the crowded hotel, few locations were available for a confidential meeting with the incoming president. After waiting alone for what seemed an eternity, Seward heard Lamon call out. He stepped out of the room in time to see Lincoln coming down the hallway. Seward later wrote: "After a few words of friendly greeting, with inquiries about my father and matters in Washington, he sat down by the table under the gas-light to peruse the letter I had brought. Although its contents were of a somewhat startling nature, he made no exclamation, and I saw no sign of surprise in his face. After reading it carefully through, he again held it to the light and deliberately read it through a second time."

Lincoln asked Seward if he knew how the information had been obtained. Had Seward ever heard the name Pinkerton? The young courier said no. Lincoln seemed to be evaluating the testimony he had been given, as if he were in a courtroom. Seward later remembered Lincoln's words: "If different persons, not knowing of each other's work, have been pursuing separate clues that led to the same result, why then it shows there may be something in it. But if this is only the same story filtered through two channels and reaching me in two ways, then that don't make it any stronger. . . . You need not think I will not consider it well. I shall think it over carefully and try to decide it right, and I will let you know in the morning." Outside the Continental Hotel, Philadelphia celebrated on into the night with a band concert and fireworks. For Lincoln, it had been another day in a never-ending stream of stressful days. He finally went to sleep.

Allan Pinkerton did not have time to sleep. It was II P.M., and a competent plan had to be conceived, set in place, and executed in the next thirty hours. He left Judd's room and tried to find his friend Thomas A. Scott, vice-president of the Pennsylvania Railroad, to arrange for a special train to bring Lincoln back to Philadelphia from Harrisburg. Scott was in Harrisburg. Pinkerton then searched for another friend, G. C. Franciscus, a Pennsylvania Railroad division superintendent. After looking in three places, he found Franciscus in his West Philadelphia Station office, and the men returned to the Continental Hotel to meet with Judd and Sanford.

The four men worked out the details of secretly getting Lincoln back to Philadelphia. Specific tasks were assigned. Sanford would see to the isolation of Harrisburg by telegraph. Franciscus would arrange a secret train, clear the tracks of other trains, and have Lincoln back in Philadelphia no later than 10:30 in the evening. It was a complicated task. Philadelphians who had gone to the state capital to participate in the president-elect's welcome would be returning home, and the railroad had scheduled a number of special trains leaving Harrisburg that evening. Franciscus would assure that all these trains left Harrisburg before Lincoln's train, but he would sidetrack them along the way, allowing Lincoln's train to pass. Only after Lincoln departed Philadelphia for Baltimore at 11:50 P.M. would the other trains from Harrisburg arrive in Philadelphia.

Pinkerton left the hotel and went to George H. Burns's house. Captain Burns was a Philadelphian—and Sanford's confidential agent. Pinkerton told Burns to find a telegraph climber and to go with him to Harrisburg on the president-elect's 9:30 A.M. train. The climber, under Burns's direction and with Sanford's authority, was to cut all telegraph lines necessary to totally isolate Harrisburg from 6 P.M. on the evening of the twenty-second until 7 A.M. the following morning. Only one telegraph line was to be kept "live" for the control of the trains, and it was to be staffed by hand-picked men. At 6 A.M. Pinkerton gave instructions to a different agent, George R. Dunn, to purchase tickets for the entire last two sections of a sleeping car on the 11:50 P.M. train going from Philadelphia, through Baltimore, to Washington, D.C. Pinkerton told Dunn to give the tickets to agent Kate Warne when she arrived at the station.

Abraham Lincoln awoke at the Continental Hotel on Friday, February 22, 1861, the one hundred twenty-ninth anniversary of Washington's Birthday. He had slept for less than six hours. Lincoln and his son Tad left the hotel at 6:50 A.M. and rode down Chestnut Street in an open carriage, escorted by Scott's Legion. These men were veterans of the Mexican War of 1846–48, and they carried the ragged banner that had accompanied them from Vera Cruz to Mexico City.

In this detail of the flag-raising ceremony at Independence Hall, February 22, 1861, the president-elect, left of center, holds his stovepipe hat. The Philadelphia Inquirer, *February 22, 1861, reported that during his February 21 reply to Mayor Henry on the Continental Hotel balcony, he held his hat in front of him, that time with both hands. Did his hat hold notes for his speeches? Tad Lincoln is the indistinct small figure,* front right. *Photograph. Courtesy of the Print and Picture Collection, the Free Library of Philadelphia.*

Lincoln had seen Independence Hall in 1848. He had attended the Whig National Convention in Philadelphia that year, and there had been a Whig political rally in Independence Square to "ratify" the nominations of Taylor and Fillmore, but this was Lincoln's first opportunity to go inside the building. At 7 A.M. the president-elect was ushered into the hall's east wing, site of the signing of the Declaration of Independence, where he found members of the city council, who had begun assembling at 5:30 A.M. After a welcome by Theodore L. Cuyler, president of Philadelphia's Select Council, Lincoln made "a wholly unprepared speech," in a low, barely audible voice.

> I am filled with deep emotion at finding myself standing here in the place where were collected together the wisdom, the patriotism, the devotion to principle, from which sprang the institutions under which we live. . . . All the political sentiments I entertain have been drawn . . . from the sentiments which originated, and were given to the world from this hall in which we stand. I have never had a feeling politically that did not spring from the sentiments embodied in the Declaration of Independence. I have often pondered over the dangers which were incurred by the men who assembled here and adopted that Declaration of Independence—I have pondered over the toils that were endured by the officers and soldiers of the army, who achieved that Independence. I have often inquired of myself, what great principle or idea it was that kept this Confederacy so long together. It was not the mere matter of the separation of the colonies from the mother land; but something in that Declaration giving liberty, not alone to the people of this country, but hope to the world for all future time. . . . If this country cannot be saved without giving up that principle—I was about to say I would rather be assassinated on this spot than to surrender it.

Because his speech was extemporaneous, the president-elect worried aloud that he might have been indiscreet but defended his words saying, "I have said nothing but what I am willing to live by, and, in the pleasure of Almighty God, die by." Very few understood, as did Allan Pinkerton, that Lincoln's pledge to stand fast even in the face of assassination was not just an idle boast.

Kansas had been admitted to the Union as a free state on January 29, but Philadelphia delayed its flag-raising ceremony for the new thirty-four-star flag until the president-elect could participate. Workmen constructed a six-foot-high wooden platform between Independence Hall and Chestnut Street and decorated it with American flags on the front and both sides. People began gathering around the platform long before sunrise; eventually it became necessary to form Scott's Legion between the platform and the crowd in order to secure the area. Philadelphian Washington H. Penrose wrote in his diary, "February 22. somewhat cloudy but pleasant . . . went to the State House in the morning before 7 o'clock to see Abraham Lincoln (President-elect) raise a flag above the State House at 7 o'clock, and swing to the breeze, the stars and stripes. Such a dence [sic] crowd I was never in before; and never wish to be again."

Long, sustained cheering greeted the president-elect when he exited Independence Hall and appeared on the platform. After brief introductory remarks by Stephen Benton, chairman of the Committee on City Property, Lincoln spoke. He stood by the wooden railing at the front of the platform, holding his hat in his left hand. He turned, half toward the dignitaries who stood with him and half toward the expectant crowd below. The first American flag to fly atop Independence Hall, he said, had thirteen stars. As the number of stars increased, so too, did the nation's size, prosperity,

This row of buildings on Chestnut Street stood opposite Independence Hall and the February 1861 speakers' platform. During Lincoln's 1865 Funeral Train, people attempted to jump ahead in the viewing line by entering the rear of these buildings and exiting from the front. This photograph looks east from Sixth Street, circa 1859. Courtesy of the Print and Picture Collection, the Free Library of Philadelphia.

and happiness. "Its [the nation's] welfare in the future, as well as in the past, is in your hands," Lincoln told the Philadelphians. Permanent prosperity would come, he hoped, by "cultivating the spirit that animated our fathers, . . . cherishing that fraternal feeling that has so long characterized us as a nation, excluding passion, ill-temper and precipitate action."

Lincoln removed his overcoat, and the Reverend Dr. Henry Steele Clark said a prayer. Everyone except the president-elect and two or three designated council members left the platform. The police stood quietly, and Scott's Legion presented arms. A signal gun fired. Lincoln gripped the ropes firmly and hoisted. As the thirty-four-star flag rose higher and higher above Independence Hall, a stiff breeze caught it, and it spread out full length in the wind. The crowd cheered. The band played "The Star-Spangled Banner" and dedicated "The Stars and Stripes Are Still Unfurled" to Mrs. Robert Anderson, wife of Major Robert Anderson, Fort Sumter's commander. Cannon in Independence Square boomed, and the program ended.

Lincoln returned to the Continental Hotel to eat breakfast and to get ready to leave for Harrisburg. At 8:10 A.M. Pinkerton arrived for a brief, final meeting with Norman Judd. Judd approved Pinkerton's arrangements and said that the telegraph company and the Pennsylvania Railroad were ready. He advised Pinkerton to expect Lincoln to return to the West Philadelphia Railroad Station sometime after 10 P.M. that evening. Judd mentioned that the secret trip was sure to cause a political uproar, but he was ready to take responsibility. Elsewhere in the hotel, Ward Hill Lamon found Frederick Seward in a hallway, took him aside, and told him that Lincoln had decided to do as he had been advised.

Pennsylvania Railroad passengers usually left central Philadelphia from the Eleventh and Market Street Station. Because locomotive engines were fire hazards and therefore banned inside city limits, mules pulled the rail cars over street rails the twenty-block distance from the downtown Eleventh and Market Street Station to the West Philadelphia Station. There workmen attached an engine and assembled the train.

That day, however, Lincoln went directly to West Philadelphia after leaving the Continental Hotel at 8:30 A.M. Surrounded by mounted police, the open carriage with Lincoln, Colonel Sumner, Norman Judd, and William P. Hacker, president of Philadelphia's Common Council, traveled west on Walnut Street and then north on Twenty-third Street to Market. As Lincoln's procession rounded the corner from Twenty-third Street onto Market, the crowd at the Pennsylvania Railroad Station was surprised. They had not expected Lincoln to come to West Philadelphia directly by carriage. Seeing him, they rushed through the Market Street covered bridge over the Schuylkill River. Police had difficulty opening a passage through the crowd, but eventually Lincoln and his party were able to reach the station and board the train. As cannon fired and people cheered, Lincoln stood on the last railcar's rear platform and bowed. The three-car special train pulled away. It was 9:30 A.M.

The welcome that Abraham Lincoln experienced in Philadelphia was not created for him alone; it was instead the result of long-term evolution of public ritual. The parade form was centuries old. Military units, trade associations, and civic groups, such as fire companies, marched in an organized display that reinforced or elevated social status. Nineteenth-century America built the public welcome of a visiting dignitary, the public funeral (welcome of the dignitary's remains), and the celebration of nation (patriotic holidays) around the framework of the organized parade.

By the time president-elect Lincoln arrived, Philadelphia's welcome rites were well established. Philadelphia had greeted the Marquis de Lafayette (1824), President

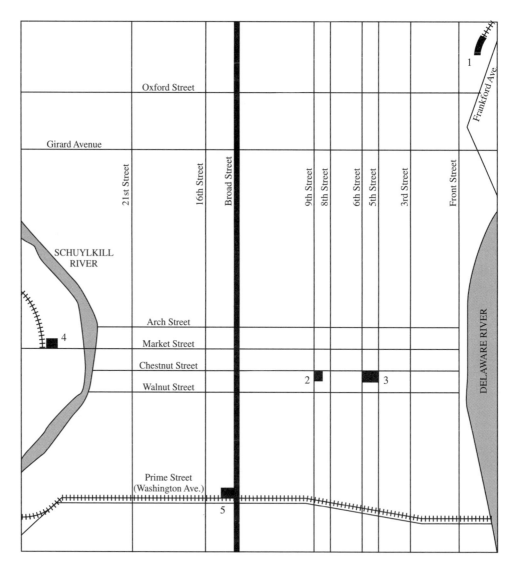

PHILADELPHIA, 1861–65. (1) *Kensington Railroad Station* (2) *Continental Hotel* (3)*Independence Hall* (4) *Pennsylvania Railroad Station* (5) *Southern and Western Railroad Station, also known as the Broad and Prime Street Station*

Andrew Jackson (1833), and President John Tyler (1843) in similar fashion. The visiting dignitary arrived at a crowded depot and entered a barouche drawn by a team of matched, white horses. Dignitary and carriage joined an organized parade and processed to the hotel. Along the way, cheering crowds, waving flags, ringing bells, saluting cannon, and perhaps exploding fireworks added excitement. At the hotel there was an official welcome, often by the mayor. It was all very straightforward.

February 22, Washington's Birthday, was one of the public celebrations that defined the nation and the American experiment. Once again the parade form provided structure. On the one-hundredth anniversary of Washington's birth in 1832, fifteen thousand city officials, policemen, volunteer militia, firemen, and tradesmen marched through Philadelphia's streets. Most Washington's Birthday celebrants also expected a flag-raising and a public reading of Washington's Farewell Address, in addition to parades, flags, bunting, and cannon salutes. Such rituals also operated at different social levels. The average citizen watched the public observances and parades and participated

The Cadwell House Hotel stood on the southeast corner of North Queen and East Chestnut Streets, Lancaster. Later renamed the Imperial Hotel, it hosted a commemoration of speeches made from its balcony. Photograph, circa 1911–15. Courtesy of the Lancaster County Historical Society.

in private outings. Organized groups held private parties, marched in the parades, and participated in the ceremonies. The upper class organized, directed, participated in, and funded the shared events. Lincoln's 1861 visit combined Philadelphia's public welcome of a visiting dignitary with her Washington's Birthday festivities. After the president-elect's morning departure, Philadelphia continued the celebration.

When Lincoln's train left Philadelphia, it headed west on the Pennsylvania Railroad's main line. This would be a four-hour trip, and the railroad took special precautions to see that it would be uneventful. Locomotive Number 161 was one of the new coal-burning smoke consumers. Its stack emitted neither sparks nor smoke. It was tastefully decorated with flags and evergreens, and in case of a breakdown, alternate locomotives were held in reserve at Parkesburg and at Lancaster. Flagmen were positioned every mile along the train route, and a telegrapher with equipment rode the train. In an emergency, he could tap into the wires to send a message.

While traveling through eastern Pennsylvania, Judd spoke privately with Lincoln and briefed him on the preparations of Pinkerton, Felton, Sanford, and Franciscus. Lincoln approved. Judd felt that they needed to inform the other members of Lincoln's inner circle as soon as the president-elect felt it was appropriate. Judd remembered Lincoln responding, "I reckon they will laugh at us, Judd, but you had better get them together."

The curious and the enthusiastic gathered at stations along the route. At Haverford College, a Quaker institution, students turned out en masse to see the president-elect. When the train stopped for four minutes at Downingtown, an immense throng of well-wishers surrounded it. At Coatesville flags and banners hung over the rail line. At Parkesburg a woman held a banner reading "LIBERTY—NATIONAL. SLAVERY—SECTIONAL." Halfway to Harrisburg the train stopped at Leaman Place, just east of Paradise, for four minutes to take on water. Lincoln came to the rear platform and said "he was too unwell to say much." He went on that he "had merely come out to see them and let them see him," adding that he "thought he had the best of the bargain!" The people protested good-naturedly and called for Mrs. Lincoln. When she came out, the president-elect explained that here was "the long and the short of it!" He 6'4", she 5'3"—the crowd laughed and cheered, and the train moved on.

Enthusiastic onlookers and American flags filled Lancaster's streets leading to the North Queen Street train station. Cadwell House Hotel rooms that fronted on Chestnut Street across from the station had been sold out for days. When Lincoln's train stopped, he appeared on the rear platform of his car. Amid shouts and cheers he moved into the crowd through an aisle cleared by police and a local military unit, the Jackson Rifles, and crossed Chestnut Street. As he entered the Cadwell House Hotel and walked up the steps to the second-floor balcony, he passed beautiful, well-dressed Lancaster women strategically placed along his route by the reception committee. By the time he got to the balcony, he refined his remarks "to see and be seen" and decided to mention the ladies who brightened his day. "I come before you to see and be seen and, as regards the ladies, I have the best of the bargain; but, as to the gentlemen, I cannot say as much."

On the way out of Lancaster, Lincoln asked someone to point out James Buchanan's home, Wheatland. As the train passed, he was able to see it in the distance. At Mount Joy, Elizabethtown, and Middletown more cheering crowds, friendly smiles, and waving flags welcomed the train.

As Lincoln traveled toward Harrisburg, people in the state's capital were getting ready for his visit. Oldtimers remembered that George Washington traveled through Harrisburg during the Whiskey Rebellion of 1794. Now a president-elect was coming on Washington's Birthday, and the town was going to celebrate! It was a perfect, sun-filled February day. American flags were everywhere. A reporter for the *Harrisburg Pennsylvania Daily Telegraph* wrote, "They waved from lofty flag-staffs—from ropes suspended across streets—and from poles jutting out from windows of private residences." At ten o'clock more than two thousand men, from hometowns as far away as Philadelphia and Bethlehem, paraded from Market Square to the State Capitol via Front and State Streets. At 12:30 P.M. veterans of the War of 1812 raised an American flag over the capitol dome. As the flag rose above the cornice of the building, a breeze caught it, and it unfurled. Cannon fired, and bands played. E. H. Raush, chief clerk of the Pennsylvania House of Representatives read George Washington's Farewell Address aloud, and the procession marched back downtown to the Pennsylvania Railroad Station to await the president-elect. A huge crowd had already gath-

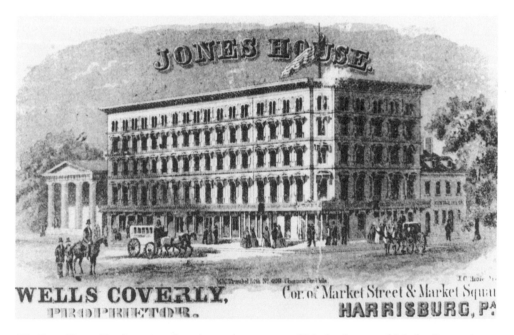

The Jones House Hotel once stood on the southeast corner of Market Street and Market Square (near Second Street). The building on the left still exists. Lincoln left this hotel at dusk on Friday, February 22, 1861, to travel secretly to Washington, D.C. Engraving. Courtesy, the Historical Society of Dauphin County.

ered. "Every balcony, window, tree and available point of observation was thickly studded with humanity anxious to obtain the first glance of 'Honest Old Abe.'" One newspaper estimated the number of people at thirty thousand.

Lincoln's train arrived in Harrisburg at 1:30 P.M. He and two of his aides were "escorted to a barouche drawn by six elegantly comparisoned grey horses, which proceeded, followed by the entire procession, to the Jones House." The Jones House Hotel stood on the southeastern corner of Market and Second Streets. "A beautiful arch, covered with spruce, was erected at the edge of the sideway opposite one of the entrances on the Market Square front of the Jones House." "The triumphal arch . . . was gaily trimmed with small American flags, and a banner contained the words, 'Welcome President to our Capitol.'" Through this, it was understood, the president-elect would enter the hotel.

Lincoln and Governor Andrew Curtin met at the entrance to the Jones House, went upstairs, and appeared on an outside balcony. The crowd of five thousand people in Market Street applauded and cheered. During his welcome remarks the governor said: "You undertake, sir, no easy task. You must restore fraternal feeling. You must heal up discord. You must produce amity in place of hostility and restore prosperity, peace and concord to this unhappy country. And future generations will rise up and call you

Before burning in 1897, the old Pennsylvania State Capitol Building stood at Third and State Streets, Harrisburg. The state offset its construction costs by the 1816 sale of Independence Hall to Philadelphia for $70,000. Courtesy, the Historical Society of Dauphin County.

blessed." Lincoln replied that he felt "the weight of that great responsibility." He trusted in the support of "the strength of the arms and wisdom of the heads of these masses." He believed that he possessed "an honest heart" for the work but realized, "I dare not tell you that I bring a head sufficient for it. If my own strength should fail, I shall at least fall back upon these masses, who, I think, under any circumstances will not fail."

After Lincoln received a number of guests in his hotel suite, Governor Curtin, senators, members of the House of Representatives, and a military guard escorted him three blocks north from the Jones House to the State Capitol building. Lincoln entered the House of Representatives at 2:30 P.M. and was formally greeted by Speaker of the Senate Robert M. Palmer and Speaker of the House Elisha W. Davis. Lincoln addressed the combined Pennsylvania General Assembly and told the lawmakers,

> Allusion has been made to the fact—the interesting fact perhaps we should say—that I for the first time appear at the Capitol of the great Commonwealth of Pennsylvania, upon the birthday of the Father of his Country. . . . This morning in the ceremonies at Philadelphia . . . I was for the first time allowed the privilege of standing in old Independence Hall. . . . Our friends there had provided a magnificent flag of the country. They had arranged it so that I was given the honor of raising it to the head of its staff; and when it went up, I was pleased that it went to its place by the strength of my own feeble arm. When, according to the arrangement, the cord was pulled and it flaunted gloriously to the wind without an accident, in the bright glowing sunshine of the morning, I could not help hoping that there was in the entire success of that beautiful ceremony, at least something of an omen of what is to come. Nor could I help, feeling then as I often have felt, that in the whole of that proceeding I was a very humble instrument. I had not provided the flag; I had not made the arrangement for elevating it to its place; I had applied but a very small portion of even my feeble strength in raising it. In the whole transaction, I was in the hands of the people who had arranged it.

Abraham Lincoln's address to the General Assembly was very revealing. During his trip from Philadelphia to Harrisburg he obviously had thought about the significance of his appearance that morning at Independence Hall and about his presence, later that afternoon, in the capital of Pennsylvania. He hoped that the success of the flag-raising ceremony was an "omen of what is to come." He declared that he felt that day as he often had felt, "a very humble instrument. . . . I was in the hands of the people who had arranged it."

After Senator Palmer delivered a lengthy oration, Lincoln went back to the Jones House, arriving shortly after 4 P.M. At that point Lincoln informed Curtin of the assassination plot. The president-elect attended a 5 P.M. dinner hosted by the governor at the hotel. Col. Thomas A. Scott of the Pennsylvania Railroad, Col. E. V. Sumner, Ward Hill Lamon, Dr. William Wallace, and David Davis were among those present. During dinner, talk eventually turned to the Baltimore assassination plot alleged by General Winfield Scott and Frederick Seward. Alexander K. McClure, Republican ally

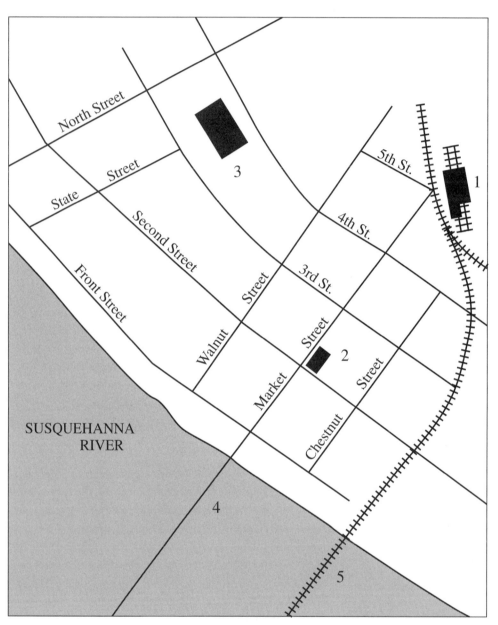

HARRISBURG, 1861–65. (1) *Pennsylvania Railroad Station* (2) *Jones House Hotel* (3) *Capitol Building* (4) *Market Street Bridge* (5) *Cumberland Valley Railroad Bridge*

of Governor Curtin, was an eyewitness. "The question of a change of route was discussed for some time by everyone with the single exception of Lincoln. He was
the one silent man of the party, and when he was finally compelled to speak he
unhesitatingly expressed his disapproval of the movement. . . . 'What would the nation think of its President stealing into the Capital like a thief in the night?'"

Eventually Lincoln agreed to drop out of public view and board the waiting train.
McClure continued.

> There was a crowd of thousands around the hotel. . . . Scott directed that Curtin, Lin-
> coln, and Lamon should at once proceed to the front steps of the hotel, where there was
> a vast throng waiting to receive them, and that Curtin should call distinctly, so that the
> crowd could hear, for a carriage, and direct the coachman to drive the party to the
> Executive Mansion. That was the natural thing for Curtin to do—to take the President
> to the Governor's mansion as his guest, and it excited no suspicion whatever. Before
> leaving the dining-room Governor Curtin halted Lincoln and Lamon at the door and
> inquired of Lamon whether he was well armed. . . . Lamon at once uncovered a small
> arsenal of deadly weapons, showing that he was literally armed to the teeth. In addition
> to a pair of heavy revolvers, he had a slung-shot and brass knuckles and a huge knife
> nestled under his vest. The three entered the carriage, and, as instructed by Scott, drove
> toward the Executive Mansion, but when near there the driver was ordered to take a
> circuitous route and to reach the railroad depot within half an hour. When Curtin and
> his party had gotten fairly away from the hotel I accompanied Scott to the railway depot,
> where he at once cleared one of his lines from Harrisburg to Philadelphia, so that there
> could be no obstruction upon it, as had been agreed upon at Philadelphia the evening
> before in case the change should be made. In the meantime he had ordered a locomotive
> and a single car to be brought to the eastern entrance of the depot, and at the appointed
> time the carriage arrived. Lincoln and Lamon emerged from the carriage and entered the
> car unnoticed by any except those interested in the matter, and after a quiet but fervent
> "Good-bye and God protect you!" the engineer quietly moved his train away on its
> momentous mission.

McClure's account was corroborated by Governor Curtin, who later wrote: "He put
on his overcoat and hat (it was a felt hat such as were in common use at that time)
and taking my arm we passed through the hall of the hotel and downstairs to a carriage in waiting at the door. We drove down the street and by the house in which I
lived to the train. The halls, stairways and pavements in front of the house were much
crowded, and no doubt the impression prevailed that Mr. Lincoln was going to the
Executive Mansion with me. To avoid inquiries I remained in the house when repeated
calls were made by persons who supposed he was there."

Lincoln's special train of one locomotive and one passenger car left Harrisburg bound
for Philadelphia. It was decided not to light the passenger car's interior lights, and the

occupants traveled to Philadelphia in darkness. At Downingtown the train stopped to take on water for the locomotive. Tea and a roll were brought on board for the president-elect.

Telegraph company superintendent W. P. Westervelt had arrived in Harrisburg late in the afternoon. He, George H. Burns, and climber Andrew Wynne drove two miles south of Harrisburg and grounded the telegraph wires along the Northern Central rail line. Col. Thomas A. Scott disabled other telegraph lines leading out of the city. Communication by telegraph was now impossible save for the one secure line. Scott himself controlled access to the line in Harrisburg, and telegraph office manager H. E. Thayer secured it in Philadelphia. Harrisburg was isolated.

In Philadelphia, Pinkerton and Samuel Felton had been busy all afternoon. Felton sent William Stearns, master machinist for the Philadelphia, Wilmington, and Baltimore Railroad, to Baltimore. Stearns's mission was to wait in Baltimore for the 11:50 P.M. train from Philadelphia. If the train secretly bearing Lincoln from Philadelphia was delayed, Stearns was to go to the superintendent of the Baltimore and Ohio Railroad and demand that its night train to Washington be held. In the unlucky event that the train from Philadelphia was late, Felton did not want Lincoln stuck in Baltimore overnight, having missed the connecting train to Washington. If the train was on time, Stearns would do nothing.

Felton also ordered the conductor of the evening train from Philadelphia to delay his departure until he had received an important package bound for Washington. Felton introduced Pinkerton to Henry F. Kenney, superintendent of the Philadelphia, Wilmington, and Baltimore Railroad. Kenney was given a bogus package and was told to meet Pinkerton and Lincoln at the Pennsylvania Railroad's West Philadelphia Station. From West Philadelphia Kenney would accompany them to the P.W. & B.'s Broad and Prime Street Station, arriving just before the scheduled departure. After Lincoln was safely on board, Kenney would give the bogus package to the conductor.

Pinkerton went back to the St. Louis Hotel and made last-minute arrangements with agent Kate Warne. Pinkerton instructed her to tell George Dunn, when he gave her the train tickets later that evening, to obtain the key to the rear door of the very last sleeping car on the train, and to unlock it when Pinkerton arrived. Everything was ready. Pinkerton rested and waited.

At 9:15 P.M. the Chicago detective received a dispatch from Harrisburg, to "J. H. Hutcheson, St. Louis Hotel Philadelphia. Nuts left at six—Everything as you directed—all is right. Geo. H. Burns." Soon afterward, Pinkerton and Kate Warne left the St. Louis Hotel. He put her in a carriage for the Broad and Prime Street Railroad Station. Pinkerton himself got in a carriage and went to the West Philadelphia Railroad Station at Thirty-second and Market Streets. At 10:03 P.M. Lincoln arrived at the West Philadelphia Station accompanied by Ward Hill Lamon, railroad general superintendent Enoch Lewis, and division superintendent G. C. Franciscus. Lincoln wore a soft, brown, cloth hat. An overcoat was draped over his shoulders. Lincoln, Pinkerton, and Lamon got inside the waiting carriage. Superintendent Kenney, who was waiting at the station, rode up top with the driver.

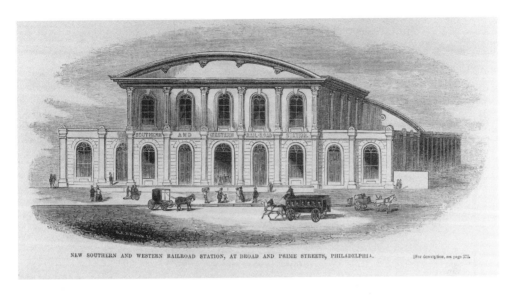

NEW SOUTHERN AND WESTERN RAILROAD STATION, AT BROAD AND PRIME STREETS, PHILADELPHIA.   [For description, see page 575.]

The Southern and Western Railroad Station of the Philadelphia, Wilmington, and Baltimore Railroad stood on the northwest corner of Broad and Prime Streets (now Washington Avenue) and had a large, roofed enclosure that allowed passenger access to trains without exposure to rain or snow. Courtesy, the Print and Picture Collection, the Free Library of Philadelphia.

Because Pinkerton felt that it was too early to arrive at the Broad and Prime Street Station, Mr. Kenney told the driver that he was looking for someone and wanted to drive around the city. They drove slowly east on Market, north on Nineteenth, east on Vine, and then south on Seventeenth Street toward the station. During the carriage ride, Lincoln told Pinkerton of Seward's visit the previous night with letters urging a change in his route. He had put Seward off, he said, telling him that he would make up his mind in Harrisburg. Later he reconsidered and let Seward know that he would change his route. He said that he found it impossible to get away from the crowd in Harrisburg without the help of Governor Curtin and Colonel Sumner. Lincoln said that his wife had insisted on burly Lamon coming along, and that the military officers wanted to accompany him just in case Pinkerton was setting a trap to kidnap him and sell him to Southern agents. Lincoln told them that Pinkerton was loyal.

While the carriage was driving around the streets of Philadelphia, Kate Warne was at the Broad and Prime Street Station. George Dunn gave her the tickets he had purchased at Pinkerton's instruction. He obtained a key to the rear door of the last sleeping car by telling a conductor that one of the passengers was an invalid gentleman and could enter only through the rear. Dunn was nervous. There were men standing around the outside of the car, and they appeared to be looking for someone. Kate Warne entered the car, picked out the last three berths, stood by them to save them, and gave the conductor fifty cents to help her. What Dunn and Warne did not know was that the men outside, who later filled the rest of the car, were also Pinkerton agents.

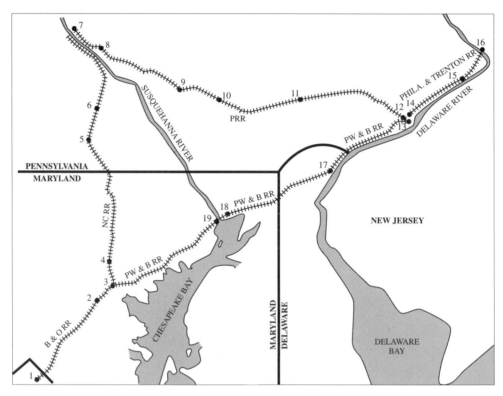

TRAIN ROUTES, FEBRUARY 21–23, 1861 (1) *Washington, D.C., depot at New Jersey and C Streets* (2) *Washington Junction/Relay House (B & O)* (3) *Baltimore, Maryland—Camden Street, President Street, and Calvert Street Stations* (4) *Relay (Northern Central Railroad)* (5) *Hanover Junction* (6) *York* (7) *Harrisburg* (8) *Middletown* (9) *Lancaster* (10) *Leaman Place* (11) *Downingtown* (12) *Philadelphia—West Philadelphia Station* (13) *Philadelphia—Broad and Prime Station* (14) *Philadelphia—Kensington Station* (15) *Bristol* (16) *Trenton, New Jersey* (17) *Wilmington, Delaware* (18) *Perryville, Maryland* (19) *Havre de Grace, Maryland.*

Pinkerton wrote in his daily record book for February 23, 1861, "Lincoln was cool, calm, and self possessed—firm and determined in his bearing." Nearing the depot, the party left the carriage in the shadows of Carpenter Street. Pinkerton walked into the depot with Lincoln and Lamon behind. Agent George Dunn showed the group to the sleeping car, and they entered unnoticed through the rear door. Kate Warne was already inside saving sleeping berths. "In about three minutes from the time we got aboard the train started. . . . Mr. Lincoln soon laid down in his Berth, and when the Conductor came around for his Tickets, I [Pinkerton] handed him the Tickets for Mr. Lincoln. He did not look in the Berths at all—left and did not return again during the trip."

The train arrived in Baltimore at the President Street Station of the P.W. & B. Railroad at 3:30 A.M. Kate Warne got off, and William Stearns got on and whispered in Pinkerton's ear "all is right" in Baltimore. Horses transported the sleeping cars over the city's street rail system to the Baltimore and Ohio's Camden Street Station. The train left Baltimore at 4:15 A.M. and arrived in Washington, D.C., at 6 A.M. Lincoln went to Willard's Hotel.

Back in Harrisburg, anxious hours came to an end. A. K. McClure wrote that on the evening of the twenty-second, he and Colonel Scott had cut Harrisburg telegraph lines by 7 P.M. Together they monitored the lines to make sure that none were repaired. "No one attempted to sleep. . . . Scott, who was of heroic mould, several times tried to temper the severe strain of his anxiety by looking up railway matters, but he would soon abandon the listless effort, and thrice we strolled from the depot to the Jones House and back again, in aimless struggle to hasten the slowly-passing hours, only to find equally anxious watchers there and a wife whose sobbing heart could not be consoled." Near dawn Scott reconnected the lines and soon received an unsigned telegram "from Washington, saying, 'Plums delivered nuts safely.' He whirled his hat high in the little telegraph office as he shouted, 'Lincoln's in Washington,' and we rushed to the Jones House and hurried a messenger to the Executive Mansion."

Mrs. Lincoln and the remainder of Lincoln's party left Harrisburg on Saturday, February 23, on the Northern Central Railroad and traveled to Baltimore. The crowd of five thousand waiting in York, the smaller crowd at Hanover Junction, and, of course, the conspirators, if there were any, in Baltimore were disappointed. Lincoln was not on the train. He was already in Washington.

Lincoln's entrance into the capital was a source of political embarrassment, to say the least. Loyal newspapers winced. The opposition press had a field day, and Southern doubts about Northern courage grew. The *New York Tribune* hoped to see proof of "imminent and great" danger. The *New York Herald* wrote that Lincoln feared to ride in his own carriage because it was not "bomb proof." The *Boston Post* thought that the whole idea of a plot was concocted "to direct the public mind from Mr. Lincoln's crude speeches." Political cartoonists drew Lincoln disguised in a tam and kilts. The president came to regret his actions.

In retrospect, however, all was not despair. During those extraordinary thirty-six hours from Thursday evening, February 21, to Saturday morning, February 23, 1861, the president-elect found an omen of success. He allied himself with the Founding Fathers, "I have never had a feeling politically that did not spring from the sentiments embodied in the Declaration of Independence." He grasped the personal dangers faced by men who had signed the Declaration, and he publicly pledged his life to the nation's preservation—and to liberty and equality for all. It was a Washington's Birthday quite unlike any other. Ten days later Abraham Lincoln became the sixteenth president of the United States.

The Mordecai Lincoln homestead in Exeter Township, Berks County, Pennsylvania, was home to Mordecai Lincoln from 1733 until his death in 1736. Photograph, nineteenth century. Courtesy of the Historical Society of Berks County.

2

"Mystic Chords of Memory"

Lincoln Ancestors

The mystic chords of memory, stretching from every battlefield, and patriot grave, to every living heart and hearthstone, all over this broad land, will yet swell the chorus of the Union, when again touched, as surely they will be, by the better angels of our nature.

—Abraham Lincoln, First Inaugural Address, March 4, 1861

Abraham Lincoln did not have a great interest in his own genealogy, yet Lincoln's ancestry shaped his life more than perhaps he knew. The story of Lincoln's ancestors in the seventeenth and eighteenth centuries is a story of the growing iron industry in the Colonies. It is a story of frontier life and of westward migration. And it is a story closely interwoven with the Boone family. The iron industry brought Lincolns to Pennsylvania, and Daniel Boone took them away. Lives lived and decisions made long ago predestined the birth of Abraham Lincoln into poverty in Kentucky in 1809.

The story of Lincoln's ancestors was not an unusual one in eighteenth-century America. They followed a commonly used migration route, moving south from central Pennsylvania through the Cumberland and Shenandoah Valleys. From the Shenandoah Valley they moved to North Carolina and then northwest through the Cumberland Gap into Kentucky. From Kentucky many families continued a northward migration into Indiana, Illinois, and other states of the Northwest Ordinance.

More than a century earlier, President Lincoln's paternal ancestor Samuel Lincoln (1619–90) had migrated across the Atlantic. He left England and landed at Salem, Massachusetts, on June 20, 1637. Lincoln, his wife Martha, and their eleven children lived in Hingham, Massachusetts, just east of Braintree. Iron and processed iron products of that era were mainly imported from England, but in time England found it increasingly difficult to meet her own needs, let alone supply her colonies. Local blacksmiths moved to increase production, and entrepreneurs built the first iron furnaces and forges in 1644 at Lynn and at Braintree, Massachusetts, using forge hammers and other machinery imported from England. Samuel Lincoln was a skilled weaver and mariner, but in time he built his own ironworks and taught his sons the new trade.

The fourth son of Samuel and Martha Lincoln was born on June 14, 1657, in Hingham. Mordecai Lincoln became a blacksmith and an ironworker. He married Sarah Jones in 1685 and about 1691 moved east to Scituate, Massachusetts. An ambitious and innovative man, he not only owned a gristmill and a sawmill, but also dammed the west branch of Bound Brook near Scituate to power a trip hammer for his iron forge. At his death on November 28, 1727, his estate was valued at 3,099 pounds.

Mordecai and Sarah Lincoln's first son was also named Mordecai. He was born in 1686 in Hingham and died in 1736 in Pennsylvania. He was President Abraham Lincoln's paternal great-great-grandfather. Sometime between 1710 and 1714 he moved to Freehold Township near Clarksburg in Monmouth County, New Jersey, where his brother Abraham owned a blacksmith shop and forge. Central New Jersey's bogs provided a commercially profitable source of iron ore, and the two brothers decided to join the emerging mid-Atlantic iron industry. By 1714 twenty-eight-year old Mordecai Lincoln had married Hannah Salter, the daughter of a prominent local mill owner. The new Lincoln family had one son and five daughters.

Mordecai Lincoln hoped to profit by bringing his knowledge and experience of iron manufacture from New England to the growing New Jersey markets. A hardworking blacksmith using high-grade iron ore could produce as much as one hundred pounds of iron per day at a daily profit for himself of fifty shillings. But, iron manufacture in New Jersey was established thirty-five years before Lincoln's arrival, and New Jersey's bog iron ore was not high grade. Although demand for his product was ample, profits were not as he expected.

The Schuylkill Valley west of Philadelphia, in contrast, was an ideal site for development as a colonial iron center. Pennsylvanians had capital, knowledge, and experience. Abundant high-grade iron ore, extensive forests for charcoal production, and plentiful local limestone were in close proximity to each other. Large local population centers provided a ready market for the product, and streams that powered the iron plantation's waterwheels doubled as a pathway to the waiting customer. Everything came together, and Pennsylvania's iron industry exploded into the eighteenth century.

In 1716 Thomas Rutter constructed the first iron furnace in the Schuylkill Valley. In 1718 Samuel Nutt Sr. built the area's second furnace. Coventry Iron Works (Forge) was located on French Creek and was named after Samuel Nutt's hometown in England. Nutt's bloomery furnace did not differ significantly in design from that of tenth-century Spain. In a charcoal-heated hearth, iron ore slowly became a molten mass. Workers with long iron poles worked the mass and, at the appropriate time, brought out molten iron that they then shaped into iron blooms, also known as ingots. Blacksmiths bought the cooled ingots and worked them into pots, pans, kettles, nails, horseshoes, and other items of everyday life.

Mordecai Lincoln saved his money, and the death of his wife's uncle brought a small inheritance. Lincoln was interested in Nutt's iron works, and the family decided that Pennsylvania might be the right move. On October 21, 1720, 150 acres of land were surveyed for Mordecai and Hannah Lincoln "Near ye Branches of the ffrench Creek & the Branches of Brandywine" in Coventry Township, Chester County, Pennsylvania. For five years beginning in 1720, Mordecai Lincoln, William Branson, and Samuel Nutt Sr. were associated in the Coventry Iron Works. Samuel Nutt Sr., "ironmonger," was the creative force, experience, and capital in the partnership. William Branson, "merchant of Philadelphia," was the major investor. Junior partner Mordecai Lincoln, "ironmonger," had experience and some capital. With the additional capital provided by the partnership, Coventry Iron Works added a blast furnace and a refining forge. The three partners "at their joint charge lately erected, Built, and provided one Dwelling House and a Forge with Engines belonging to their Iron Works besides other Buildings and Erections Situate, Lying, and being on a Certain Tract of Land at French Creek." With the addition of the forge, the large water-powered hammer could process the ingots produced by the blast furnace into a higher quality, stronger iron product.

Mordecai and Hannah Lincoln were intimately involved in iron production for some five years. Things went well. Coventry Forge prospered, and partner Samuel Nutt became Chester County's representative to the Pennsylvania provincial assembly in 1723. But on December 14, 1725, Mordecai Lincoln sold his one-third interest in Coventry Forge to partner William Branson for 500 pounds and prepared to return to New Jersey. Perhaps Hannah Lincoln missed her relatives, or perhaps she became ill. In any case, after Hannah died in 1727, Mordecai decided to stay in Pennsylvania.

Mordecai Lincoln left Coventry Township and moved to Amity Township, Philadelphia County, later known as Exeter Township, Berks County. In 1727 he, Benjamin Boone, and others were appointed to oversee Tulpehocken Road construction from the Schuylkill River to Oley. His father died that same year, and Mordecai sold the gristmill and ironworks in Massachusetts, thus acquiring additional capital. In 1729 he married Mary Robeson. The couple leased a 1,000-acre tract of land in Exeter Township, Berks County, Pennsylvania, that had been granted to Andrew Robeson—probably Mary Robeson's father—by the London Company in 1718 for a rent of one beaver pelt payable on March first forever. In May 1730 Mordecai and Mary Lincoln purchased the land.

Their first home on the site was a log cabin. In time they built a two-story stone farmhouse four-tenths of a mile from the Schuylkill River. The house was originally one room wide and two rooms deep and was built on the side of a hill. This "bank" type construction allowed ground level entry on both floors of the home. A stone wall in the gable end of the home was inscribed "M.L.—1733." Mordecai Lincoln died on May 12, 1736, at age fifty. Estate appraiser Squire Boone valued the family's two slaves "Negro Will" at 20 pounds and "Negro John" at 10 pounds. Family oral tradition remembered their nicknames as "Quick" and "Dead."

The Lincoln family and the Boone family were pioneer neighbors, living only four miles apart, and attended the same Quaker meeting. Squire and his wife Sarah purchased their farm in 1730, and on November 2, 1734, their sixth child, Daniel, was born in their log cabin home. Squire Boone was expelled from Quaker meeting in 1748, and two years later, when Daniel was fifteen, the Boone family left Pennsylvania.

Mordecai and Hannah Salter Lincoln's only son, John L. Lincoln (1716–88), was born on May 3, 1716, in Freehold, New Jersey. John was eleven when his mother died and the family moved to the Amity area. He was twenty when his father died. In Pennsylvania, John Lincoln worked as a farmer, weaver, and tax collector. On July 5, 1743, he married widow Rebecca Flowers Morris, whose parents and grandparents were Quakers. On October 9, 1746, he purchased 50 acres of land in Caernarvon Township, Lancaster County. The land was one-half mile east of Birdsboro and in present-day Union Township, Berks County. Later he purchased 150 adjoining acres, which he sold in 1762.

In 1765 John and Rebecca Lincoln sold the remaining Pennsylvania land and migrated to Virginia with the Josiah Boone family and others. They followed the Allegheny Trail westward from Berks and Lancaster Counties. Travelers, often in Conestoga wagons, crossed the Susquehanna River by ferry at Harrisburg and took the Virginia Road southwest through the Cumberland Valley. The valley towns of Carlisle, Shippensburg, and Chambersburg grew up one to two days' journey apart by Conestoga wagon. After the travelers crossed the Potomac River and entered Virginia, they noticed that the valley had changed its name. From Exeter Township in Pennsylvania to the Shenandoah Valley in Virginia was, on average, a one-month trip.

The Lincolns settled in the beautiful Shenandoah Valley at Linville Creek, Augusta County (now Rockingham County), Virginia, north of present-day Harrisonburg.

Conestoga wagons like "Philadelphia to Pittsburgh 20 Days" were popular from 1750 to 1855. A Conestoga wagon and team of four or six horses could haul as much as nine thousand pounds of freight up to fourteen miles each day. Photographs, MG-286, Penn Central Railroad Collection, Pennsylvania State Archives.

Possibly they learned of this area from Daniel Boone, for he and his father's family had spent one or perhaps two growing seasons at Linville Creek some fifteen years earlier. John Lincoln bought 600 acres of land in June 1768. He and his mother were Baptist, and he donated land for a new church to be built near his home. John died in Virginia in 1788. To later generations of Lincolns, he was known as "Virginia John."

The president's paternal grandfather, also named Abraham Lincoln (1744–86), was born in Pennsylvania on May 13, 1744, the first child of John and Rebecca Lincoln. He moved with his parents to Linville Creek, Virginia, in 1765, and in 1770 he married Bathsheba Herring. In August 1773 John and Rebecca Lincoln deeded 210 acres of land to son Abraham. He later purchased an adjacent 50 acres for his farm. Abraham and Bathsheba Lincoln's fourth child, Thomas Lincoln, was born at Linville Creek, Virginia, on January 6, 1778.

The Lincoln and Boone families continued their close relationship from their years together as Pennsylvania neighbors. Including distant relatives, there were four Lincoln-Boone marriages in the eighteenth century, and Daniel Boone maintained contact with the folks back home in Pennsylvania and at Linville Creek, Virginia, for many years. In 1755 during the French and Indian War, twenty-year-old Daniel was in southwestern Pennsylvania with the North Carolina militia, fighting in British General Edward Braddock's expedition against Fort Duquesne, when he learned of an Indian trail through the North Carolina mountains to the Kentucky grasslands. Boone entered the region in 1767, founded Boonesborough in 1775, and guided several parties of settlers through the Cumberland Gap to the new lands. In 1775 the Josiah Boone family left Linville Creek and moved to Kentucky, and in July 1776 Daniel Boone listed 1,000 Kentucky acres surveyed for Abraham Lincoln.

On February 18, 1780, Abraham and Bathsheba sold their 262-acre farm in Linville Creek for 5,000 pounds. On March 4, 1780, Lincoln was in Kentucky to pay 160 pounds for a land warrant to 400 acres. About 1782 Abraham Lincoln, wife Bathsheba, sons Mordecai, Josiah, Thomas, and two daughters migrated from the Shenandoah Valley in Virginia to North Carolina in preparation for their journey through the Cumberland Gap into Kentucky. By 1785 they had settled on 400 acres of land near Long Run, ten miles east of Louisville, Kentucky. Eventually Lincolns owned 5,544 acres of Kentucky land.

In May 1786 an Indian shot and killed Abraham Lincoln while he was working in a cornfield with his three sons at Long Run in Kentucky. Thomas Lincoln was a small child when he saw his father murdered. His older brother Mordecai ran and, using the family rifle from inside the cabin, killed the Indian as he approached Thomas, who was still beside his father's body.

Thomas Lincoln (1778–1851) did not significantly benefit from his father's estate. By law the bulk of the estate went to Abraham's oldest son Mordecai. Left without a father and without financial stability, Thomas struggled. On June 12, 1806, he married Nancy Hanks; and in December 1808 they bought 300 acres of land, known as

American frontiersman Daniel Boone was born in Pennsylvania in 1734 near the Mordecai Lincoln homestead. He, more than any other man, was responsible for the Lincoln family's migration to Kentucky. Engraving by J. B. Longacre, 1835, from a painting by Chester Harding, 1820 (the only known portrait of Boone done from life). Courtesy of the author.

the farm at Sinking Spring, three miles from Hodgenville, Kentucky. There on February 12, 1809, future president Abraham Lincoln was born.

Why would people like the Lincolns choose to leave the relative security of settled lands and go into the unknown? Some said it was a migration fever, an intangible wanderlust. America seemed to be filled with adventurers and risk-takers, a people on the move. From 1790 to 1840, 2.47 percent of the population moved west each year. Some said that the population was genetically selected for the traits of restlessness, survival, and courage. After all, didn't it take a dreamer to make that first Atlantic crossing in a tiny, leaking ship? Weren't all white Americans of that era descended from wanderers who had risked everything? People said that the Atlantic crossing and early survival hardships "sifted the grain" and created an especially hardy stock, with remarkable characteristics.

Population growth in an agrarian society was one of the more tangible forces that drove western migration. A farming family with eight or ten children needed land in order to give each son a farm of his own. If land could not be purchased nearby, the most viable option to keep the extended family together was to move. They migrated west, usually in groups of families, and often to an area already known by some acquaintance. The availability of a seemingly unlimited supply of land empowered the American spirit. Fields and forests, mountains, lakes, and rivers seemed to go on forever; and a man could always find freedom, opportunity, and equality just a little farther west, just beyond that horizon.

Governmental policy influenced human behavior too. Clear land titles in the Northwest Ordinance territories might have had as much to do with people moving in, as unclear land titles in Kentucky had to do with people moving out. Beginning in the early nineteenth century, President Thomas Jefferson's visionary policies of land acquisition, exploration, and internal improvements catalyzed American expansion. After the Louisiana Purchase, the Lewis and Clark Expedition, enhanced access to the mouth of the Mississippi River, and construction of the National Road, America had a new horizon.

Many Easterners chose to move west, and by 1860 so many Pennsylvanian males had migrated out of state that there were more females than males in the fifteen- to twenty-nine-year age group. Numerous friends and acquaintances of Abraham Lincoln had Pennsylvania ancestors, just as he did. Mary Todd's grandparents, David and Hannah Owen Todd, lived near Pequea, Lancaster County, Pennsylvania. They had three children—John, who became governor of the Illinois Territory; Levi; and Robert, who settled in Lexington, Kentucky. Mary Todd, born in 1818, was one of Robert and Eliza Parker Todd's four daughters.

Frances Todd, another of Robert Todd's daughters, married Dr. William Smith Wallace, a graduate of Jefferson Medical College in Philadelphia. His parents owned a general store in East Earl, Lancaster County, Pennsylvania. After medical school Dr. Wallace returned to East Earl to practice out of his home, but he later moved to Springfield, Illinois. In time he became Lincoln's brother-in-law and physician.

Abraham Lincoln wrote an autobiographical sketch on December 20, 1859, at the request of Illinois friend and Republican Party politician Jesse W. Fell. Edward J. Lewis, formerly of Pennsylvania, edited a section of Fell's newspaper, the *Bloomington Daily Pantagraph.* They sent Lincoln's information back home to Lewis's brother. On February 11, 1860, the *Chester County Times* published West Chester attorney Joseph J. Lewis's expanded political biography of candidate Lincoln. In his sketch Abraham Lincoln wrote: "My paternal grandfather, Abraham Lincoln, emigrated from Rockingham County, Virginia, to Kentucky, about 1781 or 2, where, a year or two later, he was killed by Indians, not in battle, but by stealth, when he was laboring to open a farm in the forest. His ancestors, who were Quakers, went to Virginia from Berks County, Pennsylvania."

3

"Struck Blind"

Lincoln in Congress

The other day, one of the gentlemen from Georgia (Mr. Iverson) an eloquent man, and a man of learning, so far as I could judge, not being learned, myself, came down upon us astonishingly. He spoke in what the Baltimore American calls the "scathing and withering style." At the end of his second severe flash, I was struck blind, and found myself feeling with my fingers for an assurance of my continued physical existence. A little of the bone was left, and I gradually revived.

—Abraham Lincoln, The Presidential Question, speech in the House of
  Representatives, July 27, 1848

Abraham Lincoln spent his early years in the backwater of frontier subsistence farming. Once released into adulthood he drifted on, at various times shopkeeper, postmaster, surveyor, and militia captain. In time he discovered politics, and his life's journey quickened. Beginning in 1834 he represented his district in the Illinois state legislature, first in Vandalia and later in Springfield. His friend John Todd Stuart suggested that he study law, and the young legislator took the advice. In 1837 attorney Lincoln began the practice of law with Stuart in Springfield; in 1841 Lincoln joined in partnership with Stephen T. Logan; and in 1845 Lincoln formed his third and last law practice, this time with William H. Herndon. After Lincoln and Mary Todd married on November 4, 1842, the family interest in politics doubled. Family size increased also: Robert Todd Lincoln was born on August 1, 1843, and Edward Baker Lincoln on March 10, 1846. The young lawyer was riding the fast current in midstream.

On August 3, 1846, the people of the Seventh Congressional District of Illinois elected thirty-seven year-old Abraham Lincoln to the United States House of Representatives. Lincoln, the Whig candidate, captured 56 percent of the vote, defeating Democrat Peter Cartwright and Elihu Walcott of the Liberty Party, 6,340 votes to 4,829 and 249 votes, respectively. Lincoln was elected to the Thirtieth Congress, which began on December 6, 1847, sixteen months after his election.

Lincoln filled this time practicing law and politics. Improvements to rivers and harbors were a central theme of the Whig Party and were essential to Lincoln's vision

Abraham Lincoln was about thirty-eight years old in this daguerreotype taken in 1846–47, possibly by Nicholas H. Shepherd of Springfield, Illinois. Courtesy of the Library of Congress.

This daguerreotype of Mary Todd Lincoln, 1846–47, was taken at the same time as that of her husband. She is about twenty-eight years old and soon to travel to Washington, D.C. Courtesy of the Library of Congress.

of developing the United States economically, Illinois in particular. When Democratic President James K. Polk vetoed a Whig-sponsored internal improvements bill, outraged Whig politicians organized the Chicago River and Harbor Convention in protest. Lincoln purchased railroad stock on May 20, 1847, and thereby qualified to be a convention delegate. Horace Greeley, editor of the *New York Tribune* attended, as did politician Thurlow Weed, editor of an Albany, New York, newspaper. Lincoln spent two days at the convention and delivered an address on July 6, rebutting a speech made by a moderate New York delegate.

On October 25, 1847, Lincoln, his wife, and their two sons left Springfield and, journeying by stagecoach, ferry, steamboat, and train, traveled the 800 miles to Lexington, Kentucky, in about a week. They arrived at Mary Todd Lincoln's parents' home in Lexington around November 2, 1847. Their journey brought troubled memories to Lincoln. As he wrote to his friend Joshua Speed years later: "In 1841 you and I had together a tedious low-water trip, on a Steam Boat from Louisville to St. Louis. You may remember, as I well do, that from Louisville to the mouth of the Ohio there were, on board, ten or a dozen slaves, shackled together with irons. That sight was a continual torment to me; and I see something like it every time I touch the Ohio, or any other slave-border."

In 1848 Charles Fontayne and William S. Porter photographed an eight-daguerreotype panorama of the Cincinnati riverfront, looking across the river from Newport, Kentucky. This view is plate 3 in the panorama that contains the earliest known photographs of American steamboats. The side-wheeler Brooklyn advertises its route from Pittsburgh to St. Louis, while riverfront businesses cater to steamboat traffic. From the Collection of the Public Library of Cincinnati and Hamilton County.

On November 25, after spending three weeks with the Robert Todd family, the Lincolns continued on to Washington. They traveled by stagecoach to Maysville, Kentucky, where they boarded a steamboat and traveled northeast, up the Ohio River. They passed Wheeling, Virginia, and entered Pennsylvania for the first time, bound for Pittsburgh. (See Appendix A. This account of their journey from Lexington to Washington, D.C., is based on circumstantial evidence.)

What was steamboat travel on the Ohio River like for the Lincoln family in 1847? Probably it was very much like what Charles Dickens experienced in his voyage on the Ohio River from Pittsburgh to St. Louis. Dickens published his account in 1842.

In the first place, they have no mast, cordage, tackle, rigging, or other such boat-like gear; nor have they anything in their shape at all calculated to remind one of a boat's head, stern, sides, or keel. Except that they are in the water, and display a couple of paddle-boxes, they might be intended, for anything that appears to the contrary, to perform some unknown service, high and dry, upon a mountain top. There is no visible deck, even: nothing but a long, black, ugly roof, covered with burnt-out feathery sparks; above which tower two iron chimneys, and a hoarse escape-valve, and a glass

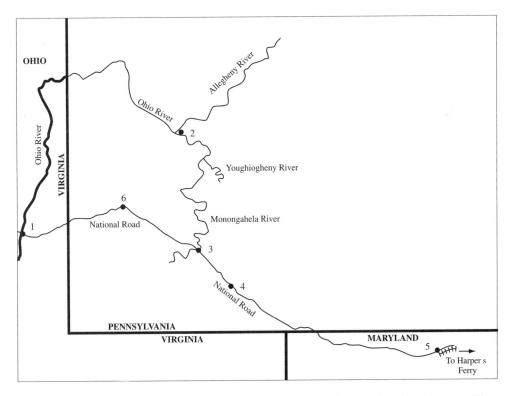

SOUTHWESTERN PENNSYLVANIA, 1847. (1) *Wheeling, Virginia* (2) *Pittsburgh* (3)*Brownsville* (4) *Uniontown* (5) *Cumberland, Maryland* (6) *Washington*

steerage-house. Then, in order as the eye descends towards the water, are the sides, and doors, and windows of the state-rooms, jumbled as oddly together as though they formed a small street, built by the varying tastes of a dozen men: the whole is supported on beams and pillars resting on a dirty barge, but a few inches above the water's edge: and in the narrow space between this upper structure and this barge's deck, are the furnace fires and machinery, open at the sides to every wind that blows, and every storm of rain it drives along its path.

Travel by steamboat in the first half of the nineteenth century was not completely safe. From 1807, when scheduled commercial steamboat navigation appeared in the United States, until 1853 at least 7,013 people died in accidents.

Terrible Steamboat Accident—Burning of the *Clarksville*—Twenty Lives Lost! . . . The steamboat, *Clarksville*, running between New Orleans and Memphis, was wholly destroyed by fire on the evening of Saturday the 25th ult. [May 1848]. . . . In a very few minutes after the discovery of the fire, the boat struck the ground, when any of the passengers might have gotten on the forecastle, and thence reached the Island. As soon as she struck, the flames, hitherto driven back by the current of air, burst through up into the cabin. . . . One of the boilers burst soon after she struck; and, subsequently, three kegs of powder in the hold exploded.

The most common type of fatal accident was a boiler explosion. The boiler pressure gauge was not invented until the 1850s. Before its invention, men stoking the boiler had no idea how much pressure they were building, nor did they know the amount of pressure a boiler would tolerate. Boilers exploded, simultaneously blowing boiling water onto those nearby and sending fire that had been beneath the steam boiler into many sections of the wooden craft. As Dickens wrote: "Passing one of these boats at night, and seeing the great body of fire, exposed as I have just described, that rages and roars beneath the frail pile of painted wood: the machinery, not warded off or guarded in any way, but doing its work in the midst of the crowd of idlers and emigrants and children, who throng the lower deck; under the management, too, of reckless men whose acquaintance with its mysteries may have been of six months' standing: one feels directly that the wonder is, not that there should be so many fatal accidents, but that any journey should be safely made."

Dickens described what he saw as he steamed down the Ohio from Pittsburgh.

A fine broad river always, but in some parts much wider than in others: and then there is usually a green island, covered with trees, dividing it into two streams. Occasionally, we stop for a few minutes, maybe to take in wood, maybe for passengers, at some small town or village (I ought to say city, every place is a city here); but the banks are for the most part deep solitudes, overgrown with trees, which, hereabouts, are already in leaf and very green. For miles, and miles, and miles, these solitudes are unbroken by any sign of human life or trace of human footstep; nor is anything seen to move about them but the bluejay, whose colour is so bright, and yet so delicate, that it looks like a flying flower. At lengthened intervals a log cabin, with its little space of cleared land about it, nestles under a rising ground, and sends its thread of blue smoke curling up into the sky. It stands in the corner of the poor field of wheat, which is full of great unsightly stumps, like earthy butchers'-blocks. Sometimes the ground is only just now cleared: the felled trees lying yet upon the soil: and the log-house only this morning begun. As we pass this clearing, the settler leans upon his axe or hammer, and looks wistfully at the people from the world. The children creep out of the temporary hut, which is like a gypsy tent upon the ground, and clap their hands and shout. The dog only glances round at us; and then looks up into his master's face again, as if he were rendered uneasy by any suspension of the common business, and had nothing more to do with pleasurers.

It is likely that Lincoln and his family docked at Pittsburgh and arranged passage to Brownsville. The route up the Monongahela River had been improved only three years earlier, in 1844, by a series of dams and locks. At Brownsville the steamboat route connected with the National Road. Thomas Jefferson signed legislation in 1806 creat-

The river wharf at Pittsburgh, circa 1876, was crowded. According to Louis C. Hunter, in Steamboats on the Western Rivers *(page 53) an average of 265 steamboats arrived at Pittsburgh each month in 1847. Engraving. Courtesy of the Carnegie Library of Pittsburgh.*

ing the United States' first federally funded highway. Known as the National Road, the Cumberland Road, and the National Pike, it was a vital link to the American West. Although it utilized established roads from Baltimore to Cumberland, Maryland, beyond Cumberland it paralleled buffalo trails, Indian trails, and Braddock's Road. Using only hand tools, workmen cleared a sixty-six-foot-wide strip through the wilderness. The actual road surface was a central thirty-two-foot width that was macadamized with stone. The macadam process began by laying large stones to form a base. This was topped with smaller and smaller hand-crushed stone and gravel, until a smooth, hard surface appeared. The section from Cumberland, Maryland, to Uniontown, Pennsylvania, was completed in 1817 at a cost of $9,745 per mile. By 1847 the National Road's western limit neared Indianapolis, Indiana.

After docking at Brownsville, Lincoln would have had to purchase stagecoach tickets from a local agent. Stagecoach fares averaged four cents per mile; and a fare from Brownsville to Cumberland, about seventy-five miles, averaged three dollars. The ticket included payment for all passenger tolls at Searight's, Mt. Washington, and Petersburg tollhouses. Prior to departure, the agent for the stagecoach line gave the driver a trip roster that included the name of each passenger, his destination, the fare paid, and the time of departure. At each stop the driver gave the roster to the local landlord who filled in the time of arrival and departure of each passenger.

The National Road Stage Company and the Good Intent Stage Line operated scheduled passenger service on the National Road in southwestern Pennsylvania. Stagecoaches were brightly colored and had exotic names, such as "Stars and Stripes," "Columbia," "Highlander," and "Ivanhoe." Entry to the coach compartment was often through a front door. Inside there were bench seats along the sides and the rear, three in all, seating nine passengers. A tenth passenger rode up top with the driver. The coach compartment rested on large leather straps that acted crudely to cushion the ride. Regular mail and passengers traveled at an average speed of eight miles per hour, and a good trip from Washington, D.C., to Wheeling took two days and eleven hours. Express runs, made in "gutbusters" and used primarily for important news, such as the declaration of war against Mexico in 1846, could average twelve miles per hour. They covered the distance from Washington, D.C., to Wheeling in twenty-four hours.

Once underway, stagecoach passengers found the National Road to be a very busy thoroughfare. Families migrated west over the National Road, and peddlers hawked their wares—better to buy now than to do without in the wilderness. After nightfall travelers' campfires along the road lit a ribbon of life that was visible for miles. Conestoga wagons were everywhere, moving finished goods west, furs and agricultural goods east. One traveler on the road described seeing twenty-four Conestoga wagons in his view at one time. In a single year at one of the five Wheeling freight warehouses, 1,081 wagons unloaded shipments averaging 3,500 pounds each.

Stagecoach passengers ate and slept at one of the many taverns that sprang up to accommodate the traffic. Mt. Washington Tavern, Brownfield House, and the United States Hotel were a few of the many nineteenth-century National Road inns that provided food, drink, and lodging. Each had its own special quality and was linked with a particular stagecoach line. Tavern food was always home-cooked and tasted great. Andrew Jackson loved the cured hams, and Henry Clay's favorite was buckwheat cakes.

Stagecoach travel, like steamboat travel, was not hazard free. On his trip down the Ohio, Charles Dickens met two newlyweds on their way to live in the West: "They were both overturned in a stage-coach the other day (a bad omen anywhere else, where overturns are not so common), and his head, which bears the marks of a recent wound, is bound up still. She was hurt too, at the same time, and lay insensible for some days; bright as her eyes are, now."

On his arrival in Cumberland, Maryland, Lincoln purchased Baltimore and Ohio Railroad tickets to Washington, D.C. The two-hundred-mile train journey was an adventure in 1847. An Englishman described his journey from Cumberland, Maryland, to Harpers Ferry, Virginia, in 1854.

> I arrived in Cumberland on Saturday and proposed proceeding . . . on Monday morning at eight o'clock and was in readiness with fourteen other passengers at the proper time. . . . Ten o'clock arrived but no train; accordingly three cars and a baggage-car were prepared for our conveyance. The first car was set apart for the colored portion of our party, consisting of three women and two men slaves. The second car was allotted to gentlemen and the third and last to ladies. . . . As soon as we had taken our seats the bell rang and we dashed off. In a few minutes the conductor . . . informed us that we were very late in starting and that it would take smart work to make up the time. To effect this required additional speed, which I had every reason to believe could not be maintained without serious danger. . . . The line after leaving Cumberland follows the windings of the Potomac, describing sharp curves. Round these the engine darted with rocket-like impetuosity, the car in which we were seated swaying in a manner rendering it necessary to hold on. . . . With blind if not willful recklessness it [the train's speed] was maintained and at length . . . a terrific crash and a series of dislocatory heavings and collisions, terminating in deathlike silence and the overthrow of the car which we occupied, gave certain evidence that we had gone off the line. I have no distinct recollection of how I crawled out of the car, for I was half stunned. . . . With the exception of about half the middle car and engine there was scarcely a portion of the train that was not more or less broken. The wheels were whirled to great distances and the rails for the length of many yards either wholly wrenched from the sleepers or converted into snakeheads. . . . After a detention of five hours, we resumed our journey and fortunately reached Harper's Ferry without further accident.

The convention described in this 1854 account of a separate rail car for women (and their companion travelers) was popular in the South. After leaving Cumberland, Maryland, the Lincoln family probably traveled together in the women's car as the train

The intersection of "Market Street at Eighth—North Side, 1846" was three blocks northeast of the Chinese Museum Building and was typical of the Philadelphia Lincoln visited in 1848. Note the sentry box with gas lamp at the corner. Courtesy of the Print and Picture Collection, the Free Library of Philadelphia.

moved along at about twelve miles per hour. On the evening of December 2, 1847, after traveling for a week, Lincoln and family arrived in Washington, D.C.

Although Lincoln arrived in Washington as a Henry Clay supporter, he gradually became convinced that Clay could not win the 1848 presidential election. As the 1848 Whig National Convention neared, Congressman Lincoln threw his support to a Louisiana planter and Mexican War hero, Zachary Taylor. Lincoln joined a congressional Taylor club called the "Young Indians," and these young men resolved to improve Taylor's chances of winning the Whig presidential nomination. The club was organized by Alexander Stephens of Georgia and included Stephens, Robert Toombs of Georgia, Truman Smith of Connecticut, Lincoln of Illinois, and three Virginians— William Preston, Thomas Flournay, and John Pendleton. The group wrote letters, lobbied colleagues, and gave campaign speeches in the Washington area.

The Chinese Museum Building, on the northeast corner of Ninth and Sansom Streets, Philadelphia, hosted the June 1848 Whig National Convention. The building originally exhibited a local merchant's Chinese artifacts. Engraving. Courtesy of the Print and Picture Collection, the Free Library of Philadelphia.

The Whig National Convention began at noon on Wednesday, June 7, 1848, on the second floor of Philadelphia's Chinese Museum Building on the northeast corner of Ninth and George (Sansom) Streets. Lincoln was not an official delegate, but as he later wrote, "In my anxiety for the result, I was led to attend the Philadelphia convention." He was not the only nondelegate to attempt to influence the convention's outcome. Thurlow Weed, Horace Greeley, John Crittenden, Schuyler Colfax, and Millard Fillmore were also there. During the convention, someone introduced Lincoln to Pennsylvania's Thaddeus Stevens as the lone Whig star of Illinois. Lincoln also saw Mary Lincoln's acquaintance, Thomas W. Newton from Arkansas. Lincoln wrote to his wife that Newton "was a sort of Trinity, three in one, having the right, in his own person, to cast the three votes of Arkansas."

On the first ballot, no candidate had a winning majority. Taylor had 111 votes, Henry Clay 97, Winfield Scott 43, and Daniel Webster 22. On Friday, June 9, 1848, Zachary Taylor won the nomination on the fourth ballot with 171 votes. Millard Fillmore of New York was nominated for vice-president. Later that evening the delegates adjourned to Independence Square, a few blocks away on the south side of Independence Hall, for a "ratification meeting." There were speeches from three stands "and a dozen stumps."

> The main stand was erected immediately over the entrance into the Hall. It was about 20 feet high, and decorated with a profusion of the stars and stripes. In front was an eagle bearing in his beak the names of the nominees. Above all, and against the wall of the building, was a large transparency containing the following, "Democratic Whig Nomination—Zachary Taylor for President—Millard Fillmore for Vice President of the United States." Besides all this, there were 18 large glass lamps, appropriately arranged around the stand. . . . In different parts of the yard, lamps fastened in strips of wood, were strung from tree to tree, and thus presented a lively, interesting and agreeable appearance. There were two other stands erected in various sections of the yard, all of which gemmed with brilliant lights, banners, flags, etc. etc., presented a most splendid appearance. It is now half-past eight o'clock, the yard is full—every street presents a moving mass of human beings—music comes from every quarter—tremendous cheers from the State House yard rend the air, and fairly strip the foliage from the trees—cannon are fired at intervals from the main staging—the boys following suit, are firing off crackers a la Fourth of July—cheer after cheer ascends for old Rough and Ready, Palo Alto, Buena Vista.

On Saturday, June 10, Lincoln and three of his colleagues from the House of Representatives, William Haskell of Tennessee, Edward Cabell of Florida, and John Houston of Delaware left Philadelphia and rode to Wilmington, Delaware, to address an evening Whig Party ratification meeting. Lincoln wrote to his wife that after the meeting, he rode all night (by horseback or train?) and arrived in Washington, D.C., on Sunday morning.

Lincoln continued to write letters on behalf of candidate Taylor:

Hon: Thaddeus Stevens
Washington,

Dear Sir: Sept. 3. 1848

You may possibly remember seeing me at the Philadelphia Convention—introduced
to you as the lone whig star of Illinois. Since the adjournment, I have remained here,
so long, in the Whig document room. I am now about to start for home; and I desire
the undisguised opinion of some experienced and sagacious Pennsylvania politician,
as to how the vote of that state, for governor, and president, is likely to go. In casting
about for such a man, I have settled upon you; and I shall be much obliged if you will
write me at Springfield, Illinois. The news we are receiving here now, by letters from
all quarters is steadily on the rise; we have none lately of a discouraging character.
This is the sum, without giving particulars. Yours truly

A Lincoln

*"The Assassination of the Sage of Ashland" depicts Daniel Webster, editor James W. Webb, former
New York mayor William V. Brady, David Wilmot, John J. Crittenden, and Thurlow Weed
knifing Henry Clay in the back at his Kentucky home. The implication is that this symbolically
occurred at Philadelphia's Whig Convention when Clay lost the nomination to Taylor. Engraving, 1848. Courtesy of the Library of Congress.*

On or about September 9, 1848, after the first session of the Thirtieth Congress ended, Lincoln and his family left Washington by train to campaign for Zachary Taylor in New England. They entered Pennsylvania while traveling from Baltimore on the Philadelphia, Wilmington, and Baltimore Railroad. Two miles south of Philadelphia, the locomotive was unhitched, and a team of horses pulled the railcars over the Schuylkill River, through the covered bridge at Gray's Ferry, and proceeded to the railroad station on the southeastern corner of Eleventh and Market Streets. From there, the Lincolns traveled by public conveyance the two and one-half miles to the Philadelphia and Trenton Railroad's Kensington Station. At this depot they boarded a train to Trenton, New Jersey, and points north.

By September 12 Lincoln and his family were in Massachusetts, and the young congressman met New York's William H. Seward. After Lincoln had done his best for Zachary Taylor, he went home by way of Albany, New York. While there he talked with Thurlow Weed who took him to meet Millard Fillmore, comptroller for New York State and now the Whig vice-presidential candidate.

During the visit, Weed might have given Congressman Lincoln information on how to get to Chicago by way of Buffalo, Niagara Falls, and the lake steamships. Or perhaps Lincoln heard about the route during the Chicago River and Harbor Conven-

Zachary Taylor, twelfth president of the United States, won the Whig nomination for president in June 1848, won the presidency on November 7, 1848, and died in office on July 9, 1850. Photographs, MG-264, I.U. International Political Memorabilia Collection, Pennsylvania State Archives.

tion in 1847 or at the 1848 Whig National Convention in Philadelphia. However he learned of the lake excursion to Chicago, he and his family traveled 325 miles from Albany to Buffalo by rail and booked passage home by lake steamer. The voyage between Buffalo and Chicago lasted five or six days and covered 1,013 or more miles, depending on the number of stops. Many companies regularly scheduled the trip; and in the year prior to 1848, ninety-eight steamers and thirty-five propeller steamships operated on the Great Lakes.

After visiting Niagara Falls, the Lincoln family boarded the lake steamship *Globe* on October 1, 1848, to travel from Buffalo to Chicago. The *Globe* was a propeller steamship of average displacement—319 tons. At some point during their passage on Lake Erie, the Lincolns traveled along Pennsylvania's lakefront, although perhaps at a distance of three to six miles off shore. The *Globe* did not stop in Erie. The Lincolns' lake voyage was probably very much like the one taken by Thurlow Weed in 1847 on his way to the Chicago River and Harbor Convention. Weed traveled on the 1,140-ton steamer *Empire* and sent dispatches back to his newspaper in New York, the *Albany Evening Journal.*

> July 2—At 8:30 o'clock this morning we came alongside a dock upon the Canada shore, to wood. An hundred-and-six cords of wood (hickory, maple, beech and oak) were seized by the deck hands, steerage passengers, etc., and soon transferred from the dock to the boat, and at 12 o'clock we were under way. I learn that the *Empire,* in a single trip, consumes over 600 cords of wood. This requires for each trip the clearing up of over ten acres of well-wooded land. The wood which was taken on board today cost $1 per cord. . . . July 4—This is the 71st anniversary of the Declaration of American Independence. Its sun dawns upon us in the middle of Lake Michigan, "the blue sky above and the blue waters beneath us," but no land in sight. It is a bright day. We are steaming onward rapidly, headed for Milwaukee, yet some seventy miles distant. . . . Though nearly three hundred passengers draw around the table, the fare continues as abundant and extensive as it could be if Fulton Market was at hand every morning.

By October 5, 1848, Lincoln was in Chicago. He spent the next two months in Springfield with his family.

On November 7, 1848, Zachary Taylor won the presidential election with 1,360,099 popular votes and 56 percent of the electoral votes. His democratic opponent Lewis Cass received 1,220,544 votes. At the end of November, Lincoln traveled back to Washington, D.C., to attend the second session of the Thirtieth Congress. He was late in arriving, but he needn't have hurried. A controversy was stirring, and Horace Greeley was the brewmaster.

Congressional pay in the 1840s was meager. It was common practice for a congressman to lawfully augment his pay by collecting round-trip mileage reimbursement between his hometown and Washington. The longer the route the better. This practice was the subject of an exposé in the *New York Tribune* on December 22, 1848. Horace

Greeley wrote that the routes taken were "exceedingly crooked even for a politician." The *Tribune* printed the mileage claimed by each of the more than 290 members of Congress, and Abraham Lincoln's name was on the list. Lincoln charged the government $1,300.80 for an 1847–48 round-trip distance of 3,252 miles (1,626 miles each way). The *Tribune* noted that the shortest postal route from Springfield to Washington, D.C., was 780 miles each way; and it calculated Lincoln's excess charge to be $676.80. After Greeley's article, Congress debated the issue and established a committee to make recommendations, but the Thirtieth Congress did not change the law. In spring 1849 Lincoln traveled back to Illinois after his term of office in the House ended. Once again Lincoln's request for reimbursement showed 1,626 miles traveled each way, to Washington in December 1848 and home again in March 1849. This controversy publicized the number of miles that Lincoln traveled to Congress; and this, along with the known duration of his trips and the known average speeds of stagecoaches, steamboats, and railroads, established his route through Pennsylvania.

Abraham Lincoln made other trips east too, other than for sessions of Congress. In June 1849, he traveled from Springfield to Washington to lobby for appointment to the patronage post of commissioner of the General Land Office. He went by stagecoach at least as far as Indianapolis. His route from there is unclear; but geographically speaking, an eastbound stagecoach traveler going from Indianapolis to Washington had a direct route over the National Road to the rail head at Cumberland, Maryland. Lincoln did not get the appointment.

On July 21, 1857, Lincoln was in Springfield. On July 24, 1857, he and wife Mary registered as guests at the Cataract House in Niagara Falls, New York. To travel from Springfield to Niagara Falls in four days, he must have gone by rail; and the only reasonable train route was through Erie, Pennsylvania. The Lincolns visited Niagara Falls, Canada, and New York and probably returned home the same way. By August 5, 1857, he was back in Springfield.

Abraham Lincoln was elected to Congress in 1846, and he was struck blind, but not in a way that he knew or understood. The next fourteen years, from 1846 to 1860, witnessed his transition from a man of regional influence to a leader of national import. During the same fourteen-year period Lincoln became acquainted with Pennsylvania. Unnoticed, he traveled Pennsylvania's roads, rails, rivers, and Great Lake. With the coming of 1860, Lincoln began to play a major role in the lives of Pennsylvanians. Never again would he be inconspicuous.

4

"Dare to Do Our Duty"

Lincoln and the Pennsylvania Politicians

Let us have faith that right makes might, and in that faith, let us, to the end, dare to do our duty as we understand it.

—Abraham Lincoln, address at Cooper Institute, New York City, February 27, 1860

Late in 1859 James A. Briggs, Salmon P. Chase's eastern presidential campaign manager, invited Lincoln to speak at Henry Ward Beecher's Plymouth Church in Brooklyn. Briggs offered $200 and expenses. Lincoln believed that this was an attempt by Chase's organization to divert support away from New Yorker William H. Seward and his presidential bid. In November Lincoln agreed to "make a political speech of it." Lincoln's suspicions were reinforced when the Young Men's Republican Club of New York City assumed sponsorship and moved the event to the Cooper Institute. Horace Greeley and William Cullen Bryant, both anti-Seward men, were club advisers.

Abraham Lincoln departed Springfield on February 23, 1860, and traveled by train to New York City and the Cooper Institute. As he traveled through Pennsylvania, no doubt he was aware of that state's importance to any would-be presidential candidate. The Commonwealth was the second-most populous state in the Union, and its twenty-seven electoral votes were highly prized. In 1856, Pennsylvania went to favorite son Democrat James Buchanan who rolled up 230,686 votes in the state to Republican John C. Frémont's 147,286. Republicans lost the national election but felt they could have won had a swing state like Pennsylvania gone their way. One year later the party's David Wilmot lost the gubernatorial election. In 1860 Pennsylvania had a Democratic governor, but the state's Republican Party had gained remarkable strength in only six years. Change was in the air.

Pennsylvania was somewhat different from Lincoln's home state. In 1860 it was more populous, more urbanized, and more industrialized than Illinois. Railroads were a catalyst in transforming Pennsylvania. Railroad construction stimulated the state's lumber and mining industries, and completed railroads carried her manufactured goods throughout the nation and brought western agricultural products to compete with those from less efficient eastern farms. These forces encouraged migration into cities and towns.

This daguerreotype of Abraham Lincoln, age fifty-one years, was taken May 20, 1860, in Springfield, Illinois, two days after Lincoln's nomination. Joseph H. Barrett, Cincinnati Gazette *editor and 1860 Republican Convention delegate, requested this image in order to publicize Lincoln's candidacy. Courtesy of the author.*

In 1860 the population of Pennsylvania was 2,906,215, with 40 percent under the age of sixteen. More than 30 percent lived in urban environments. Of the 430,505 Pennsylvanians born outside of the United States, more than 200,000 had been born in Ireland, and slightly more than 138,000 had been born in Germany. The state's population of 56,849 African Americans (40 percent of whom lived in Philadelphia) was fifteenth in the nation. Philadelphia's 585,529 inhabitants (29 percent were foreign-born) ranked her as the second largest American city. Pittsburgh and Allegheny City together (across the river from each other) had 77,919 inhabitants.

Pennsylvania had 151,145 farm workers, but almost 38 percent of her labor force worked in construction, manufacturing, mining, or transportation. She supplied almost 75 percent of the nation's coal, especially anthracite coal, and employed 13,164 ironworkers at 177 industrial sites. Her manufacture of men's clothing, leather goods, iron products, and machinery was significantly ahead of Illinois's output.

The population of Illinois had doubled in the preceding ten years, to 1,711,951, and included 7,628 African Americans. Her largest city, Chicago, was home to 109,260 people, 50 percent of whom were foreign-born. Illinois was an agricultural state. Her corn production was five times that of Pennsylvania, and her wheat production was double that of the Keystone State. Only in production of rye, oats, potatoes, and butter did Pennsylvania significantly outpace Illinois.

Perhaps Lincoln wondered how Pennsylvania would affect his future and that of the Republican Party as his train traveled across the state. When he reached Philadelphia on February 25, someone gave him the cards of Simon Cameron and David Wilmot, two of the state's foremost Republicans. Both men were staying at the Girard House Hotel at 825–27 Chestnut Street. Etiquette of the day required some type of response, either a social call or a note. Lincoln tried to visit, but he had very little time between trains and also had to change stations. He detoured to the Girard House but found neither man in his room. He left quickly, traveled several miles through city streets to the Philadelphia and Trenton Railroad's Kensington Station, and was just in time to catch his train for New York. Most probably, Lincoln was very disappointed that he had missed an opportunity to meet with the two men. He wrote each a note:

Hon: Simon Cameron: New-York.
Dear Sir   Feb. 26. 1860

    I write this to say the card of yourself, and Hon. David Wilmot, was handed me yesterday at Philadelphia, just as I was leaving for this city [New York]. I barely had time to step over to the Girard, where I learned that you and he were not at your rooms. I regret that being so near, we did not meet; but hope we may yet meet before a great while.

    Will you please forward the enclosed to Mr. Wilmot, as I do not remember his address?
Yours truly
A. Lincoln.

On Monday evening, February 27, 1860, Lincoln addressed 1,500 people gathered at the Cooper Institute. Lincoln emphatically declared that the Founding Fathers had marked slavery for extinction in the United States, and he supported his case with examples of laws that they had enacted. The Republican Party, he reasoned, was simply furthering the work of the forefathers. He called for all clear-thinking men to resist Southern threats, to "dare to do our duty." The speech was a stunning success, and the crowd and the nation exploded. *New York Tribune* reporter Noah Brooks said, "He's the greatest man since St. Paul." Many daily newspapers printed the text in its entirety. The *New York Tribune,* the *Illinois State Journal,* and others published the speech as a pamphlet, and the Young Men's Republican Club of New York City and the Republican Executive Congressional Committee in Washington, D.C., published it as campaign literature.

Lincoln next traveled to New England, ostensibly to visit his son Robert at boarding school in Exeter, New Hampshire. Along the way he scheduled political appear-

The new Girard House Hotel, 825–27 Chestnut Street, Philadelphia, was featured in a Boston publication in February 1852. Gleason's Pictorial *reported, "The halls of entrance, both public and private, are large and elegant in design; the vestibule and other doors enriched with gorgeous stained glass; the walls highly ornamented, and the floors laid in encaustic tile-work." Courtesy of the Print and Picture Collection, the Free Library of Philadelphia.*

ances almost every night. On February 28 he spoke in Providence, Rhode Island. On February 29 he arrived at Exeter. His tour became exhausting. He spoke in Manchester, Concord, Hartford, and New Haven but declined offers to speak in Pittsburgh and Philadelphia. On March 12 he left New York City on the Erie Railroad to return to Illinois. The Erie line, sometimes known as the New York and Erie, carried him through southern New York to Lake Erie at Dunkirk, New York. From there, Lincoln's train route paralleled the lakefront and passed through Erie, Pennsylvania. He arrived in Springfield on the Great Western Railroad on March 14, 1860, and the next day deposited $604 in his bank account.

Lincoln's Cooper Institute speech was a political manifesto for the Republican Party and the Union. But his visit to the East that February and March had an additional purpose: it was a campaign trip designed to test the political waters and to whip up support for his presidential bid. He fashioned his speech and his opportunity with great care. Once back in Illinois, Lincoln focused on the upcoming Republican National Convention.

The Republican Party rose out of the turmoil of the 1850s. Two major wounds had festered in the American political soul since the birth of the Republic. The Founding Fathers had left the issues of slavery and states' rights (state versus national sovereignty) unresolved. During the nation's early years, opinions diverged and pride hardened hearts. Flames of conflict erupted here and there, but somehow cooler heads prevented

Thaddeus Stevens, the Great Commoner, wielded power as chairman of the House Ways and Means Committee. His wit was as sharp as his oratory was brilliant. Graphic Material, MG-17, Samuel Bates Papers, Pennsylvania State Archives.

general conflagration. The nation, however, moved inexorably toward a time when a fatal spark would ignite the tinderbox.

The Compromise of 1850 dealt with the issue of slavery in lands acquired from Mexico as a result of the Mexican War of 1846–48. One of its provisions was a fugitive slave law that mandated legal action against any individual who aided a fugitive slave. American resolve for disobeying "unjust" laws stiffened, and travel on the Underground Railroad continued. In September 1851 forty individuals attacked a Maryland slave owner who was in Pennsylvania to recover one of his former slaves. Two months later in a Philadelphia courtroom on the second floor of Independence Hall, Thaddeus Stevens and others successfully defended those involved in the Christiana riot.

Pennsylvania's Thaddeus Stevens was a brilliant, inscrutable, and contentious man who championed the oppressed. He lived twenty-six years of his life in Gettysburg and as a member of the Pennsylvania House of Representatives became known as the savior of the state's free public education law. Lincoln met him at the 1848 Philadelphia Whig National Convention and later corresponded with him. During the years 1849 to 1853 Whig Stevens represented his Lancaster constituency in the U.S. House of

David Wilmot, author of the Wilmot Proviso and twice chairman of the Republican Party's platform committee, finished Simon Cameron's United States senatorial term from 1861 to 1863. After a lithograph by M. H. Traubel in the Century Magazine, *February 1887, page 542. Courtesy of the author.*

Representatives. After 1853 Stevens cast about for a political party more in line with his views. Already a new political party was beginning to form.

In 1854 Congress passed the Kansas-Nebraska Act, written by Illinois Senator Stephen A. Douglas. The act organized the two new territories west of the Mississippi River and north of Missouri and provided for popular sovereignty in deciding whether the territories would be slave or free. In doing so, it violated the Missouri Compromise of 1820 and set the stage for the Supreme Court's Dred Scott decision three years later. Regional war broke out, and Abraham Lincoln's interest in politics was reborn.

Pennsylvania's David Wilmot was between jobs. In 1851 he served his last year in Congress as a Democratic representative from Pennsylvania. Wilmot was famous in political circles as the author of the Wilmot Proviso. In 1846, anticipating the end of the war with Mexico, President James K. Polk requested passage of an appropriations bill authorizing $30,000 for negotiating expenses with Mexico and $2,000,000 to compensate that nation for the loss of any territory that the United States might wish to

Musical Fund Hall, 810 Locust Street, Philadelphia, was the site of the Republican National Convention in June 1856. Comparison of this drawing with the photograph in chapter 10, page 146, reveals that even in 1856 political artists took liberties. Courtesy of the Print and Picture Collection, the Free Library of Philadelphia.

keep. House antislavery members Hannibal Hamlin of Maine, Preston King of New York, and Robert McClelland of Michigan authorized David Wilmot to write a proviso to be attached to the appropriations bill that would prohibit slavery's introduction into any new territory. On August 8, 1846, Wilmot introduced: *"Provided,* That as an express and fundamental condition to the acquisition of any territory from the Republic of Mexico by the United States, by virtue of any treaty that may be negotiated between them, and to the use by the Executive of the moneys herein appropriated, neither slavery nor involuntary servitude shall exist in any part of said territory, except for crime, whereof the party shall first be duly convicted."

The House passed the Wilmot Proviso on February 15, 1847, but it died in the Senate. Thereafter it was reintroduced several times but never again passed the House. Abraham Lincoln, exaggerating somewhat, said that as a member of Congress, he had voted for the Wilmot Proviso about forty times. Actual count was much lower.

In the mid-1850s David Wilmot was one of the driving forces behind the state and national organization of the Republican Party. At the Pennsylvania Republican State Convention in Pittsburgh on September 5, 1855, Wilmot became chairman of the Republican State Committee. He and other state chairmen summoned political leaders to attend a Republican Party national organizing convention at Lafayette Hall in Pittsburgh. The two-day meeting began on Washington's Birthday, February 22, 1856, and was held "for the purpose of perfecting the National Organization." Twenty-four states sent delegations. Riding the political storm, former Whigs, former Democrats, Know-Nothings, Free Soilers, and abolitionists found common ground. The convention established a National Executive Committee, and David Wilmot, as Pennsylvania's state chairman, became a member. The Pittsburgh convention also chose June 17, 1856, as the starting date of the full Republican National Convention in Philadelphia, where the party would adopt a party platform and nominate candidates for president and vice-president.

David Wilmot and Thaddeus Stevens were members of the eighty-one-man Pennsylvania delegation to the first Republican National Convention, held in Musical Fund Hall at 810 Locust Street in Philadelphia on June 17–19, 1856. The *New York Tribune*'s Horace Greeley was there, as was Preston King, allied with David Wilmot since their days together in the House of Representatives. Abraham Lincoln did not attend.

The platform committee chaired by Wilmot produced a document that called for adherence to the principles contained in the Declaration of Independence and the federal Constitution and maintained that all men had a right to "Life, Liberty, and the Pursuit of Happiness." The party proclaimed that Congress had a right and a duty to regulate slavery and polygamy in the territories, and it demanded admission of Kansas to the Union as a free state. Republicans also proposed construction of a transcontinental railroad and supported river and harbor improvements.

Colonel John C. Frémont of California won the Republican presidential nomination. When Pennsylvania's John Allison nominated Abraham Lincoln as a potential vice-presidential candidate, delegates applauded. Someone shouted, "Who is he?" and Allison answered, "An old line Whig, and the prince of good fellows." In a nonbinding canvass of the convention, William L. Dayton received 259 votes, Abraham Lincoln 110 votes, Nathaniel P. Banks 46 votes, David Wilmot 43 votes, and Charles Sumner 35 votes. All thirty-three of Illinois's votes went to Lincoln. When the formal vote was taken, Lincoln received only 23 votes, while Dayton's total was overwhelming. The convention declared the former New Jersey senator its unanimous choice for vice-president. Lincoln's supporters lost but gained valuable convention experience.

In Cincinnati the Democrats nominated Pennsylvania's James Buchanan on the seventeenth ballot. In other cities the Know-Nothings and the Whigs nominated Millard Fillmore. Republican Party strategists immediately began to publish campaign literature that targeted the Democratic nominee. Campaign strategy focused on Buchanan's Southern sympathies, acceptance of slavery, support for the Democratic Party platform, defense of Preston Brooks's attack on Charles Sumner in the House of Representatives, desire to annex Cuba as slave territory, and endorsements by Southern leaders. Nevertheless, in the 1856 presidential election, Buchanan won 174 electoral votes, Frémont 114, and Fillmore 8.

President-elect James Buchanan possessed impressive credentials as a public servant. He had been a three-term Federalist member of the U.S. House of Representatives from

"Presidential Portrait of James Buchanan, the Fifteenth President of the United States" by John C. Buttre (who also engraved Lincoln's image). Buttre's work hung in Buchanan's Wheatland library. Photographs, MG-264, I.U. International Political Memorabilia Collection 1786–1972, Pennsylvania State Archives.

Lancaster, and in 1828 he was elected on the Democratic Party ticket. President Andrew Jackson appointed Buchanan minister to Russia in 1832. In 1834 the Pennsylvania General Assembly elected him to the U.S. Senate. He resigned from the Senate to become secretary of state from 1845 to 1849. In April 1853 President Franklin Pierce appointed him minister to Great Britain.

Although Buchanan was from a Northern state, he was sympathetic to the South. He saw slavery as a property issue rather than as a crime against mankind. "That the Constitution does not confer upon Congress power to interfere with slavery in the States, has been admitted by all parties and confirmed by all judicial decisions ever since the origin of the Federal Government. . . . Hence, it became necessary for the abolitionists, in order to furnish a pretext for their assaults on Southern slavery, to appeal to a law higher than the Constitution." In his legalism Buchanan disdained this appeal to a law higher than the Constitution. Regarding the Fugitive Slave Act he wrote, "Without this law [Fugitive Slave Act] the slaveholder would have had no remedy to enforce his Constitutional right. There would have been no security for his property."

Simon Cameron was a Pennsylvania political boss who was adept at trading favors. After Lincoln's death, he aided Mary Lincoln and later supported her pension bill in the United States Senate. Courtesy of the Library of Congress.

Buchanan wrote further that the Wilmot Proviso, first introduced when he was secretary of state, "was a firebrand recklessly and prematurely cast among the free and slave States, at a moment when a foreign war was raging, in which all were gallantly fighting, side by side, to conquer an honorable peace."

James Buchanan's presidency began on March 4, 1857. Two days later Chief Justice Roger B. Taney handed down the Dred Scott decision. One portion of the decision ruled that African Americans were not citizens of the United States and therefore had no right to sue in federal court. Another section declared that the Constitution granted citizens the right to own property; and thus all congressional laws restricting slavery—viewed by the Court as a property issue—in the territories were unconstitutional.

From August through October 1858, Abraham Lincoln debated Stephen A. Douglas in the Senate race in Illinois. A year later, on October 16, 1859, John Brown attacked the federal armory at Harpers Ferry, Virginia, and after being apprehended and tried, was executed on December 2, 1859. On February 27, 1860, in New York City, Lincoln's Cooper Institute speech roused the nation.

When the Republican National Convention began in Chicago, Illinois, on Wednesday, May 16, 1860, Pennsylvania's delegation was studded with colorful, powerful men. Thaddeus Stevens, a Republican member of the House of Representatives since 1859, was there. Simon Cameron was the state's favorite son. He was a senator from Pennsylvania and also a master at creating, organizing, and exploiting the political party machine.

Andrew Gregg Curtin was not an official delegate but attended as the Republican gubernatorial candidate. He had been secretary of the Commonwealth under Governor James Pollock. In 1855 Curtin had opposed Simon Cameron for the Know-Nothing Party nomination for senator. At the party caucus Cameron received a one-vote majority for the party's nomination—until it was noticed that the votes added to a total of one vote more than the number of electors present. More than twenty-five caucus members left in protest; and on the next quickly taken ballot, Cameron won by a large majority. Because of this perceived theft of the nomination, Curtin and Cameron became lifelong enemies.

Republican Party platform and credentials issues filled the first two days of the national convention, delaying the first ballot for president until Friday. The party's platform, written by David Wilmot's committee, affirmed support for the principles set forth in the Declaration of Independence and the Constitution and declared that the normal condition of the United States was freedom. Republicans denounced disunion and the perceived governmental policies that elevated sectional interests above national priorities. The party attacked the Dred Scott decision; and it called for admission of Kansas as a free state, adjustment of taxes, passage of a Homestead Act, passage of significant appropriations for rivers and harbors, and a transcontinental railroad.

Various factions used the convention's first two days to maneuver for votes. New York's William Seward was the front-runner. Pennsylvania's ninety-five-man delegation had fifty-four votes. Except for a pledge to vote for favorite son Simon Cameron on the first ballot, Pennsylvania delegates were divided as to whom they should support. Nondelegate

Andrew Gregg Curtin was the two-term Republican war governor of Pennsylvania. Curtin's father owned an iron furnace near Bellefonte, and his grandfather was a former United States senator. Photo Album, MG-218, General Photo Collection, Pennsylvania State Archives.

Andrew Curtin felt strongly that a Seward nomination would doom his own chances in the October election because Seward had alienated many Know-Nothing Party members, and Curtin needed their votes to win. The gubernatorial candidate and his followers gradually settled on Lincoln as their choice. Cameron's supporters were said to have made a deal in the early morning hours of Friday, May 18. Allegedly Lincoln campaign managers David Davis and Leonard Swett met with a Cameron representative and agreed upon a cabinet post for Cameron in return for Pennsylvania's votes after the first ballot. If true, Lincoln was not aware of the deal at the time.

On the first ballot, Seward received 173 ½ votes, Lincoln 102, Cameron 50 ½, Chase 49, and Edward Bates 48 votes. On the second ballot, Seward received 184 ½ votes and Lincoln 181. Pennsylvania gave 48 votes to Lincoln. On the third ballot, Seward received 180 votes and Lincoln 231 ½. Fifty-two of Lincoln's votes were from Pennsylvania. The number of votes necessary to nominate was 233. Immediately after the third ballot, many delegates requested to change their votes to Lincoln, and his final total became 354. The election was declared unanimous. David Wilmot later wrote to Simon Cameron, "It was perfectly clear to every man, that your friends, by their votes on the 2nd ballot, nominated him [Lincoln]."

In the presidential election of 1860, Lincoln and the Republican Party ran against Stephen Douglas of Illinois and the Northern Democrats, John C. Breckinridge of Kentucky and the Southern Democrats, and John Bell of Tennessee and the Constitutional Union Party. Given their experience in 1856, Republican insiders felt that Pennsylvania was a key state, and they were watching closely when, on October 9, 1860, Curtin defeated Democrat Henry O. Foster for the governor's seat by 32,000 votes. This augured well for a Republican national victory. On November 6, 1860, Lincoln carried Pennsylvania easily with 268,036 votes—almost 60,000 votes more than the combined total of his opponents. Lincoln went on to win the national election with 1,866,452 popular votes and 59.41 percent of the electoral vote.

To the last days of his presidency, Buchanan attempted to preserve the Union through moderation and compromise, appealing to reason and constitutional authority. Many Republicans despised his policies of appeasement and deference to sectional interests and felt that his administration worsened Lincoln's predicament when he took office in March 1861. One individual heard Lincoln say that Buchanan was "giving away the case," a reference to an attorney who lost the verdict because of his ill-considered and unnecessary disclosures during a trial. At the end, neither abolitionists nor secessionists saw Buchanan as friend.

In his visits to the Keystone State Lincoln encountered not only her land but also her people. Pennsylvania's politicians, as a group, played a significant role in Lincoln's life from 1860 to 1865. Such men as Republicans Simon Cameron, David Wilmot, Thaddeus Stevens, and Andrew Gregg Curtin, and Democrat James Buchanan dominated Pennsylvania's political scene. Pennsylvania Republicans and the political forces that they marshaled were influential in nominating Lincoln at the Republican National Convention of 1860 and were crucial in electing him to the presidency later that year. The president-elect's inauguration was four months away.

5

"To See and Be Seen"

The Inaugural Train

I come before you to see and be seen and, as regards the ladies, I have the best of the bargain; but, as to the gentlemen, I cannot say as much.

—Abraham Lincoln, Remarks, Lancaster, Pennsylvania, February 22, 1861

After his election as president of the United States on November 6, 1860, Lincoln began preparations for his trip to Washington, D.C., and his inauguration. The president-elect decided to turn the journey into a grand railroad tour of Northern cities. Lincoln wanted to cement the people's loyalty to the Union and to himself. Those along the way wanted a first glimpse of the new leader, an opportunity to see the man on whom they placed their hopes. The Inaugural Train would be the first of its kind, and in concept, it was exceptional.

Lincoln boarded the train at the Great Western Railroad depot in Springfield, Illinois, at 8 A.M. on February 11, 1861. He spoke from the train's rear platform.

My friends—No one, not in my situation, can appreciate my feeling of sadness at this parting. To this place, and the kindness of these people, I owe every thing. Here I have lived a quarter of a century, and have passed from a young to an old man. Here my children have been born, and one is buried. I now leave, not knowing when, or whether ever, I may return, with a task before me greater than that which rested upon Washington. Without the assistance of that Divine Being, who ever attended him, I cannot succeed. With that assistance I cannot fail. Trusting in Him, who can go with me, and remain with you and be every where for good, let us confidently hope that all will yet be well. To His care commending you, as I hope in your prayers you will commend me, I bid you an affectionate farewell.

Lincoln traveled east—often changing railroad lines, often giving and listening to speeches, always with immense numbers of people crowding, pushing, shaking hands. At 5 P.M. on the eleventh he arrived in Indianapolis. Mary Lincoln joined him there. The next day was his fifty-second birthday, and he arrived in Cincinnati at 3 P.M.

On February 13, 1861, while Lincoln traveled on, the American constitutional process played out its own, different drama in Washington. Amid rumors of coup d'états, assassination, secession, and other intrigues, Congress quietly but officially counted the presidential electoral votes, state by state. A strong police force was on duty in the House gallery and throughout the Capitol as the votes were counted in the House of Representatives. As members of the House and Senate watched, Vice President John C. Breckinridge announced that Abraham Lincoln of Illinois was duly elected President of the United States for a four-year term beginning March 4, 1861; and that Hannibal Hamlin of Maine was elected Vice President of the United States for the same term. At 2 P.M. Lincoln arrived in Columbus, Ohio.

At 8 A.M. the next morning, Valentine's Day, Lincoln left Columbus. His destination was Pittsburgh. In Steubenville, Ohio, Lincoln met a select committee from Allegheny City, Pennsylvania, that had arrived by train to escort him to their city. Across the Ohio River from Steubenville lay Virginia, but the Inaugural Train would not pass through that state. After visiting Steubenville and Wellsville on the western bank of

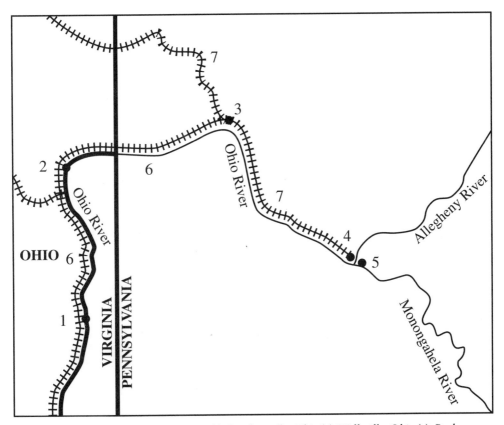

SOUTHWESTERN PENNSYLVANIA, 1861. (1) *Steubenville, Ohio* (2) *Wellsville, Ohio* (3) *Rochester* (4) *Allegheny City* (5) *Pittsburgh* (6) *Cleveland and Pittsburgh Railroad* (7) *Pittsburgh, Fort Wayne, and Chicago Railroad*

the Ohio, the Inaugural Train entered Pennsylvania for the first time. It traveled on the Cleveland and Pittsburgh Railroad.

Accompanying Lincoln were his wife Mary Todd Lincoln, seventeen-year-old Robert Todd Lincoln, thirteen-year-old William Wallace Lincoln, and seven-year-old Tad Lincoln. His brother-in-law, Dr. William S. Wallace, who traveled with them, was also the family physician. John Nicolay and John Hay were Lincoln's private secretaries. Norman B. Judd and Judge David Davis were political allies and friends. Military officers guarding the president-elect included Colonel Edwin V. Sumner, Major David Hunter, Captain George W. Hazzard, and Colonel Elmer E. Ellsworth (who would be killed in May 1861 after tearing down a Confederate flag in Virginia). George C. Latham was Robert Todd Lincoln's college friend. Lockwood M. Todd was Mary Lincoln's cousin. W. S. Wood of Springfield was in charge of the Inaugural Train's day-to-day arrangements. Ward Hill Lamon was friend, former law associate, and personal bodyguard. The Lincolns' paid African-American servant William Johnson rode the train, as did nine reporters for various Northern newspapers and the Western Union Telegraph.

At 4 P.M., the Inaugural Train arrived at Rochester, Pennsylvania. People from throughout the neighboring countryside gathered at the station to see the president-elect. Flags waved; music played; and a cannon announced the train's arrival. Lincoln appeared at the rear platform in response to the crowd's cheers, bowed, and said that he did not have a speech to make.

> A voice in the crowd inquired, "What will you do with the secessionists then?" Turning toward the direction of the voice, Mr. Lincoln replied, "My friend, that is a matter which I have under very grave consideration." Mr. L. continued for some time longer conversing with various persons who approached the car. . . . Mr. Henry Dillon, a very enthusiastic Republican, and withal a most excellent fellow, who stands some six feet three or four inches in his boots, cried out to Mr. Lincoln that he (Dillon) was taller than the president. "Let us see about that," responded Old Abe, reaching forth his hand to Mr. Dillon, who in a moment was by his side; then turning their backs to each other, while prolonged and enthusiastic cheers rent the air, Old Abe demonstrated that he was a little the tallest man in the crowd yet. However, some of Mr. Dillon's friends maintain that the president was not quite as tall as Mr. Dillon. Perhaps this, like many other vexed questions, will remain an unsettled one; but of one thing we are sure, that Mr. Lincoln has not a stronger supporter in the State.

During the heat of the contest one man allegedly said to the other, "Oh, I could lick salt off the top of your head." Witnesses disagreed as to whether the statement came from Lincoln or from Dillon.

The planned twenty-minute stop in Rochester turned into a two-hour delay. The tender car of a freight train had broken an axle and derailed near Freedom, Pennsylvania, blocking the rail line between Rochester and Pittsburgh. An hour passed before the train could be moved from the tracks, and another hour more until the backlog of waiting trains cleared.

While the Inaugural Train waited at Rochester, a welcoming committee from Pittsburgh met with Lincoln. A six-member legislative delegation of the Pennsylvania house and senate also boarded. While the train traveled from Rochester to Allegheny City, the legislators invited Lincoln to visit Harrisburg to address a joint session of the Pennsylvania General Assembly on Washington's Birthday, February 22, 1861. The president-elect accepted.

Throughout the afternoon Allegheny City and Pittsburgh prepared for Lincoln's visit. Flags appeared; shops closed; and people from nearby towns swelled the cities' populations. They and local townspeople lined streets and blocked the depot. At 5 P.M. a line of carriages carrying Pittsburgh's mayor and other dignitaries arrived at the Pittsburgh, Fort Wayne, and Chicago Railroad Station on Federal Street in Allegheny City. Crowds packed Federal Street and St. Clair Street from the depot, across the windswept suspension bridge over the Allegheny River, and on into Pittsburgh. A cannon brought from the United States Arsenal began firing a salute from a nearby hill.

The Inaugural Train arrived and departed from this two-story, brick Pittsburgh, Fort Wayne, and Chicago Railroad Station in Allegheny City. In this April 21, 1902, photograph, Federal Street is in the foreground, and the rail line is on the opposite side of the station. The wooden shed on the right may be the one that sheltered Lincoln's carriage from the rain. Courtesy of the Carnegie Library of Pittsburgh.

The Inaugural Train was scheduled to arrive at the Fort Wayne depot at 5:20 P.M. It did not. At 6 P.M. a light rain began falling and then increased in intensity. The temperature was thirty-nine degrees Fahrenheit, and many chilled, wet people left. Open carriages designated for Lincoln and other dignitaries were brought onto the roofed depot platform to shelter from the rain. Orders were given, and a file of soldiers moved into position on each side of the waiting carriages, with officers to the front and to the rear. Nearby, the cannon's powder supply was exhausted, and its firing stopped.

Finally at 8 P.M. the locomotive engine "Comet," decorated with American flags, pulled three passenger cars and one baggage car into the station in Allegheny City. Lincoln's party occupied the second and the third cars, preferred because they were farther away from the wood-burning engine and its cinders. With the arrival of the train, the Washington Infantry cleared a passageway on the train platform. Lincoln

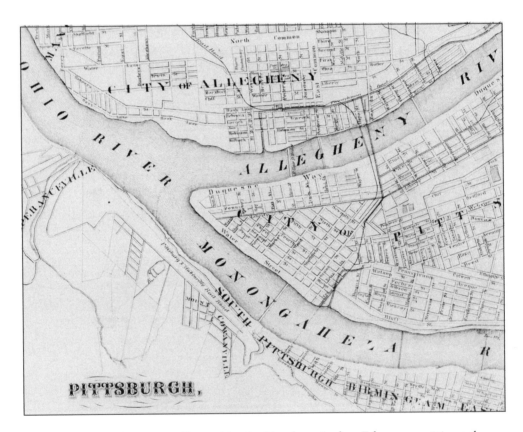

PITTSBURGH AND ALLEGHENY CITY, 1860–61. *Lincoln arrived on February 14, 1861, at the Pittsburgh, Fort Wayne, and Chicago Railroad Station in Allegheny City. He traveled along Federal Street, over the suspension bridge on St. Clair Street, to Market, Fifth, and Smithfield Streets to arrive at the Monongahela House Hotel. On February 15, 1861, he traveled Smithfield, Fourth, Grant, Fifth, Wood, Liberty, Hand, Penn, and St. Clair to Federal Street and the depot for departure. Courtesy of the Carnegie Library of Pittsburgh.*

and Allegheny City Mayor Simon Drum walked from the train to a waiting open carriage drawn by six horses. Even though a cold February rain was pouring down, the crowd erupted in cheers when they saw the president-elect. To cries of "Speech! Speech!" Lincoln stood in the carriage. Illuminated only by lamplight, he spoke briefly of the delay in arrival, of problems with the weather, and of the need to change plans. The crowd cheered "Old Abe" as the procession moved off.

Lincoln traveled in the downpour toward the Monongahela House Hotel at One Smithfield Street in Pittsburgh by way of Federal, St. Clair, Market, Fifth, and Smithfield Streets. The remainder of Lincoln's party followed in other carriages. The Pennsylvania Dragoons, the Jackson Independent Blues, the Washington Infantry, the committees of reception, city council members, a band, and local citizens walked behind. At 9 P.M. they arrived at the Smithfield Street entrance of the Monongahela House. The crowd, estimated at four thousand people, was so dense that soldiers needed bayonets to clear a passage for Lincoln to walk from his carriage into the hotel.

The president-elect entered a packed Monongahela House Hotel lobby. Amid cries for a speech, someone found a chair. Lincoln removed his coat, gave it to a friend, and

The Monongahela House Hotel was located at One Smithfield Street, on the northwest corner of Smithfield and Water Streets, Pittsburgh, from 1847 to 1935. The hotel's Water Street (Fort Pitt Boulevard) side, facing the viewer, overlooked the Monongahela River. On the right is Smithfield Street and a balcony from which Lincoln spoke on February 14 and 15, 1861. Photograph, 1896. Courtesy of the Carnegie Library of Pittsburgh.

stood on the chair in the midst of the lobby. "I have a great regard for Allegheny County. It is 'the banner county of the Union,' and rolled up an immense majority for what I, at least, consider a good cause. . . . I could not help thinking, my friends, as I traveled in the rain through your crowded streets, on my way here, that if all that people were in favor of the Union, it can certainly be in no great danger—it will be preserved."

Lincoln went to his room to get his notes for his intended speech but was persuaded to postpone it until morning. He appeared briefly on the hotel's Smithfield Street balcony "only to afford you [the crowd] an opportunity of seeing, as clearly as may be, my beautiful countenance! In the morning at half-past eight o'clock I purpose speaking to you from this place. Until then, I bid you all good night." The crowd below roared back, "Good night!" Inside the hotel again, Lincoln was introduced to a few local citizens and then retired to his room. Half an hour later and slightly drier, he was finally able to eat supper with family and friends.

On Friday morning, February 15, 1861, Lincoln visited Illinois friend Leonard Swett who had become ill while traveling to Washington, D.C., and who had been staying at the Monongahela House Hotel for a number of weeks. Lincoln also spent half an hour in his room with members of Pittsburgh Common Council and other guests. Near 8:30 A.M. Pittsburgh Mayor George Wilson escorted Lincoln from his room. The *Pittsburgh Evening Chronicle* reported: "He wore a black dress suit, rather fashionably made, with large turndown collar and black tie. A judiciously cultivated beard and whiskers hides the hollowness of his jaws to some extent, and takes away the prominence of the cheek bones, given him in engravings." They walked through a double file military guard into a parlor and from there out onto the Smithfield Street balcony. Although it had rained until 8 A.M., the street below was filled with people. From the balcony it appeared that all of Smithfield Street, from Water Street to Second Street, was filled with umbrellas. Mayor Wilson introduced Lincoln, and he moved to the railing of the balcony.

> Notwithstanding the troubles across the river, there is really no crisis, springing from anything in the government itself. In plain words, there is really no crisis except an artificial one! What is there now to warrant the condition of affairs presented by our friends "over the river"? Take even their own view of the questions involved, and there is nothing to justify the course which they are pursuing. I repeat it, then—there is no crisis, excepting such a one as may be gotten up at any time by designing politicians. My advice, then, under such circumstances, is to keep cool. If the great American people will only keep their temper, on both sides of the line, the troubles will come to an end, and the question which now distracts the country will be settled just as surely as all other difficulties of like character which have originated in this government have been adjusted. Let the people on both sides keep their self-possession, and just as other clouds have cleared away in due time, so will this, and this great nation shall continue to prosper as heretofore.

Lincoln spoke to the Pittsburgh audience of war and of Pennsylvania's special interest—a tariff on foreign goods, especially iron products. He ended the longest speech of his inaugural journey just before 9 A.M. Military guards pushed people out of the way to allow Lincoln to move through the parlor and hallway to return to his room. A few minutes later he walked outside onto Smithfield Street and a waiting carriage. Pittsburgh's *Saturday Dollar Chronicle* reported, "Men seemed perfectly wild, and it was only by the utmost exertions of the military and police that a narrow passage was kept open for him to pass through. Mayor Wilson held one arm, and Colonel Hunter the other, and it was amusing to observe the attempts of Mr. Lincoln to conceal his hands, which were seized every second by some ardent citizen, and squeezed very vigorously." He sat down beside Mayor Wilson, but cries of "Stand up!" persuaded him to stand and bow to the crowd. The people loved it and cheered even more.

Lincoln's departure was behind schedule. He ordered John Nicolay to get the procession moving even though the military was not yet ready. Later he apologized to General James S. Negley for the "urgent necessity" that required this action. The *Chronicle* continued: "Some two minutes of necessary delay expired before the driver in charge of the president could safely move his horses. . . . It is fortunate that no one was injured. Several were, however, knocked down by the horses, but managed to extricate themselves before being trampled on." The Inaugural Train party, the mayors and city councils of Pittsburgh and Allegheny City, and the military moved north on Smithfield Street, to Fourth, Grant, Fifth, Wood, Liberty, Hand, Penn, and St. Clair Streets; over the suspension bridge on St. Clair Street; and up Federal Street to the Allegheny City Fort Wayne Railroad Station.

> There was a solid mass of humanity about the depot, almost impenetrable, and the enthusiasm exceeded anything we ever before witnessed. The rain had ceased to fall, and old and young, male and female, crowded around the depot by thousands. Gen. Negley and staff made no effort here to press back the crowd, as it seemed next to impossible to obtain a passageway. Gen. Negley, however, upon appealing to the people, succeeded in getting Mr. Lincoln from the carriage, and the party reached the platform one by one in Indian file. . . . In a few minutes the special train approached the depot, and the party embarked amidst the shouts and cheers of the excited multitude.

The Inaugural Train left Allegheny City depot at 10 A.M. It retraced its path out of Pennsylvania through Rochester, Pennsylvania, and Wellsville, Ohio. During the trip Lincoln spent more time than usual by himself, reading newspapers, and thinking. The train was scheduled to arrive in Cleveland at 4 P.M. It arrived in a snowstorm.

Back in Pittsburgh, townspeople noticed that Lincoln had not been their only visitor. A band of pickpockets followed the Inaugural Train, preying on the large crowds. William Hall had his wallet stolen. It contained a certificate of deposit for $50. William Ward of Common Council had his wallet removed from his pants. He lost $450 and a note for $500. Judge Warner had his wallet stolen. It contained a note for $5,000. Apparently the professional pickpockets had a problem: how were they to dispose of so many stolen wallets? Too many empty wallets lying on the ground would have alerted the crowd. One pickpocket with a sense of humor found a practical solution. On the day following Lincoln's visit, one local man told police that he found three wallets in his pants pockets. All three were empty.

On Saturday morning at 9 A.M., Lincoln and the Inaugural Train left Cleveland. They traveled east on the Cleveland, Painesville, and Ashtabula Railroad. More local dignitaries rode the Inaugural Train out of Cleveland, and the train increased in size to a locomotive, tender car, baggage car, and three passenger cars. For this leg of the trip a Buffalo, New York, company loaned Lincoln the use of their new luxury railroad car. The president-elect's first stop in northwestern Pennsylvania was at Girard, where *New York Tribune* editor Horace Greeley boarded the train. The *Tribune*'s editor had a speaking engagement in Meadville, Pennsylvania, and decided to travel to Girard to ride with Lincoln. Greeley boarded "with a valise and his well-known red and blue blanket." When he entered Lincoln's car, Lincoln recognized him immediately and came forward to greet him. Together they rode the eighteen miles to Erie.

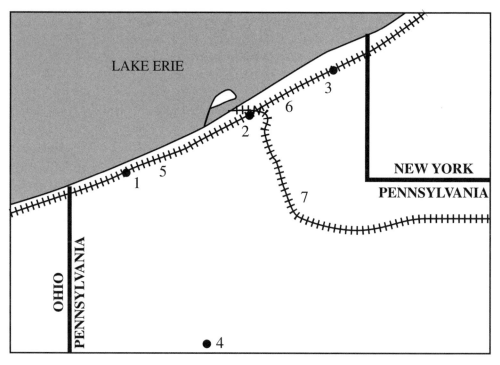

NORTHWESTERN PENNSYLVANIA, 1861. (1) *Girard* (2) *Erie* (3) *North East* (4) *Meadville* (5) *Cleveland, Painesville, and Ashtabula Railroad* (6) *Erie and North East Railroad* (7) *Sunbury and Erie Railroad*

At 12:22 P.M. the train arrived in Erie at an unassuming frame station at Fourteenth and Peach Streets. Flags decorated the depot and the dining room, and there was an arch over the tracks. Evergreens wrapped the sides of the arch, and an American eagle adorned the top. A sign on the arch's crosspiece said, "The Union, the Constitution, and the Laws." The train was not scheduled to stop in Erie for lunch, but rail station dining room cooks Thomas Moore and his wife had prepared a feast. It was rumored that Mr. Lincoln was unable to resist a very tearful Mrs. Moore when she asked him to just "try a piece of my home-made mince pie." After Lincoln and his party ate the lunch, he was directed to a balcony on the depot's eastern side. "Being hoarse and fatigued, he excused himself from speaking at any length or expressing his opinions on the exciting questions of the day. He trusted that when the time for speaking, fully and plainly, should come, he would say nothing not in accordance with the Constitution and the Laws and the manifest interests of the whole country. Counseling all to firmness, forbearance, and patriotic adherence to the Constitution and the Union, he retired amidst applause."

A group of individuals climbed onto a roof of a nearby building in order to get a better view of Lincoln. While he was speaking, the roof collapsed because of the added weight. The sudden disappearance of the roof and everyone on it looked comical, and men laughed even as they rushed to find out if anyone was hurt. Luckily, no one was. After a half-hour layover, the Inaugural Train left on the Erie and North East Railroad. As Lincoln's train pulled away from the Erie depot, the president-elect stood on the last car's platform and held the staff of the American flag in his right hand. At North East, Pennsylvania, Lincoln spoke briefly to the assembled crowd. A correspondent for the *New York Tribune* wrote that Mr. Lincoln's hoarseness caused him to speak less on the sixteenth than on any day since he left Springfield.

At 4:30 P.M. the Inaugural Train arrived in Buffalo, New York. Former President Millard Fillmore waited to welcome his old acquaintance. The crowd of ten thousand pushed and shoved so forcibly that Major David Hunter's shoulder dislocated. On February 18 as Lincoln traveled through New York State on his way to Albany, Jefferson Davis took the oath of office as provisional president of the Confederate States of America in Montgomery, Alabama. On February 19, Lincoln arrived in New York City. He left at 8 A.M. on February 21 and traveled southwest through New Jersey. In Trenton he addressed the New Jersey state legislature. The Inaugural Train left the state capital just after 2 P.M., with a welcoming committee from Philadelphia on board.

The Inaugural Train entered Pennsylvania for the third and last time on Thursday afternoon, February 21, 1861. Traveling southwest on the Philadelphia and Trenton Railroad, it crossed the Delaware River and headed for Philadelphia. Crowds gathered at each depot. Farmhouses displayed American flags, and one farmer wedged the pole of an American flag into his woodpile. One thousand gathered at Bristol's depot, and after the train stopped, Lincoln came to the rear platform and acknowledged their presence and support. By the time the train entered the outskirts of Philadelphia, the streets were filled with people who had waited for hours in the cold just to see the train go by. They stood in doorways; they waited inside windows; they sat on awnings and on roofs.

Lincoln arrived in Philadelphia at Kensington Station at 3:45 P.M. An artillery squad of Minute Men placed in a nearby vacant lot fired a salute, announcing his arrival. Invited guests and their carriages filled the depot enclosure. As at many previous stops, the president-elect again faced an excited, immense crowd. Lincoln, the chairman of the reception committee, and the president of Select and Common Councils of Philadelphia rode away from the depot in a barouche (an open carriage with two bench seats facing each other, a high front driver's seat, and a folding top at the back) drawn by four white horses. Police on horseback and on foot surrounded the carriage. Pennsylvania Dragoons, city council members, other members of Lincoln's party, members of the committees from New Jersey and the Pennsylvania state legislature, members of the press, and invited citizens followed. From Kensington Depot, the procession

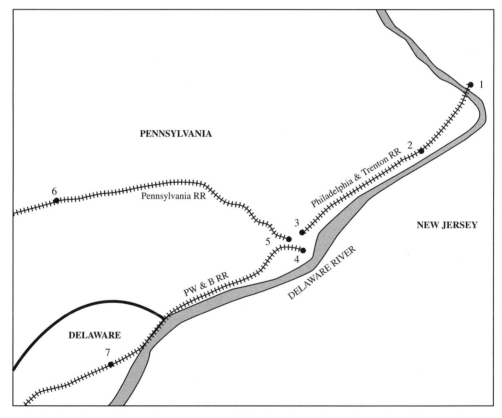

SOUTHEASTERN PENNSYLVANIA, 1861. (1) *Trenton, New Jersey* (2) *Bristol* (3) *Kensington Station, Philadelphia and Trenton Railroad, Philadelphia* (4) *Broad and Prime Station, Philadelphia, Wilmington, and Baltimore Railroad, Philadelphia* (5) *West Philadelphia Station, Pennsylvania Railroad, Philadelphia* (6) *Downingtown* (7) *Wilmington, Delaware*

traveled south on Frankford Avenue to Girard Avenue; west on Girard to Sixth Street; south on Sixth to Arch Street; west on Arch to Sixteenth Street; south on Sixteenth to Walnut Street; east on Walnut to Ninth Street; and north on Ninth Street to the Continental Hotel (see chapter 1, page 12).

American flags and bunting decorated houses and businesses along the entire parade route. Near Girard Avenue a military squad fired a one-hundred-gun salute. At Frankford Avenue below Girard, the William Penn Hose Company fire hall was decorated with flags, and the fire truck was parked in the street. When the procession passed, the fire bell in the cupola and other smaller bells rang in tribute. At Sixteenth and Chestnut Streets, the building owned by artificial limb manufacturer Dr. B. Frank Palmer had a huge thirty-four-star American flag flying overhead. As Lincoln's barouche passed, the flag caught a stiff breeze and billowed over the president-elect's head. The crowd gave "three cheers for Lincoln," and he stood up in the barouche and bowed in acknowledgment.

In Philadelphia, as in other cities, pickpockets worked the crowd. Reverend J. O. Blythe had his pocket picked of $300 in gold. Police watched and then arrested three individuals who tried to pick a woman's pocket at Ninth and Chestnut Streets.

When Lincoln arrived at the Continental Hotel's Ninth Street entrance, he found city police controlling the sidewalk, and for once he had no problem getting to the hotel door. Inside he walked upstairs to the Chestnut Street balcony. Philadelphia Mayor Alexander Henry appeared on the balcony, followed by Mr. Hacker, the chairman of the reception committee. With the crowd below watching, Mr. Hacker introduced president-elect Lincoln to Mayor Henry. There was thunderous and prolonged applause. In his welcoming remarks the Mayor said, "I tender to you the hospitality of this city. I do this as the official representative of 90,000 hearths, around which dwell 600,000 people, firm and ardent in their devotion to the Union."

The crowd inside the hotel overflowed out onto the balcony so forcefully that several times while he was speaking, Lincoln had to elbow people in order to maintain his place. As Lincoln replied to the mayor's welcome, he stood very erect with his two hands holding his hat in front of him. He ignored the crowd below and looked directly at Mayor Henry as he replied. Lincoln admitted, "there is great anxiety amongst the citizens of the United States at this time." This "artificial panic" he believed, "has done much harm." The president-elect hoped that he could "restore peace and harmony and prosperity to the country." He pledged to "do nothing inconsistent with the teachings of those holy and most sacred walls" wherein the nation's founders drafted the Declaration of Independence and the Constitution of the United States.

Lincoln met privately with Judge James Milliken who represented Pennsylvania coal and iron interests, Morton McMichael of the Philadelphia *North American* who represented the press, and several other individuals. There was great pressure on Lincoln to appoint Simon Cameron to his cabinet. Illinois German-American political leader Gustave Koerner later wrote that on January 6, 1861, Lincoln had said to him, "There has been delegation after delegation from Pennsylvania, hundreds of letters, and the cry is 'Cameron, Cameron!' Besides, you know I have already fixed on Chase, Seward, and Bates, my competitors at the convention. The Pennsylvania people say: 'If you leave out Cameron you disgrace him.' Is there not something in that?" Later in the conversation Lincoln asked, "Can I get along if that state should oppose my administration?"

The Pennsylvania Republican Party, however, was split into two factions, and Governor Andrew Curtin had been trying to block Cameron's appointment to the Lincoln cabinet. Lincoln found himself in the middle of the dispute. During the meeting on the evening of the twenty-first, Judge Milliken, an ironmaster and a Cameron ally, told the president-elect that he was authorized to speak on behalf of Governor Curtin. Milliken informed Lincoln that the Curtin faction had withdrawn all opposition to the Cameron appointment. The next day Milliken wrote to Cameron that at their meeting Lincoln said, "It relieved him greatly [that Curtin's opposition was withdrawn]. . . . He was not, however, prepared to decide the matter and would not until he should reach Washington; that it had been suggested it would perhaps be proper and desirable to retain some of the present cabinet officers, for a short time, at least, if they would consent to remain."

Titian J. Coffey, a Pennsylvania lawyer and politician, was also present. He wrote Simon Cameron to report that Lincoln said, "All along, the preponderance in Pennsylvania was so largely in your [Cameron's] favor that he did not consider the opposition from Pennsylvania to you sufficient to prevent your appointment. . . . The kind of hostility expressed to General Cameron by those who opposed him in Pennsylvania has spread to other states, and it is from those states that the greatest opposition is made."

Philadelphia held a private reception for Lincoln at 8:30 P.M. in the hotel's second-floor parlor. A reception line was formed, and Lincoln shook hands with the guests, most of whom were members of the city council. While Lincoln sat on a long couch, a few special guests were presented. William S. McCaulley and a committee from Wilmington, Delaware, extended an official invitation to visit Wilmington. Lincoln replied warmly, "Soon after the nomination of Gen. Taylor I attended a political meeting in the city of Wilmington, and have since carried with me a fond remembrance of the hospitalities of the city on that occasion." But going to Wilmington was "an impossibility."

Lincoln was directed to a colonnade overlooking the main staircase of the hotel. As reserve infantrymen stood guard, the public entered the hotel through the Ninth Street door, filed up the stairs, and moved past the president-elect as he stood bowing. They were close enough to see him well but could not reach him. Once past Mr. Lincoln, the people were moved quickly toward the exit. Hurrahs for "Honest Old Abe" were heard often. A German who was employed in a local jewelry factory, his wife, and son Abe were in the crowd. Their child was born on election day and named after the successful candidate. They asked Lincoln to hold their son and to give him his blessing.

The densely packed crowd outside the Continental Hotel was enormous. From time to time a Lincoln impostor appeared on the hotel's Chestnut Street balcony and entertained the throng below. When the ruse was discovered, yells and groans greeted the tall, black-bearded man. At 9 P.M. the United States Cornet Band played "The Star-Spangled Banner" and several other tunes from the hotel balcony. At 10 P.M. fireworks began, and at 10:15 P.M. officials lit a special display created for the president-elect's visit. A shield of red, white, and blue fire surrounded a silver center and its words, "Welcome Abraham Lincoln. The Whole Union." As the special effects burned, the band played "Hail Columbia." The crowd gave three cheers for the Union, three groans for South Carolina, and three cheers for Abraham Lincoln. February twenty-first ended. Next day was Washington's Birthday, February 22, 1861. The celebration was to begin at Independence Hall.

6

"Looked at Through a Fog"

Lincoln and the Railroads

When birds and animals are looked at through a fog they are seen to disadvantage . . . .
I can only say that my visit to West Point did not have the importance which has been
attached to it.

—Abraham Lincoln, reply to crowd, Jersey City, New Jersey, June 25, 1862

As public memory fades, time obscures, forms distort, and comprehension of past
reality blurs. Clarity improves as information increases. Lincoln often traveled by rail,
and his experience was very much different from that of today. When looked at through
the "fog" of time, Lincoln's image passes in and out of focus. So too does the reality of
nineteenth-century railroads. An unobstructed view of early rail travel is important
to understanding Lincoln's life.

When the president-elect arrived in Washington, D.C., in February 1861, he met
with President James Buchanan at the White House. The Pennsylvania Democrat did
not believe that the federal government had constitutional authority to force Southern states to remain in the Union, nor had he done anything of practical value to put
the United States on a war footing. Buchanan did believe, however, that if war began,
its inevitable conclusion would be victory for the North.

On March 4, 1861, Buchanan and Lincoln rode in an open carriage from Willard's
Hotel at Fourteenth Street and Pennsylvania Avenue to the Capitol Building.
General Winfield Scott placed armed soldiers on rooftops and streets to guard their
parade route and to ensure an orderly transfer of constitutional power. In the Senate
chamber the two men watched as John C. Breckinridge of Kentucky, the outgoing vice-
president, administered the oath of office to Hannibal Hamlin of Maine. After being
introduced on the Capitol portico at 1 P.M., Lincoln delivered his inaugural address.
Chief Justice Roger B. Taney administered the oath of office. Buchanan and Lincoln
rode back to the White House where the outgoing president told Lincoln, "If you are
as happy in entering the White House as I shall feel on returning [home] to Wheatland,
you are a happy man indeed."

The first months of the Lincoln presidency were chaotic. Lincoln had to create a new administration, learn to run a national government, confront the disintegration of the country, and formulate practical policies to stabilize and reunite the nation. Several Pennsylvanians were in key positions. Simon Cameron resigned his Senate seat and became Lincoln's secretary of war. Pennsylvania Governor Andrew Curtin met with Lincoln at least three times in April 1861, once in May, and once in September. Discussions revolved around men, materials, and political support. In 1861 the Pennsylvania General Assembly elected David Wilmot to fill the unexpired portion of Cameron's Senate seat. Thaddeus Stevens, a Republican member of Congress since December 1859, became chairman of the House Ways and Means Committee on July 8, 1861. Over the next year he successfully guided bills through Congress to empower the federal government to print paper money, to tax income, and to fund Lincoln's call-up of troops. Some said that Stevens cleared away the underbrush while Lincoln sowed the seeds. The two were very different, but they shared several common goals.

Simon Cameron found himself in the midst of the whirlwind. On March 1, 1861, Lincoln offered him the secretary of war cabinet post, and Cameron accepted. It was a controversial appointment as rumors of corruption surrounded the Pennsylvanian. According to one member of the House of Representatives, President-elect Lincoln asked Thaddeus Stevens, "You don't mean to say you think Cameron would steal?" Stevens replied, "No, I don't think he would steal a red-hot stove." Lincoln told Cameron what had been said, and an unhappy Senator Cameron approached Stevens in the House chamber and demanded a withdrawal of the statement. Stevens sought out Lincoln and announced, "Well, he is very mad and made me promise to retract. I will now do so. I believe I told you he would not steal a red-hot stove. I will now take that back."

Cameron and the nation were ill prepared for civil war. With an army of fewer than 17,000 men, no military experience, and seemingly little direction from within his department, Cameron faced the daunting task of readying the North to fight a war. Military contracts awarded by the War Department diverted rail traffic from the Philadelphia-Baltimore corridor to the Philadelphia-Harrisburg-Baltimore route. Cameron was linked to both railroads that profited, the Pennsylvania and the Northern Central. Cameron's enemies became incensed and publicized his old ties. In what was perhaps the last straw, Cameron's annual department report included an unauthorized recommendation to free and arm the slaves in states then in rebellion. The printer's office informed Lincoln who had the report withdrawn and rewritten, but national newspapers discovered and printed the original report.

Scandals apart, Cameron was not up to the job, and in January 1862 the president appointed him minister to Russia. The secretary was shaken and hurt. Alexander K. McClure was with Assistant Secretary of War Thomas A. Scott of Pennsylvania when Cameron burst in. McClure wrote: "Cameron was affected even to tears, and wept bitterly over what he regarded as a personal affront from Lincoln. . . . Colonel Scott, who was a man of great versatility of resources, at once suggested that Lincoln did not intend personal offense to Cameron, and in that I fully agreed; and it was then and there arranged that on the following day Lincoln should be asked to withdraw the offensive letter; to permit Cameron to antedate a letter of resignation, and for Lincoln to write a kind acceptance of the same. The letter delivered by Chase was recalled; a new correspondence was prepared, and a month later given to the public."

During Lincoln's first fifteen months in office, the news was unsettling if not downright depressing. Fort Sumter surrendered in April 1861. Arkansas, North Carolina, Tennessee, and Virginia seceded in April and May. The Union was defeated at the first battle of Bull Run in July 1861. On February 20, 1862, Lincoln's son Willie died from "bilious fever." A slight glimmer of hope appeared in April 1862 when the Union declared victory after heavy casualties at the battle of Shiloh. Expectations rose when General George B. McClellan and the Army of the Potomac began the Peninsula campaign, southeast of the Confederate capital, Richmond, Virginia.

At 4 P.M. on Monday, June 23, 1862, Lincoln left Washington on a special train bound for West Point. The president, traveling with General John Pope, entered Pennsylvania on the Philadelphia, Wilmington, and Baltimore Railroad and arrived in Philadelphia at the Broad and Prime Street Station. Lincoln and his group traveled three and a half miles through city streets to the Kensington Station of the Philadelphia and Trenton Railroad without being noticed. They departed Philadelphia by train and arrived in New York City at midnight. Lincoln reached Cozzens's Hotel at West Point at 3 A.M. on the morning of the twenty-fourth.

The reasons for Lincoln's rapid, secretive night journey were not known, and the newspapers were flooded with conjecture. The *Philadelphia Inquirer*'s New York correspondent was amused.

> The town [New York City] rolled up its eyes today when, about noon, it was discovered that President Lincoln and General Pope had passed through the jetty, before daybreak, and had arrived, by special train, at West Point. Everybody asked, "What did it mean!" "What was in the wind!" "What was up!" etc., etc., but nobody could give even an intelligible guess. The sensation reporters went to the Hudson River Railroad Office and subjected the Conductor of "the special train" there, to a series of close cross-questionings, but nothing was elicited save the bare fact that the President had really gone to West Point. Rumor had it that he was gone there to consult with the veteran General Scott—that new military combinations were on foot of a most startling character—that the emergency was a most urgent one, else Mr. Lincoln would never have undertaken so long and so rapid a journey on a rainy night. But as rumor is oftener wrong than right, it is difficult to say how far the jade, in these allegations, can be relied upon. Doubtless, we shall know all about it tomorrow, however, as a powerful detachment of the press gang go up to West Point by this afternoon's train, with instructions to sound the President, General Scott, General Pope, Cozzens, the hotel keeper, and, in short, everybody else who can tell what is afoot.

The New York papers didn't know anything more. The *New York Express* speculated that perhaps General Scott was to return to Washington to be reinstated as head of the armies, or that perhaps General McClellan was to be given command of all the armies. The *New York Evening Post* thought that the trip was "evidently connected with some new military movement," and the *Commercial Advertiser* reported that the visit was solely for the purpose of consultation with General Scott. Lincoln wasn't talking.

The president and General Scott, now retired from active duty not quite one year, spent the morning of the twenty-fourth meeting in private. Later that day Lincoln toured the military academy, attended a dinner party, visited a cannon foundry, and received guests at the hotel. At midnight the academy's military band serenaded him. It was a long day.

On Wednesday, June 25, the president, director of military railroads Colonel Daniel C. McCallum, and others left West Point at 10:10 A.M. At 11:10 A.M. they boarded a ferry in New York City and landed in New Jersey twenty minutes later. In Jersey City when asked about the purpose of his trip, the chief executive remarked to a crowd, "The Secretary of War [Stanton], you know, holds a pretty tight rein on the Press, so that they shall not tell more than they ought to, and I'm afraid that if I blab too much he might draw a tight rein on me."

When Lincoln's party arrived in Philadelphia, Samuel M. Felton, president of the Philadelphia, Wilmington, and Baltimore Railroad joined the group. The president's special train arrived back in Washington, D.C., at 6:50 P.M., having established a new record time between New York City and Washington of only seven hours and twenty minutes.

On June 26, 1862, his first full day back in Washington, Lincoln created the Army of Virginia by combining the commands of Generals Nathaniel P. Banks, John C. Frémont, and Irvin McDowell. He placed General Pope in command. One of the new army's prime directives was to protect the national capital from Confederate attack. That same day the Seven Days' Battle began in Virginia. It signaled the end of McClellan's lackluster Peninsula campaign.

Publicly Lincoln may not have placed much importance on his excursion to West Point, but the trip demonstrated Lincoln's use of available railroad technology. The president fashioned a mobility unknown to previous generations. He was able to make a journey of hundreds of miles in order to consult with a general he trusted in record time. For the general public, train speeds averaging thirty to forty miles per hour would not be achieved until after the Civil War.

Abraham Lincoln most frequently experienced the Commonwealth as a rail passenger (see appendix B). What was Lincoln's 1862 rail journey really like? Of course as president, his experience was no doubt a cut above that of the average traveler. But passenger Lincoln was probably well acquainted with early passenger trains that consisted of a locomotive—with no shelter for the engineer, a tender car for wood, and usually one or two passenger cars. A typical passenger car was thirty-six feet long, eight feet wide, and six feet four inches high. It had a center aisle, seating for thirty to forty people, and a two-foot by three-foot lavatory closet. A stove heated the car in winter-time, and a single candle at either end provided light at night. Luxurious directors' cars provided to the president would have had a sitting room arrangement with sofas and an area to lie down. Lamps replaced candles, and over the years improvements provided more light and less fumes.

Early rail travel involved inconveniences other than the crudity of the passenger cars. In Lincoln's lifetime there was no railroad bridge over the mouth of the Susquehanna River between Philadelphia and Baltimore. As congressman and president, Lincoln made that trip several times. To cross the Susquehanna River, passengers had to get off the train, cross the river on the ferry *Susquehanna,* and board a different train waiting on the opposite riverbank. In 1854 the iron steamboat ferry *Maryland* began service across the Susquehanna River between Havre de Grace and Perryville, Maryland. The

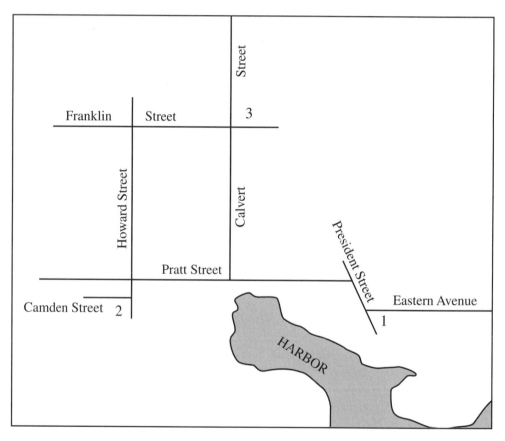

BALTIMORE RAILROAD STATIONS. (1) *President Street Station. Philadelphia, Wilmington, and Baltimore Railroad trains approached from the east.* (2) *Camden Street Station. Baltimore and Ohio Railroad trains approached from the south.* (3) *Calvert Street Station. Northern Central Railroad trains approached from the north.*

Maryland had rails on her deck and could transport entire railroad cars complete with passengers.

Railroad operation inside city limits also presented special challenges. Cities prohibited locomotives inside their boundaries because the fire hazard was too great. Locomotives spewed glowing embers that started track fires and sometimes house fires. Entire city blocks were at risk. Because locomotives were forbidden, horses or mules had to pull passenger and baggage cars over city street rails (similar to today's trolley car system) from the locomotive's legal limit on the outskirts of the city to the downtown passenger terminals. The distances involved were as much as two miles. An alternative transport was a horse-drawn omnibus, but that required passengers and their baggage to transfer to the bus.

Rail stations took up a significant amount of space, yet they needed to be centrally located downtown. Changing needs frequently required new construction; and in Lincoln's era, Philadelphia rail stations were in constant flux. For example, in 1851 Philadelphia had nine different train depots. Abraham Lincoln used four of Philadelphia's passenger stations.

Railroad	Depot	Dates in Service
Philadelphia, Wilmington, and Baltimore (rail service to Baltimore)	11th and Market Streets southeast corner	1843–52
Also used by the Pennsylvania Railroad		1854–64
Philadelphia, Wilmington, and Baltimore (rail service to Baltimore)	Broad and Prime Streets northwest corner	1852–81
Philadelphia and Trenton (rail service to Trenton and New York)	Kensington east side of Front Street between Berks and Montgomery Streets	1834–82
Pennsylvania Railroad (rail service to Harrisburg)	West Philadelphia 32nd and Market Streets northeast corner	1858–64

Often early rail lines did not interconnect, and rail companies needed alternative methods to move passengers between different rail systems in the same city. A passenger like Lincoln traveling from Washington, D.C., to New York City had to travel three and a half miles through Philadelphia streets from the Broad and Prime Street Station to the Kensington depot. Distance between Baltimore railroad stations figured prominently in Lincoln's decision to travel secretly through Baltimore on the evening of February 22–23, 1861. The Baltimore rail stations involved in Lincoln's deliberations were:

RAILROAD	DEPOT	DATE OPENED
Philadelphia, Wilmington, and Baltimore (rail service to Philadelphia)	President Street	1850
Baltimore and Ohio (rail service to Washington, D.C.)	Camden Street	1853
Northern Central (rail service to Harrisburg)	Calvert Street	1850

Lincoln also endured early railroad food service. As president he conceivably could have traveled on trains equipped with a kitchen. (The Funeral Train had one for its occupants.) But this was not so for the average passenger. A rail traveler in America in 1838 wrote: "At every fifteen miles of the railroads there are refreshment-rooms. The cars stop, all the doors are thrown open, and out rush all, the passengers like boys out of school, and crowd round the tables to solace themselves with pies, patties, cakes,

Early steam engine John Bull pulls a tender car and passenger cars. In September 1833 New Jersey's Camden and Amboy Railroad first attached this English locomotive to an American passenger train. After more than thirty years' active service, John Bull *retired to the Smithsonian Institution. Photograph circa 1854. Photographs, MG-286, Penn Central Railroad Collection, Pennsylvania State Archives.*

hard-boiled eggs, hams, custards and a variety of railroad luxuries too numerous to mention. The bell rings for departure, in they all hurry with their hands and mouths full, and off they go again until the next stopping-place induces them to relieve the monotony of the journey by masticating without being hungry."

Safety was an issue. Steam engine explosions and train derailments were common. From 1853 to 1859 there were 1,109 deaths as a result of more than 900 railroad accidents. One of those deaths was the only son of Franklin and Jane Pierce: eleven-year-old Benjamin Pierce died in a railroad accident near Andover, Massachusetts, on January 6, 1853. The inaugural ball, to be held two months later, was canceled. Pierce was in mourning.

In addition to unforeseen difficulties along the route, departure and arrival times were hopelessly mired in the lack of standardization of time throughout the United States. Rail schedules for average passengers were simply unreliable. In Buffalo, New York, for example, local time and New York Central railroad time were twenty minutes apart. Local time for Washington and Baltimore differed by three minutes. If more than one railroad served a city, several different railroad times were possible. Lobbying did not bring about national standardization of time for many decades.

From 1847 to 1865 Abraham Lincoln dealt with these issues as he traveled throughout Pennsylvania, most often as a rail passenger. To fully comprehend what the Commonwealth was like for Lincoln, an understanding of his rail travel is indispensable. His was an era of steam and of a developing technology. The president's 1862 Pennsylvania transit was insignificant. His next journey in the Keystone State would also be by rail, this time to dedicate a cemetery. Its significance would be far greater.

7

"Unfinished Work"

The Gettysburg Address

It is for us the living, rather, to be dedicated here to the unfinished work which they who fought here have thus far so nobly advanced.

—Abraham Lincoln, Gettysburg Address, Gettysburg, Pennsylvania, November 19, 1863

The battle raged for three days, but often the dying took a lot longer. Many men died where they fought; many others died later. The wounded were eventually moved to the relative safety of rear staging areas. The severely wounded never made it any farther. Any house, store, church, or mill that sheltered wounded men became a hospital. More than 160 hospital sites and their wounded populated Gettysburg and the surrounding area. The largest, General Hospital (also known as Camp Letterman), was a tent city east of Gettysburg on the York Road.

It was the dead and the dying and the suffering that Pennsylvania Governor Andrew G. Curtin wanted to visit on July 10, 1863. He came to see the battlefield firsthand, and he came to talk with the soldiers. As he approached Gettysburg and its battlefield, the stench of flesh rotting in the hot July sun greeted him while he was yet miles away. Dead horses lay in the streets and fields, and human bodies remained unburied or only partially buried, with arms and legs protruding. Hogs rooted men out of shallow graves and ate their fill. In town the experience was even more overwhelming. A coating of chloride of lime, put down to reduce infection, covered streets, dead horses, and human remains. The debris of battle—carts and caissons, knapsacks, weapons, papers, letters—was everywhere. Wagons rumbled through the streets transporting the dead and the wounded to the train station. Cries of suffering surrounded hospital sites; and at night when sounds carried farther, the pain of dying men filled the town. It was to this Gettysburg that Governor Curtin came on July 10. He stayed the day. It was best not to stay longer. Lee and his army were still north of the Potomac, and the rebel cavalry or a rebel straggler might have heard of his presence.

David Wills, a successful Gettysburg attorney and local Republican Party leader, guided the governor that day. Before Curtin left, he appointed Wills as his Gettysburg agent to oversee the burial of Pennsylvanians. In a July 24, 1863, letter to Curtin, Wills suggested that the State of Pennsylvania purchase land in Gettysburg for use as a cemetery. The concept was gradually broadened to include the eighteen Union states whose men fought at Gettysburg. In August, Wills successfully purchased five separate lots for $2,475.87 and combined them into one seventeen-acre plot on Cemetery Ridge, adjacent to the private Evergreen Cemetery. He hired William Saunders, a landscape gardener employed by the Department of Agriculture, to design the cemetery. By August 17 Wills felt the work had progressed sufficiently to suggest to Curtin that the cemetery be "consecrated by appropriate ceremonies." On August 28 Governor Curtin visited Lincoln in Washington, D.C. Three days later Curtin wrote to Wills, "The proper consecration of the grounds must claim our early attention." On September 23 David Wills extended a formal invitation by letter to Edward Everett to be the featured speaker at dedication ceremonies proposed for October 23, 1863.

Edward Everett, former Harvard professor of the classics, former governor of Massachusetts, former secretary of state, former vice-presidential candidate on a ticket that

"Harvest of Death" captured the horror of war. Union dead, without shoes, lie on the battlefield between Rose Farm and Devil's Den, scene of second and third days' battles. A burial detail is in the distance. Photograph, July 5, 1863, by Timothy H. O'Sullivan, assistant to Alexander Gardner. Photograph NWDNS 165 SB 36 "Harvest of Death, Gettysburg, Pa."; National Archives at College Park, College Park, Maryland.

ran against Lincoln, was the most noted orator of his day. Everett accepted but wrote that he was not available until November 19, 1863. The date of the ceremony was changed to accommodate his schedule.

On October 22 Wills opened the contractors' bids for exhumation of bodies on the battlefield and reburial at the cemetery. He awarded the contract to Frederick Biesecker who submitted the low bid of $1.59 per body. Work began on October 27, and Wills later reported that work was progressing well at a rate of about sixty bodies per day. More than one-quarter of the remains were unidentifiable. Superintendent of exhumations Samuel Weaver wrote: "The bodies were found in various stages of decomposition. On the battle field of the first day, the rebels obtained possession before our men were buried, and left most of them unburied from Wednesday until Monday following, when our men buried them. After this length of time, they could not be identified. The consequence was, that but few on the battle field of July 1st, were marked. They were generally covered with a small portion of earth dug up from along side of the body. This left them much exposed to the heat, air, and rains, and they decomposed rapidly, so that when these bodies were taken up, there was nothing remaining but the dry skeleton."

Gettysburg attorney and Republican Party leader David Wills was the individual most responsible for the creation of Soldiers' National Cemetery. Scholars still speculate as to whether Wills received the copy of the Gettysburg Address that he requested from Lincoln, and if so, what became of it. Photograph. Courtesy of the Dwight D. Eisenhower Society.

In an October 30, 1863, letter to Ward Hill Lamon, Wills confirmed Lamon as chief
marshal of the procession and master of ceremonies on November 19. Lamon accepted
and asked Washington, D.C., commissioner of public buildings Benjamin B. French
to assist him. In a November 2 letter, Wills formally invited Lincoln to say "a few
appropriate remarks." Later the Gettysburg attorney also invited the president to join
Everett and Curtin as his houseguest on the evening of November 18.

Lincoln accepted both of Wills's invitations. He wanted to come to Gettysburg. His
exact reasons are unknown, but possibilities are many. The war was in its third year,
and Lincoln hoped to strengthen waning national support. On a practical level, he
wanted to consecrate the cemetery, to honor loyal men. Their support was vital to his
administration. But Lincoln was also beyond the immediacy of Gettysburg. For some
time he had been wrestling with "ultimate questions" involving existence and sacrifice.
For what higher purpose did these men die? When would the nation's atonement end?
How much sorrow was enough? The president surely confronted and certainly wished
to answer such questions for himself and the nation.

On a regional level, Pennsylvania and Governor Curtin had been very supportive
of his administration and its war policies. Pennsylvania had supplied large numbers

*Edward Everett gave the principal
oration on November 19, 1863.
Three years earlier, he ran against
Lincoln as the vice-presidential
nominee of the Constitutional
Union Party. Photographs, MG-
264, I.U. International Political
Memorabilia Collection 1786–
1972, Pennsylvania State Archives.*

of troops and materials, and Governor Curtin had hosted the Altoona Governors' Conference in September 1862. That conference had solidified Northern governors' support for Lincoln. Pennsylvania's continued support was essential, and the chief executive clearly understood that fact.

On a more political level, Lincoln's thoughts might have turned to Thaddeus Stevens. Lincoln and Stevens were often at odds, but Lincoln had to work with Stevens. In 1863 Thaddeus Stevens was a radical Republican congressman from Lancaster, Pennsylvania, and chairman of the House Ways and Means Committee. Congressional bills necessary to finance Lincoln's policies and to fund the war effort originated in Stevens's committee. Gettysburg was formerly Stevens's hometown, and David Wills had studied law under him in Lancaster. After June 26, 1863, Thaddeus Stevens was even less inclined to be flexible in his views. Just days before the battle of Gettysburg, Confederate General Jubal Early's cavalry rode to Caledonia, fifteen miles west of Gettysburg, and destroyed Stevens's Caledonia Iron Works. What the Confederates could not carry off, they burned. Stevens estimated his loss at $90,000. He was not happy, to say the least. Lincoln the moderate needed to engage Stevens the radical, and a visit to Stevens's old home area could not hurt. It remained to be seen if it would help.

Ward Hill Lamon, Lincoln's sometime Illinois law associate, chief bodyguard, and marshal of the District of Columbia, was chief marshal of the Soldiers' National Cemetery dedication procession and ceremony. Photograph. Courtesy of the Dwight D. Eisenhower Society.

The creative process for the Gettysburg Address began long before November 1863. Abraham Lincoln's thought and style matured with time, and they were, no doubt, influenced by his cultural heritage and by his contemporaries. Whether by conscious or unconscious design, the outline of Lincoln's address imitated the Greek classical style established by Pericles' funeral oration of 431 B.C. The president's address began with praise for the dead and ended with advice for the living. The body of the address incorporated additional topics suggested by the classical model, for example, nobility of the ancestors; heroism of the dead; and that the living should take comfort in, and should prove worthy of, the deeds of the dead. Lincoln also looked to philosophers of his own day. William Herndon was sure that his former law partner had read at least one lecture of New England transcendental philosopher Theodore Parker in which Parker used his oft repeated "a government of all, by all, and for all." The president reworked his own thoughts too. In response to a serenade at the White House on July 7, 1863, the president had said, "How long ago is it?—eighty odd years—since on the Fourth of July for the first time in the history of the world a nation by its representatives, assembled and declared as a self-evident truth that 'all men are created equal.'"

William H. Seward, Lincoln's secretary of state, came to Gettysburg with a prepared address that he delivered to the crowd on the evening of November 18. The White House requested that it be included in the official record of the ceremonies published by the Commonwealth of Pennsylvania. Photograph. Courtesy of the Dwight D. Eisenhower Society.

Above all, Lincoln wanted to craft his words carefully. Journalist friend Noah Brooks remembered his reply on November 15 when asked about his speech: "Well, no, it is not exactly written. It is not finished, anyway. I have written it over, two or three times, and I shall have to give it another lick before I am satisfied. But it is short, short, short." Lincoln's troubled search for the ultimate meaning of the death and sacrifice required by the war reached a time when he was willing to verbalize his conclusions publicly. That day would be November 19, 1863.

By Tuesday, November 17, 1863, the flood of visitors coming to Gettysburg had swamped every entry to the town, which normally contained fewer than 2,500 people. All types of vehicle clogged the roads, and standing room on incoming railroad cars could not be purchased at any price. Sleeping accommodations were overwhelmed. Hotels filled, sometimes with as many as twenty people per room. States sent delegations, and hotels hung out signs, "Headquarters of Ohio" and "Headquarters of New Jersey." Pennsylvania College (now Gettysburg College) and the Lutheran Theological Seminary housed visitors. Private homes took boarders, and churches let people sleep in pews.

John P. Usher, Lincoln's secretary of interior 1863–65, was a conservative Republican from Indiana who greatly admired Lincoln. Usher spent much of his time on African-American colonization proposals, Indian resettlement, and the transcontinental railroad. Photograph NWDNS 111 B 5933 "John P. Usher"; National Archives at College Park, College Park, Maryland.

Flags waved throughout Gettysburg, and townspeople put out sidewalk tables with bullets, projectiles, and shell fragments for sale. Visitors wanted to see the battlefield. "When breakfast was over, thousands turned out from their houses to inspect the battlegrounds and the cemetery. Every horse and carriage in the place was hired at exorbitant rates, and all day long the crowds passed to and fro in ceaseless promenades." When they got to the battlefield, what they saw was graphic: "Torn knapsacks, cartridge boxes, fragments of clothing, discarded shoes and rejected equipments were scattered over the whole ground. The remains of the horses which had fallen were seen in heaps of charred and mouldering bones, where the fires that consumed them had been kindled. Scabbards and sheaths lay all along the route of the battle, and under the faded, withered autumn leaves the bleached remnants of a thousand letters, the contents of fallen soldiers' knapsacks, were peeping."

On Wednesday, November 18, 1863, Lincoln left Washington, D.C., in a special four-car train supplied by the Baltimore and Ohio Railroad. The locomotive was decorated with the American flag and wreaths of jasmine and evergreen. Lincoln traveled with personal secretaries John Nicolay and John Hay; Secretary of State William H. Seward;

As a conservative from Maryland, Montgomery Blair, Lincoln's postmaster general 1861–64, was not optimistic about the future of race relations in the United States. Photograph NWDNS III B 4294 "Montgomery Blair"; National Archives at College Park, College Park, Maryland.

Secretary of the Interior John P. Usher; Postmaster General Montgomery Blair; and Lincoln's paid African-American servant William H. Johnson. The train left about 12 noon and reached Baltimore around 1:10 P.M.

In Baltimore the special train stopped at the Camden Street Station of the Baltimore and Ohio Railroad. Teams of horses pulled the special cars over city street rails to the Northern Central rail system. During the transfer the Marine Band played several tunes. General Robert C. Schenck and his staff boarded the train to accompany the president. (Schenck was known as a hero of the battle of Bull Run, and he was also a "hero" in Lincoln's eyes for defeating antiwar advocate Clement L. Vallandigham in an Ohio congressional race.) The Second United States Artillery Regiment Band from Fort McHenry, twelve singers of the National Union Musical Association of Baltimore, and several local city officials also got on board.

Lincoln's train traveled north on the Northern Central line, which ran between Baltimore and Harrisburg. During several stops the Baltimore chorus sang or one of the bands played. Several miles south of York, Pennsylvania, the train stopped at Hanover Junction, the entrance to the Hanover-Gettysburg Railroad. Gettysburg was still thirty miles to the west. Hanover Junction had been raided by Jubal Early's cav-

WASHINGTON, D.C., TO GETTYS-
BURG, NOVEMBER 18–19, 1863.
Lincoln traveled on the Baltimore and Ohio Railroad from Washington to Baltimore, where he transferred from the B & O's Camden Street Station to the Northern Central Railroad. At Hanover Junction, Pennsylvania, his train transferred to the Hanover-Gettysburg Railroad. (1) *Washington, D.C.* (2) *Washington Junction/Relay House (B & O)* (3) *Baltimore* (4) *Relay (Northern Central)* (5) *Hanover Junction* (6) *Hanover* (7) *Gettysburg* (8) *York*

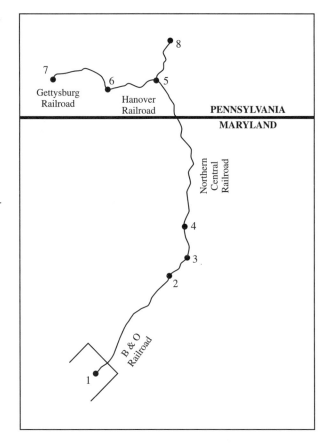

alry before the battle of Gettysburg. A railroad bridge was burned, and crucial telegraph lines destroyed. All had been repaired, and after the battle thousands of wounded
moved by rail from Gettysburg through Hanover Junction to hospitals in York, Baltimore, and Washington, D.C. Lincoln had agreed to meet Governor Curtin at Hanover
Junction, but the governor's train was not there.

Lincoln traveled west without the governor on the Hanover-Gettysburg Railroad
line. At Hanover, his train was placed on a siding for eight minutes while an eastbound
train passed. Waiting at the siding were nearly one hundred people, including the
president of the Hanover-Gettysburg Railroad Captain A. W. Eichelberger, who had
ultimate control over rail traffic scheduling. The pastor of St. Matthew's Lutheran
Church spoke, "Father Abraham, your children want to hear you." Lincoln replied,
"I trust when the enemy was here the citizens of Hanover were loyal to our country
and the stars and stripes. If you are not all true patriots in support of the Union you
should be."

*The porch on the eastern side of the railroad station seen in this wartime photograph of Hanover
Junction still exists today. Note the men in uniform, some of them wounded. Northern Central
rail tracks are in the foreground. Matthew Brady Studios. Photograph NWDNS 111 B 360
"Hanover Junction, Pa."; National Archives at College Park, College Park, Maryland.*

The president's train continued westward and arrived in Gettysburg around 5 P.M. David Wills, Edward Everett, Benjamin French, and Ward Hill Lamon met Lincoln at the station. The First Regiment of the Invalid Corps escorted the group two blocks south to David Wills's house on the square. William Johnson carried Lincoln's carpetbag.

After Lincoln's arrival, Mrs. Wills served dinner. The president sat at the head of the table, and Everett sat to his right. Dinner was interrupted several times. A telegram from Secretary of War Edwin M. Stanton reported that the war front was quiet and that he had inquired of Mrs. Lincoln as to Tad Lincoln's health. Tad was ill when Lincoln left Washington, and the secretary understood the president's anxiety, given Willie Lincoln's death in 1862. Stanton wrote that he had been told that Tad was ill but seemed somewhat improved. A telegram from Governor Curtin stated that his train experienced mechanical problems and would arrive late. At one point during the meal, Lincoln got up from the table, appeared to the cheering crowd outside, waved, and bowed. A third telegram, this time from Mrs. Lincoln, arrived after 9:40 P.M. and reported that Tad was feeling better.

That evening the Fifth New York Artillery Band, the Second United States Artillery Band, and the Marine Band took turns playing to the large crowd gathered in the

Lincoln arrived and departed from the Gettysburg train station on Carlisle Street, November 18–19, 1863, but did not enter. Empty coffins provided by the War Department were stored here at the time, awaiting exhumation of additional bodies for reburial in Soldiers' National Cemetery. Photograph by Dr. Henry Stewart 1886–87. Courtesy of the Adams County Historical Society.

square. About 10 P.M. the Fifth New York Artillery Band went to the door of the Wills House to serenade the president. Lincoln came outside and responded from the Wills House steps. In more words than were necessary, he told the crowd that he had no speech to make.

The crowd moved next door to serenade William H. Seward, and he responded with a prepared address. "I thank my God that I believe this strife is going to end in the removal of that evil [slavery], which ought to have been removed by deliberate councils and peaceful means. . . . When we part tomorrow night, let us remember that we owe it to our country and to mankind that this war shall have for its conclusion the establishing of the principle of democratic government—the simple principle that whatever party, whatever portion of the community, prevails by constitutional suffrage in an election, that party is to be respected and maintained in power until it shall give place, on another trial and another verdict, to a different portion of the people."

Abraham Lincoln was a guest at the David Wills House, built circa 1814, on the southeast corner of the Gettysburg Diamond, and spoke briefly from the steps facing York Street. Secretary of State William H. Seward and Benjamin B. French were guests at the Robert G. Harper House, seen on the right. Photograph, circa 1890. Courtesy of the Adams County Historical Society.

Lincoln went to his second-floor bedroom. He asked for paper. Around 11 P.M. he walked downstairs and requested to be taken to Secretary Seward, perhaps to get Seward's opinion on his speech revisions. Seward and Benjamin French were staying at the home of Robert G. Harper, editor of the Gettysburg Republican newspaper the *Adams Sentinel*. While the president was inside the Harper house, the Baltimore choir stood on the front sidewalk and sang "We Are Coming Father Abraham" and "Our Army Is Marching On." About 11:30 P.M. Robert Harper opened the front door, and

Abraham Lincoln received this telegram, Wednesday evening, November 18, 1863, at the Wills House. Photograph. Courtesy of the Dwight D. Eisenhower Society.

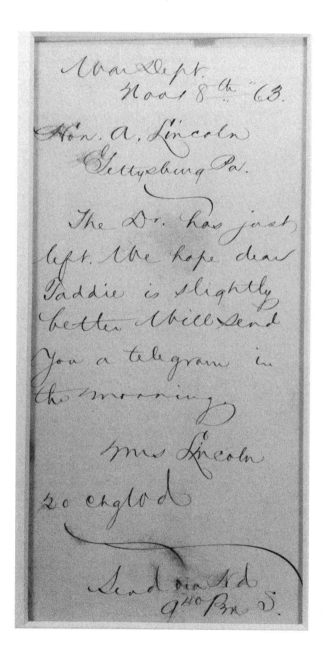

Anthony Berger photographed Abraham Lincoln and son Tad Lincoln (1853–71) on February 9, 1864, at the Matthew Brady Studios in Washington. Courtesy of the Dwight D. Eisenhower Society.

Lincoln and his escort walked back through the crowd the few feet to the Wills House. He retired for the night.

Gettysburg, however, was still very much awake. Bands guided serenading parties to the night's lodging of one distinguished guest after another. Secretary Seward, Secretary Blair, the military commanders—all were visited. Often parties serenaded several different homes in the square at the same time. "Bands of people walked the streets through the night. . . . It might have been the want of sleeping quarters, or it might have been the irrepressible enthusiasm of the visitors that kept them in the streets during the chill vapors of the night, but numbers of them never sought cover and through the morning hours 'Bonnie Blue Flag' and the 'Star Spangled Banner' echoed up and down the silent streets and lanes of the little historic town." On Thursday, November 19, Lincoln awoke early and breakfasted at the Wills House. As he was finalizing and memorizing his speech, John Nicolay dropped by his bedroom to see if he needed anything. Just after both men came downstairs, Secretary Seward arrived from next door. He and Ward Hill Lamon, who had visited the site of Major General John F. Reynolds's death, spoke with Lincoln. Then Secretary of State Seward and Lincoln's Canadian guest William McDougall accompanied the president on a morning carriage ride west of town. For one hour they inspected the first day's battlefield in the vicinity of Lutheran Theological Seminary and the woods where the highly regarded Reynolds of Pennsylvania had been shot and killed.

At 9 A.M. the parade began to form. Using the town square as the center, the military formed to the north on Carlisle Street; the civic processions were to the east on York Street; and the state delegations, with Pennsylvania in the lead, formed to the west on Chambersburg Street. Parade marshals formed in the square itself.

About 10 A.M. Abraham Lincoln emerged from the Wills House. He was dressed in a black mourning coat and a black hightop hat. So many people crowded around to touch and to speak to him that eventually Lamon, hoping to discourage them, asked the president to mount his horse. The crowd was not deterred. Just before 11 A.M. the procession began to move, with the Marine Band in the lead. Three cabinet secretaries and personal secretary Nicolay flanked Lincoln. The five of them, on horseback, followed the military. The parade marched south on Baltimore Street, right onto the Emmitsburg Road, left onto the Taneytown Road, and then left into the cemetery through the western gate. Along the parade route "every available spot on the principal streets was occupied."

At the cemetery the military had placed a cordon of soldiers around the speakers' platform, enclosing an area of two hundred square yards. When the lead elements of the procession arrived, "The military escort entered this [enclosure], guard first. The fine, steady bearing of the men forming a strange contrast with the restless masses outside the square. The other portions of the parade successively entered the enclosure, until it was completely filled and the immense audience stood confronting the stand." The remainder of the estimated 15,000 in attendance were beyond the military enclosure.

After the head of the procession arrived at the speakers' platform at 11:15 A.M., the military units in advance of Lincoln formed in line and presented arms. The president and more than forty other individuals who were to be seated on the speakers' platform passed in front. Lincoln was on the platform by 11:30 A.M. and sat in the middle of the front row. Secretary Seward sat on Lincoln's left, and Governor Curtin was to Seward's left. The twelve-foot by twenty-foot platform, and the individuals on it, faced northwest toward the graves of the 1,188 men (582 of them unknown) already interred. The work was not yet finished.

It was a cloudless day near fifty-two degrees, and Secretary Seward had to shield his eyes from the sun. Lamon went to the tent that Everett had asked to be erected near the platform. Everett had ridden to the cemetery in a barouche with Rev. Thomas H. Stockton and was already inside the tent when Lamon arrived. At 11:40 A.M. Benjamin French, in Lamon's temporary absence, directed Birgfield's Band to begin. When Everett arrived on the platform, he sat on Lincoln's right. A program of music, prayer, and speeches had been planned.

PROGRAM

Music	"Homage d'un Heros"	Composed by Adolph Birgfield, Birgfield's Band of Philadelphia
Prayer		Rev. Thomas H. Stockton Chaplain, House of Representatives, Washington, D.C.
Music	"Old Hundred"	Marine Band, Francis Scala, Director
Oration	"The Battles of Gettysburg"	Edward Everett
Music	"Consecration Hymn"	Written by Benjamin French, Chanted by the National Union Musical Association, Baltimore, Maryland
Remarks		President Abraham Lincoln
Music	Dirge	Composed by Alfred Delaney Performed by a Local Mixed Choir and Birgfield's Band
Benediction		Rev. Henry L. Baugher President, Pennsylvania College Gettysburg

Edward Everett's two-hour oration praised brave Union men, reviewed the war's history, and explained the "battles" of Gettysburg in great detail. Social custom dictated a lengthy, learned speech that would properly honor the dead. It was expected of him, but some in the crowd drifted away. At about 2 P.M. Ward Hill Lamon introduced Lincoln, "Ladies and Gentlemen, the President of the United States." Lincoln stood and addressed the crowd:

Four score and seven years ago our fathers brought forth upon this continent a new Nation, conceived in Liberty, and dedicated to the proposition that all men are created equal. Now we are engaged in a great civil war, testing whether that Nation or any Nation so conceived and so dedicated can long endure. We are met on a great battle-field of that war. We are met to dedicate a portion of it as the final resting-place of those who here gave their lives that that nation might live. It is altogether fitting and proper that we should do this. But in a larger sense we can not dedicate, we can not consecrate, we can not hallow this ground. The brave men living and dead who struggled here have consecrated it far above our power to add or detract. The world will little note nor long remember what we say here, but it can never forget what they did here. It is for us, the living, rather to be dedicated here to the unfinished work that they have thus far so nobly carried on. It is rather for us to be here dedicated to the great task remaining before us, that from these honored dead we take increased devotion to that cause for which they here gave the last full measure of devotion; that we here highly resolve that the dead shall not have died in vain; that the nation shall, under God, have a new birth of freedom; and that Government of the people, by the people, and for the people, shall not perish from the earth.

(This, with the exception of two typographical changes, was the report of Associated Press reporter Joseph L. Gilbert, who took shorthand during the address and afterwards borrowed Lincoln's two-page manuscript in order to correct his report. Gilbert's version appeared in the *New York Tribune, Times,* and *Herald.*)

The president and other procession members got a close-up view of the northeast corner of Center Square on the morning of November 19, 1863. The McClellan House was north across the Diamond, opposite the Wills House. Photograph by Dr. Henry Stewart 1886–87. Courtesy of the Adams County Historical Society.

Following the ceremony Lamon announced that the Ohio delegation would host a patriotic program in the Presbyterian Church at Baltimore and High Streets at 5 P.M. A battery of the Fifth New York Artillery fired an eight-round salute. The marshals moved to re-form the procession to go back to town. Lincoln stepped off of the speakers' platform, went to a group of fifty Union veterans who had been wounded at Gettysburg, and shook their hands. They had come by train from the military hospital in York, to be present at the ceremony. During Lincoln's address, a captain whose arm had been amputated, "sobbed aloud while his manly frame shook with no un-

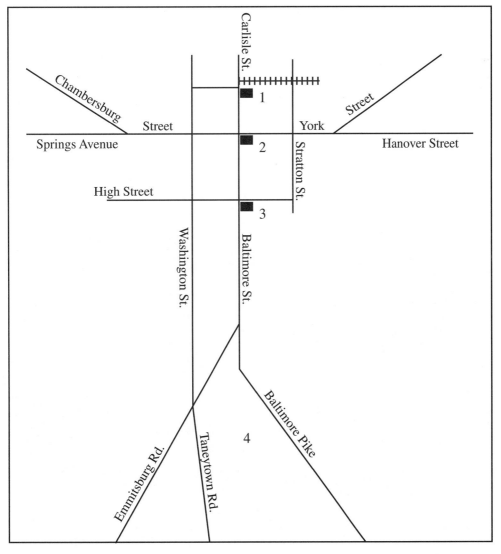

GETTYSBURG PARADE ROUTE. (1) *Train Station* (2) *Wills House* (3) *Gettysburg Presbyterian Church* (4) *Soldiers' National Cemetery*

This is the dedication ceremony procession to the Soldiers' National Cemetery as it appeared on November 19, 1863, between 11:00 and 11:30 A.M. This view looks north on Baltimore Street as the procession and the president move south and turn right onto the Emmitsburg Road. Photograph. Courtesy of the Dwight D. Eisenhower Society.

The crowd at Soldiers' National Cemetery, Gettysburg, was photographed during the dedication ceremony on November 19, 1863. Parade marshals, wearing sashes, were on their horses. Military units had cleared and cordoned off the area around the speakers' platform to provide space for procession participants, and then faced outward (Gettysburg Compiler, November 23, 1863). An enlargement of a section of this photograph (opposite) reveals the image of Abraham Lincoln. Photograph NWDNS 111 B 4975 "Crowd of Citizens, Gettysburg Pa."; National Archives at College Park, College Park, Maryland.

manly emotion. . . . He lifted his still streaming eyes to heaven and in low and solemn tones exclaimed, 'God Almighty bless Abraham Lincoln.'" To their chaplain the president said, "The men upon their crutches were orators; their very appearance spoke louder than tongues."

Philadelphian Emily Bliss Souder remembered: "It was long past noon when the procession returned. It was a magnificent sight. The long line of infantry with their bayonets gleaming in the sunlight, the artillery, the distinguished guests, the great multitude. As the president passed, every head was uncovered, and three hearty cheers were given for him. The same compliment was paid to our own Governor Curtin. The solemn pageant was over."

At 3 P.M. inside the Wills House, Mrs. Wills served dinner to Lincoln, Everett, current, past, and future governors, and others. After dinner Governor Curtin hosted a one-hour reception for the president. Ward Hill Lamon screened the entrants at the Wills House's York Street door. Lincoln stood in the hallway just beyond Lamon and greeted the guests as they entered. Governor Curtin stood at the Wills House door that opened onto the square and shook the hands of the guests as they left.

Lincoln had heard about Gettysburg resident John Burns, a seventy-year-old veteran of the War of 1812 who fought alongside Union troops during the battle. Lincoln wanted to meet him. Wills sent someone to bring Burns to the reception, and Lincoln greeted him with, "God bless you, old man."

At 5 P.M. Lincoln, Burns, Secretary Seward, and Secretary Usher walked three blocks south on Baltimore Street to attend the Ohio patriotic ceremony at the Presbyterian Church. Lamon, French, and assistant marshals escorted them. Lincoln's arm was around Burns's right arm and Seward's was around Burns's left arm. Gettysburg resident T. C. Billheimer later said: "I was standing on the pavement on the opposite side of the street when the procession came headed for this church. . . . The President was a tall man and Mr. Burns a small man and as they came along I was amused. I could not help being amused. I laughed and laughed aloud. Lincoln took enormous strides and Mr. Burns could not take strides like that. He could not keep step with the Presi-

In this enlarged detail of the dedication ceremony photograph, Abraham Lincoln is at center left. Detail of Photograph NWDNS III B 4975 "Crowd of Citizens, Gettysburg, Pa."; National Archives at College Park, College Park, Maryland.

dent. . . . Several pews had been reserved for the distinguished party. Mr. Lincoln went up the right or south aisle and stopped at the first vacant pew, instead of going to the front pew. First, he stepped aside to allow three or four of his party to enter the pew, and then took the aisle seat."

The program had already begun when they arrived, but they were in time for the main speaker. Colonel Charles Anderson, Ohio lieutenant governor-elect and brother to Major Robert Anderson of Fort Sumter fame, spoke for forty minutes. "Remember us in our fresh and bloody graves, as you are standing upon them. And let your posterity learn the value in the issues of that battlefield, and the cost of the sacrifice beneath its sod." When the address was over, the president and Secretary Seward complimented speaker Anderson. The audience was asked to remain standing while President Lincoln and his party left the church.

Lincoln and his followers walked back to the Wills House. He collected his carpetbag, said his thanks, and walked two blocks north to the train. The crowd around the train station was huge, and it was impatient. The railroad company had decided that no trains would leave until after the president's train left. Railroad executives apparently thought that he was going to leave immediately following the cemetery program. "The immense crowd manifested signs of impatience, and the management of the railroad came in for no small share of censure and abuse. Hundreds of people occupied seats in the cars at the depot for hours together without moving, fearful of losing the first chance of getting away."

The president's special train left Gettysburg sometime between 7 and 8 P.M. with Lincoln, Colonel Anderson, Ohio Governor-elect John Brough, General Schenck, and others on board.

Gettysburg's John Burns walked arm in arm with Lincoln to the Presbyterian Church on November 19, 1863, but had difficulty keeping up with Lincoln's large strides. Photograph Matthew Brady Studios, circa July 15, 1863. Courtesy of the Dwight D. Eisenhower Society.

Abraham Lincoln, John Burns, and Secretary of State Seward attended the Ohio patriotic ceremony at the Gettysburg Presbyterian Church, at Baltimore and High Streets, on Thursday afternoon, November 19, 1863. David Wills attended this church and arranged for its use and for Lincoln's visit. Photograph by Dr. Henry Stewart 1886–87. Courtesy of the Adams County Historical Society.

At Hanover Junction, the president and his party waited for several hours for a connecting train on the Northern Central line. Although the talk was lively, Lincoln seemed quiet. "Resting his elbow on the arm of his chair, he leaned his head on his hand, listened and smiled at the quaint sayings of those around him, but joined sparingly in their conversation." After waiting for several hours, an ill-appearing Lincoln left Hanover Junction on a train that took him to Baltimore and his connection with the Baltimore and Ohio Railroad. At 1:10 A.M. on November 20, the president and his party finally arrived in Washington, D.C.

Back in Gettysburg, the first passenger train left the station one hour after the president's train left. Thereafter trains departed at hourly intervals. Travel was not comfortable. A reporter for the *Philadelphia Inquirer* wrote: "The train in which your correspondent took passage left Gettysburg at nine o'clock in the evening, and reached Wrightsville, fifty-four miles distant, the next morning, at seven o'clock. The cars were crowded with a motley group of men, women and children. The cars were without lights or fire, the night was cold and chilly, and the passage home one of the most uncomfortable that can be imagined."

Once Lincoln was back at the White House, his physician diagnosed a mild case of smallpox, known as varioloid smallpox. He was quarantined for more than two weeks and joked that at last he had something that he could give to everybody. Another story that circulated at the time—possibly true, possibly false—was that Lincoln said, "There is one consolation about the matter, doctor. It cannot in the least disfigure me."

Over the next few months the president was asked for several copies of his Gettysburg Address. He responded—each time rewording the address slightly. Sometime after March 4, 1864, Lincoln wrote the last text.

> Four score and seven years ago our fathers brought forth on this continent, a new nation, conceived in Liberty, and dedicated to the proposition that all men are created equal.
>
> Now we are engaged in a great civil war, testing whether that nation, or any nation so conceived and so dedicated, can long endure. We are met on a great battle-field of that war. We have come to dedicate a portion of that field, as a final resting place for those who here gave their lives that that nation might live. It is altogether fitting and proper that we should do this.
>
> But, in a larger sense, we can not dedicate—we can not consecrate—we can not hallow—this ground. The brave men, living and dead, who struggled here, have consecrated it, far above our poor power to add or detract. The world will little note, nor long remember what we say here, but it can never forget what they did here. It is for us the living, rather, to be dedicated here to the unfinished work which they who fought here have thus far so nobly advanced. It is rather for us to be here dedicated to the great task remaining before us—that from these honored dead we take increased devotion to that cause for which they gave the last full measure of devotion—that we here highly resolve that these dead shall not have died in vain—that this nation, under God, shall have a new birth of freedom—and that government of the people, by the people, for the people, shall not perish from the earth.

Early opinions of Lincoln's address varied. Newspapers of the day divided along political party lines. Republican newspapers generally applauded the speech. Democratic papers generally did not. In a very kind letter to the president, Edward Everett wrote, "There was more in your twenty lines than in my twenty pages." Personal secretary John Hay was matter-of-fact in his eyewitness account of Lincoln's Gettysburg Address. In his diary entry for November 19, 1863, Hay wrote, "and the President in a firm free way, with more grace than is his wont said his half dozen lines of consecration and the music wailed and we went home through crowded and cheering streets."

8

"Comfort and Relief"

The Great Central Sanitary Fair

The Sanitary Commission, with all its benevolent labors, the Christian Commission, with all its Christian and benevolent labors, and the various places, arrangements, so to speak, and institutions, have contributed to the comfort and relief of the soldiers.

—Abraham Lincoln, speech at Great Central Sanitary Fair, Philadelphia, June 16, 1864

The United States Sanitary Commission was the largest civilian effort of the American Civil War. According to one conservative estimate, from 1861 to 1865 private citizens donated five million dollars in cash and fifteen million dollars in supplies to the commission. In an attempt to provide "comfort and relief" to the troops, it directed its volunteer efforts into three main areas: prevention of sickness and death in army camps, treatment of the sick and the wounded, and humanitarian aid to the soldier at other times.

To reduce the number of combat and camp deaths, the commission enlisted medical experts to study camps and hospitals. Eighteen treatises on camp sanitary conditions and on methods of improving battlefield and hospital medical care were published. Frequent site inspections encouraged the army to utilize the experts' advice. To improve treatment of the sick and wounded, the Sanitary Commission placed volunteers in ambulance corps and hospitals, designed hospital railroad cars, and subsidized hospital trains and ships. To improve nutrition, a "kettles on wheels" program provided nourishing soup to the troops.

Sanitary Commission chairman Rev. Henry W. Bellows believed that these efforts reduced mortality. At Philadelphia's Academy of Music in 1863 Chairman Bellows said: "At no time since the war began, has the average mortality been more than six per cent. Well, now, in the Crimean army, the mortality was twenty-three per cent; in the army on the Spanish peninsula under Wellington, the mortality was sixteen and one-half per cent."

To help families find their relatives, the organization published a hospital directory containing the names of all known patients. To aid furloughed soldiers traveling between home and army, the commission established lodges that were, in reality, free hotels. Eight hundred thousand soldiers received a million nights' free lodging and ate four and one-half million free meals. To aid the soldier after discharge, the commission created a claims bureau, a pension agency, and forty soldiers' homes.

This national volunteer organization was a direct outgrowth of the Women's Central Association of Relief, a New York City civilian group led by the Reverend Bellows. Secretary of War Simon Cameron formally established the United States Sanitary Commission on June 8, 1861, and appointed Bellows as chairman and Congressman Schuyler Colfax of Indiana, the surgeon general of the United States, and the chief of the U.S. Coastal Survey, among others, as commission members. Ten Northern cities formed branches under the leadership of the national organization, whose central office was at 244 F Street, Washington, D.C.

Philadelphia's branch began in December 1861, headquartered at 1307 Chestnut Street. In the first two years of operation, it raised $135,000. As war continued beyond the hope of early victory, volunteer efforts to raise money became ever more important. The commission needed new and more effective fund-raising techniques, and a number of cities turned to the charity fair. Chicago, Cincinnati, and Boston held fairs before 1864 and raised significant amounts of money. Philadelphia decided to take a serious look at such a venture.

On January 11, 1864, the Union League of Philadelphia, a group of prominent citizens banded together in support of the national government, adopted a resolution urging the Sanitary Commission to hold a fair in Philadelphia. In view of the successes of other cities, the Union League strongly recommended that Philadelphia's Sanitary Commission organize a fair with proceeds going "to promote the health, comfort, and efficiency of the soldier in active service." On January 22, 1864, the executive committee of the Philadelphia branch of the Sanitary Commission agreed with the Union League and later joined the New Jersey and Delaware commissions to sponsor the Great Central Sanitary Fair. On January 25, 1864, the executive committee of the Women's Pennsylvania Branch of the Sanitary Commission heard a firsthand report from an individual who had been involved in planning and executing the Chicago Sanitary Fair. The Philadelphia commission appointed a fair chairman, an executive committee, and eventually more than one hundred additional committees.

The executive committee wanted to hold the fair at the Academy of Music on Broad Street but abandoned this idea because previous fairs had found insufficient space to be a major problem. In time committee members agreed that Logan Square, located between Eighteenth and Logan Streets (Logan Street formerly existed between Nineteenth and Twentieth Streets) and Race and Vine Streets, was the best site. It was one of the city's five original squares designed by Thomas Holme in 1682. It had ample available space, it was close to city center, and it was beautiful. The stunning Cathedral of Saints Peter and Paul was adjacent to it, having been completed just two years earlier in 1862.

The executive committee selected architects Strickland Kneass to design the main exhibition hall and Henry E. Wrigley to design additional buildings. The committee raised money for construction by having individuals, businesses, and other organizations pledge one day's business receipts. Completed in only forty days, more than 1.5 million board feet of lumber enclosed 200,000 square feet of floor space. Total length of the buildings was 6,500 feet. Philadelphians marveled that architects had preserved and enclosed many of Logan Square's trees inside the new structures. The central exhibition hall was named Union Avenue and ran the entire length of the square from Eighteenth to Logan Streets. The avenue was 540 feet long, 64 feet wide, and 51 feet high from floor to Gothic-arched ceiling. Single-story exhibition buildings, a circular restaurant, and a spacious horticultural hall connected to the avenue and completed the complex.

The Women's Pennsylvania Branch of the United States Sanitary Commission, members of the Union League, and other interested individuals solicited items for sale, auction, special fund-raising activities, and exhibition. Unique objects that were donated included ceremonial swords, silver trophies, rare books, and autographs of famous Americans. The fair acquired the autographs of the majority of former presidents, and on May 31, 1864, President Lincoln donated his autograph to be auctioned for the benefit of the troops.

On June 7, 1864, a procession of fair executives, city officials, and delegations from New Jersey, Delaware, and Pennsylvania paraded to Logan Square for opening ceremonies. President Lincoln declined his invitation, knowing his attention would be focused on the Republican National Convention in Baltimore June 7–8. Philadelphia Mayor Alexander Henry, Delaware Governor William Cannon, New Jersey Governor Joel Parker, and Pennsylvania Governor Andrew Curtin addressed the crowd. During his opening remarks Governor Curtin said: "My friends, if there is one man more than

This view of the Great Central Sanitary Fair, Logan Square, Philadelphia, June 1864, looks southeast from the intersection of Vine and Logan Streets. Union Avenue, the restaurant, the Floral Department, and the Cathedral of Saints Peter and Paul are visible. Lithograph 1864. Courtesy of the Print and Picture Collection, the Free Library of Philadelphia.

another whom you can admit to your sincere reverence and respect, it is the private soldier. He is the true noble man of this land. He falls with unrecorded name; he serves in the army for small pay; no pageant marks his funeral; and he may fall with those who, at Gettysburg, fill the graves of the unknown."

The Great Central Sanitary Fair opened to the general public at 10 A.M. on June 8. After paying the required one-dollar admission, the visitor entered a world markedly different from the soldier's battlefield. Needlework, silverware, jewelry, Chinese goods, Japanese wares, India rubber merchandise, and fans made by Confederate prisoners hospitalized at Point Lookout could be bought. There were hats, furs, lingerie, clothing, umbrellas, canes, stoves, dry goods, perfumes, machinery, and even rare books, such as *Audubon's Birds* and *Boydell's Shakespeare*.

There were special exhibits. Fire companies demonstrated their best fire-fighting equipment. Exotic and flowering plants filled a display room 190 feet in diameter. The Pennsylvania Academy of the Fine Arts loaned its collection of paintings for exhibit along the north corridor. George Washington's state carriage, personal letters, one of his pewter spoons, and a portion of his wooden coffin were on display. Visitors could examine the bullet-shredded battle flag used at Gettysburg by the 56th Regiment, Pennsylvania Volunteers. Native Americans performed war dances, rituals, and gave interpretive demonstrations of Indian life.

The Floral Department, shown in this ground plan of the Great Central Sanitary Fair, had a one-hundred-foot-wide, canvas, canopy roof, a lake with jet fountains, and a center island with tropical plants. Courtesy of the Print and Picture Collection, the Free Library of Philadelphia.

The fair devised tempting ways to spend money. At the post office, the fairgoer could buy a piece of mail. Inside the envelope was usually "food for thought" in the form of a poetry verse or some other quote. At the tobacco department, choice Turkish blends, cigars, and pipes were sold. The purchaser could enjoy his selection on one of the several divans as he listened to the sound of a bubbling fountain in the background. At another booth Charles Leland wrote, printed, and distributed *Our Daily Fare*. Fairgoers subscribed to the daily newspaper, which contained a schedule of events and fair-related articles, as another way of donating money.

The Great Central Sanitary Fair created two special "elections." The individual with the most "votes" in each would receive an outstanding prize. Anyone could be nominated, but a "vote" sold for one dollar. Philadelphians, who had been accused for years of voting early and voting often, this time were encouraged to do so. A special $2,000 military sword had been donated to the fair. By the fair's close, the sword "election" attracted 5,541 votes and therefore raised $5,541. Voters awarded the weapon to the hero of Gettysburg, Major General George Gordon Meade. President of the Corn Exchange Edwin G. James won the second election, the Union Vase. This vase was solid silver, three feet four inches in height, on a base of Vermont marble. This election raised $10,457. Elections for a camp chest and a fire company horn raised money as well.

The Great Central Sanitary Fair operated its own restaurant on site from June 7 to June 28. Each day nine thousand people ate in the restaurant's circular seating area that was 170 feet in diameter and 40 feet in height. The restaurant employed 317 people, including 30 cooks, and utilized 400 volunteers. One hundred sixty African-American waiters wearing white jackets, white vests, and black trousers served the public. Restaurant receipts during the fair totaled $72,850.

The daily menu included:

Soup	Green Turtle 50 cents, Oyster 25 cents
Cold Dishes	Lobster Salad 30 cents, Chicken Salad 50 cents
Hot Dishes	Roast Chicken 50 cents, Roast Lamb 35 cents
Cooked to Order	Porterhouse Steak 60 cents, Chicken Croquettes 40 cents
Vegetables	Boiled Potatoes 10 cents, Tomatoes 15 cents
Pastry	English Plum Pudding 25 cents, Apple Pie 10 cents
Champagnes	Heidsick $3.50, Petiot $3.00
Ale	Philadelphia Ale 25 cents, Muir's Ale 50 cents
Liquors	Cognac $3.50, Old Rye Whiskey $2.50

Throughout the period of the Great Central Sanitary Fair, national events continued to overshadow life in Philadelphia. The Army of the Potomac under General Ulysses S. Grant started the overland campaign, pushing toward the Confederate capital of Richmond. Appomattox was still far away. The battle of the Wilderness fought on May 7–9, 1864, filled Philadelphia military hospitals with wounded. At the Republican National Convention in Baltimore Abraham Lincoln won the Republican Party nomination for a second term as president on the first ballot. Democrat Andrew Johnson of Tennessee received the vice-presidential nomination, replacing incumbent Hannibal Hamlin. On June 13, 1864, candidate Lincoln informed Sanitary Fair officials that he had decided to accept their invitation and would visit on June 16. Philadelphia and the fair had less than three days' advance notice.

The president, his wife, and a committee of Philadelphia fair officials left Washington on a Baltimore and Ohio Railroad special train the morning of Thursday, June 16, 1864. Along the route, people cheered the chief executive and fired artillery salutes in his honor. His car, decorated with flags and streamers, was transferred from the B & O Camden Street Station in Baltimore to the President Street Station of the Philadelphia, Wilmington, and Baltimore Railroad by a team of horses. At the Susquehanna River northeast of Baltimore, Lincoln's rail car transferred to the steam rail ferry *Maryland* on the western bank of the river near Havre de Grace. Riding on *Maryland*'s deck rails, Lincoln's special car crossed the river and disembarked near Perryville.

The train entered Philadelphia from the southwest, crossing over the Schuylkill River on the Gray's Ferry railroad bridge. Just east of the river in Philadelphia the train approached the Schuylkill Arsenal. Forty or fifty American flags decorated an arch over the arsenal's main south entrance. As Lincoln's train passed, a thirty-five-gun salute roared. The excited crowd watched as the train pulled into the Philadelphia, Wilmington, and Baltimore train depot in South Philadelphia at Broad and Prime Streets. The trip from Washington, D.C., had taken four hours forty-five minutes. It was 11:45 A.M.

Lincoln arrived thirty minutes early. Many who were supposed to greet him at the station had not yet arrived. Mrs. Lincoln quietly took a carriage to the hotel. The president, Governor Cannon of Delaware, and Thomas Webster of Philadelphia got into a barouche. They moved onto South Broad Street with the rest of their party following behind. A mounted police escort surrounded them as they drove north on Broad Street and east on Chestnut. At Ninth Street they turned south for one-half block before coming to the entrance of the Continental Hotel. It was a one-and-a-half-mile trip. The *Philadelphia Inquirer* testified to the excitement of the scene.

> Broad Street was packed with people from the Depot to Chestnut Street, and the greatest enthusiasm prevailed. The procession was greeted with cheers from the men and the waving of handkerchiefs by the ladies. The crowd pressed forward with the greatest anxiety to catch a glimpse of the president and his suite. Flags were displayed in profusion all along the route. At the house of the Franklin Hose and Steam Engine Company, on Broad Street, above Fitzwater, the large bell on the cupola was sounded, and the steamer and hose carriage gaily decorated with flags and displayed on the pavement. As the carriages passed this point a shrill, clear voice sung out "Three cheers for Old Abe!" These were given with a will—the shout being deafening. . . . The front windows of the La Pierre House presented a magnificent scene. The president was loudly cheered and handkerchiefs were waved from the windows by the ladies. To this mark of respect the president responded, as he did on several other

occasions along the route, by gracefully bowing to those who thus sought to do him honor. Chestnut Street presented a gay appearance when viewed from Broad Street. From almost every building flags were displayed, and the street was densely crowded. As the procession passed the Mint the employees, who were all in front of the building, gave three hearty cheers for the Chief Magistrate. At the headquarters of the Supervisory Committee for Recruiting Colored Regiments there was another demonstration. Two companies of colored troops, with presented arms and a fine band, were drawn up in line. As the barouche passed six hearty cheers were given for President Lincoln, and the band struck up the "Star-Spangled Banner." The Union League House was beautifully decorated. The Stars and Stripes were hung gracefully across the building, beneath the windows of every story, while both the State and National colors were displayed from the windows. From the flag-staff floated white streamers, each containing the name of a State. The windows of the house were occupied by ladies, who waved their handkerchiefs enthusiastically, and upon the steps were many members of the League, who cheered lustily. The president was kept quite busy in returning the salutations. The National Union Club House was also beautifully decorated, but not quite so elaborately as the League House, and the same demonstrations met the president there. Down towards the Continental the crowd increased, and it was with difficulty that the carriages could be turned into Ninth Street. The crowd at the Continental on the arrival of the escort was immense, and the air was rent with the hearty cheers from the multitude who were assembled to do homage to the distinguished guest.

An enormous crowd surrounded the hotel. City police cleared a path for Lincoln, and he walked from his carriage to the Ninth Street door. Inside Mayor Alexander Henry and a special committee of city council members formally welcomed the chief executive. Quaker Sidney George Fisher, one of the Philadelphians introduced to the president, later wrote: "He is tall, slender, not awkward and uncouth as has been represented, well dressed in black, self-possessed and easy, frank and cordial. . . . Altogether an honest, intelligent, amicable countenance, calculated to inspire respect, confidence and regard. His voice, too, is clear and manly." A short time later, Lincoln went to his room to rest and to have lunch with his wife.

At 4:15 P.M. a driver and four horses brought an empty barouche to the front of the Continental Hotel. Anticipating Lincoln, the crowd rushed the carriage to get a better look. Once again, determined police moved them back and enabled the president to move from the hotel to the barouche. His party included Mrs. Lincoln, Mayor Henry, and members of city council. As before, mounted police escorted them as they moved south on Ninth Street to Walnut Street and then turned right on Walnut Street and moved west. At Eighteenth Street the carriages turned right to move north to the fair's Eighteenth Street gate (see chapter 10, page 143).

President and Mrs. Lincoln arrived at the fair at 5 P.M. Expecting a huge crowd on the day of the presidential visit, officials had doubled the price of admission to two dollars, but still the crowd inside stood shoulder to shoulder. Police cleared Union Avenue of onlookers and lined up in single file on each side of the exhibition hall. After being welcomed by the executive committee, the Lincolns walked slowly through Union Avenue, enjoying the exhibits until they neared the entrance to the Floral Department. At that point the crowd broke through police lines, forcing the presidential party to retreat to the reception room. The president ventured out from time to time, but movement through other exhibition areas was impossible.

At 7 P.M. a banquet in Lincoln's honor began. Immediately after dinner, the president was toasted: "To Abraham Lincoln, the President of the United States." Lincoln stood to thunderous applause.

War, at the best, is terrible, and this war of ours, in its magnitude and in its duration, is one of the most terrible. It has deranged business, totally in many localities, and partially in all localities. It has destroyed property, and ruined homes; it has produced a national debt and taxation unprecedented, at least in this country. It has carried mourning to almost every home, until it can almost be said that the "heavens are hung in black." Yet it continues, and several relieving coincidences have accompanied it from the very beginning. . . . The Sanitary Commission, with all its benevolent labors, the Christian Commission, with all its Christian and benevolent labors, and the various places, arrangements, so to speak, and institutions, have contributed to the comfort and relief of the soldiers. . . . Say what you will, after all the most is due to the soldier, who takes his life in his hands and goes to fight the battles of his country. In what is contributed to his comfort when he passes to and fro from city to city, and in what is contributed to him when he is sick and wounded, in whatever shape it comes, whether from the fair and tender hand of woman, or from any other source, is much, very much; but, I think there is still that which has as much value to him in the continual reminders he sees in the newspapers, that while he is absent he is yet remembered by the loved ones at home—he is not forgotten. . . .

It is a pertinent question often asked in the mind privately, and from one to the other, when is the war to end? Surely I feel as great an interest in this question as any other can, but I do not wish to name a day, or month, or a year when it is to end. I do not wish to run any risk of seeing the time come, without our being ready for the end, and for fear of disappointment, because the time had come and not the end. We accepted this war; we did not begin it. We accepted this war for an object, a worthy object, and the war will end when that object is attained. Under God, I hope it never will until that time. Speaking of the present campaign, General Grant is reported to have said, I am going through on this line if it takes all summer. This war has taken three years; it was begun or accepted upon the line of restoring the national authority over the whole national domain, and for the American people, as far as my knowledge enables me to speak, I say we are going through on this line if it takes three years more. My friends, I did not know but that I might be called upon to say a few words before I got away from here, but I did not know it was coming just here. I have never

Architects used a series of Gothic arches to construct Union Avenue for the Great Central Sanitary Fair. By doing so, there was less need to trim branches from large trees adjacent to the building. The design also allowed some of the branches to enter the hall near the apex of the roof. Albumen photograph by R. Newell, 1864. Courtesy of the Print and Picture Collection, the Free Library of Philadelphia.

been in the habit of making predictions in regard to the war, but I am almost tempted to make one. If I were to hazard it, it is this: That Grant is this evening, with General Meade and General Hancock, of Pennsylvania, and the brave officers and soldiers with him, in a position from whence he will never be dislodged until Richmond is taken, and I have but one single proposition to put now, and, perhaps, I can best put it in form of an interrogatory. If I shall discover that General Grant and the noble officers and men under him can be greatly facilitated in their work by a sudden pouring forth of men and assistance, will you give them to me? Then, I say, stand ready, for I am watching for the chance. I thank you, gentlemen.

Three cheers for the Army of the Potomac, as well as cheers for Generals Grant, Meade, and Hancock followed applause for Lincoln's address. Major General Lewis Wallace complimented the president's speech and ended by saying, "I believe as certainly that our flag will float over Richmond, as I believe that there is an army of giants encircling it. Let us be patient. Let us sustain Mr. Lincoln. Let us sustain Grant and his army. God is on our side, and the issue is not doubtful."

America's greatest orator and Lincoln's partner at Gettysburg, Edward Everett, also attended the ceremonies and received a toast: "Edward Everett—in peace and in war, the statesman and the patriot." He responded, "I do not expect to detain the audience by anything that may fall from my lips after you have listened to the most feeling and appropriate address from the president of the United States, and from the gallant General who has breasted the shock of battle." He closed his few words with a play on the Republican campaign slogan that emphasized the need to re-elect Lincoln: "There are various modes of traffic in these Fairs—buying and subscribing. There is one kind of traffic I hope will not be protected, and that is to swap horses in crossing a stream." There was laughter and applause.

After Delaware Governor Cannon spoke briefly, former Pennsylvania Governor James Pollock rose. Lincoln had known him since their days together as Whig congressmen, and in 1861 he appointed him director of the United States Mint in Philadelphia. Pollock presented the president with a silver commemorative medal, a gift of the women's volunteer committees. Lincoln accepted the medal "as an additional token of your confidence. . . . I accept it thankfully, as another manifestation of the esteem of the ladies."

The chief executive received two additional gifts: a wooden staff made from a Trenton, New Jersey, arch under which George Washington allegedly passed in 1789 on his way to New York City and inauguration as president, and a tree branch that held two peaches. The grower had anticipated the outcome of the Republican National Convention and had placed paper letters spelling "Lincoln" on one of the peaches and "Johnson" on the other. After the peaches ripened and the paper was removed, the words "Lincoln" and "Johnson" appeared in pale yellow, while the surrounding skin was crimson red. In return Mrs. Lincoln gave fair officials a lacquered, floral Japanese vase that she had brought from Washington.

Earlier in the day, Union League members had personally invited Lincoln to visit the Union League Club at 1118 Chestnut Street and the National Union Club across the street. League members planned to escort the president from the fairgrounds that evening, but in the confusion they could not find him. The presidential party left the fair by carriage and traveled to the eleven hundred block of Chestnut Street. Gas jets illuminated both league buildings and outside the National Union Club formed the words "God and Our Country." Philadelphia attorney and league member Daniel Dougherty welcomed Lincoln to the Union League Club. Lincoln replied noting, "the extraordinary efforts of your patriotic men and lovely ladies in behalf of the suffering soldiers and sailors of our country."

After a reception inside the Union League, Lincoln stepped outside onto the building's steps and spoke. He admitted honestly that, although he felt an obligation to appear before the crowd that had waited so long, he really had nothing to say. "I came among you thinking that my presence might do some good towards swelling the contributions of the great Fair in aid of the Sanitary Commission, who intend it for the soldiers in the field."

Lincoln traveled three blocks east on Chestnut Street and retired to his rooms at the Continental Hotel. Fireworks continued until nearly midnight. Some time after

The Union League of Philadelphia met here at 1118 Chestnut Street from February 23, 1863, until moving to 140 South Broad Street on May 11, 1865. Lincoln visited on June 16, 1864, and spoke to the crowd from the steps on the far left. Political posters for the October 13, 1863, election paper an adjoining wall. Courtesy of the Print and Picture Collection, the Free Library of Philadelphia.

10 P.M. Lincoln was serenaded and responded still once more, now from the balcony of the hotel. "It did not even occur to me that a kind demonstration like this would be made to me. . . . I have really appeared before you now more for the purpose of seeing you and allowing you to see me a little while, and, to show to you that I am not wanting in due consideration and respect for you, when you make this kind demonstration in my honor."

The president and Mrs. Lincoln left Philadelphia from the Broad and Prime Street Railroad Station at 8 A.M. the next morning. The Sanitary Fair closed on June 28. An estimated 253,924 people visited a total of 442,658 times. All unsold items were auctioned on July 6, 1864. The fair's total income, including interest, was $1,154,898. Expenses were $143,922. In three weeks, the Sanitary Commission earned a net profit of more than one million dollars!

During the remainder of 1864, the Union League of Philadelphia worked tirelessly for the re-election of Abraham Lincoln. The league had been founded in December 1862 as a direct response to widespread pro-Southern sentiment in Philadelphia, especially strong during the war's first two years. A December 13, 1860, public meeting in Independence Square urged concession to the South as a means of avoiding war. Speaker Judge George W. Woodward of the Pennsylvania Supreme Court went so far as to say that slavery was "an incalculable blessing." As late as December 1862 the newspaper *North American* was still able to print, "The Union feeling in Baltimore [in a slave-holding state] is stronger at this time than it is in Philadelphia." In 1863 Judge Woodward became the Democratic Party's gubernatorial candidate. The league deemed the re-election of Pennsylvania Governor Andrew Curtin as vital to the Union cause and worked for his victory. Curtin won his bid for re-election on October 13, 1863, by 15,000 votes.

The league employed many avenues to support the Union. It spent $108,000 during the last two years of the war to enlist more than 10,000 troops. After Congress amended the Enrollment Act on February 10, 1863, the league's Supervisory Committee for the Enlistment of Colored Troops, chaired by Thomas Webster, placed 5,000 African-American troops into the Union army. In 1863 the publication committee distributed over one million pieces of pro-Union literature and in 1864, 1,044,900. Charles J. Stillé's *How a Free People Conduct a Long War* was perhaps best known. League members assisted New York and Boston when those cities founded Union Leagues. Edward Everett chaired Boston's organizing committee. And the league sponsored patriotic ceremonies. Abraham Lincoln promised to attend the league's huge parade and ceremony in Philadelphia planned for July 4, 1863, but Lee's June invasion of Pennsylvania and the July battle at Gettysburg forced cancellation of the plans.

During the 1864 presidential campaign the Union League publicized its official endorsement of President Lincoln, *An Address by the Union League of Philadelphia to the Citizens of Pennsylvania in Favor of the Re-Election of Abraham Lincoln,* authored by Quaker Sidney George Fisher. In a six-week period the organization sent out more than 560,000 campaign newspapers, the *Union League Gazette.* It distributed the fourteen-page pamphlet, *To the Soldiers of the Union.* The league held political rallies on six nights of every week for six weeks in the Concert Hall on the other side of Chestnut Street, and it canvassed every local school board chairman in the state to obtain lists of voters who were doubtful for the president.

On November 8, 1864, the president won a second term with 2,213,635 votes. His Democratic Party opponent George B. McClellan received 1,805,237 votes. Lincoln counted 212 electoral votes against McClellan's 21. The Democratic general had carried only three states. Thanks in part to the Union League of Philadelphia, Lincoln received Pennsylvania's 26 electoral votes.

In March 1865 Mrs. Mary Livermore, the wife of a Chicago Republican newspaper editor, visited the White House as she had done on a number of previous occasions. She had been the only woman newspaper reporter at the Chicago Republican National Convention in 1860. In her travels during the war she continued to send reports back to her husband's newspaper. She was heavily involved in volunteer work and had been a United States Sanitary Commission fund-raiser, nurse, and cook. The Sanitary Commission sent Mrs. Livermore to Washington to secure Lincoln's promise to attend the upcoming Chicago Sanitary Fair. This would be the second Sanitary Fair held in Chicago during the war, and Lincoln had not attended the first one. Mrs. Livermore later remembered:

Once more, and for the last time, we were admitted to the well-known audience-chamber, and to an interview with the good president. He was already apprised of this second fair, and told us laughingly, as we entered the room, that "he supposed he knew what we had come for. This time, ladies, I understand you have come for me." We confessed that no less an ambition was ours than to secure the President of the United States for our fair, and that this alone had drawn us to Washington. He said that he had been to one of these big fairs, and he didn't know as he wanted to go to another. He gave a most laughable account of his visit to the Philadelphia fair.

"Why," said he, "I was nearly pulled to pieces before I reached Philadelphia. The train stopped at every station on the route, and at many places where there were no stations, only people; and my hand was nearly wrung off before I reached the fair. Then from the depot for two miles it was a solid mass of people blocking the way. Everywhere there were people shouting and cheering; and they would reach into the carriage and shake hands, and hold on, until I was afraid they would be killed, or I pulled from the carriage. When we reached the fair it was worse yet. The police tried to open a way through the crowds for me, but they had to give it up; and I didn't know as I was going to get in at all. The people were everywhere; and, if they saw me starting for a place, they rushed there first, and stood shouting, hurrahing, and trying to shake hands. By and by the Committee had worried me along to a side door, which they suddenly opened, pushed me in, and then turned the key; and that gave me a chance to lunch, shake myself, and draw a long breath. That was the only quiet moment I had; for all the time I was in Philadelphia I was crowded, and jostled, and pulled about, and cheered, and serenaded, until I was more used up than I ever remember to have been in my life. I don't believe I could stand another big fair."

"But," we said, "there is no escape from this fair, Mr. Lincoln, and this will probably be the last of them. The Northwest won't listen to your declining; and the ladies of Chicago are circulating a letter of invitation to you, which will have ten thousand signatures of women alone. The whole Northwest proposes to come to Chicago to see you; and the desire is so general and urgent that you must not feel like declining." "Ten thousand women! What do you suppose my wife will say at ten thousand women coming after me?"

But here the ladies were ready. They had outfoxed Lincoln. Mrs. Livermore continued, "Oh, the invitation includes her; and we have already seen Mrs. Lincoln and ascertained that she would like to come." Lincoln replied, "She would? Well, I suppose that settles the matter, then."

Later in the afternoon Mrs. Livermore and a friend attended Mrs. Lincoln's reception, arriving early hoping to find her alone. The president was already there. He jokingly accused his wife of "'conspiring to get him into another big fair like that at Philadelphia, when they were both nearly suffocated.' She did not deny the charge, but begged that the letter of invitation from the ladies of Chicago might be sent to her to present to her husband. 'I told you my wife would be looking after those women!' said the President."

Five weeks later he was dead.

9

"The Heavens Are Hung in Black"

The Funeral Train

War, at the best, is terrible, and this war of ours, in its magnitude and in its duration, is one of the most terrible. It has deranged business, totally in many localities, and partially in all localities. It has destroyed property, and ruined homes; it has produced a national debt and taxation unprecedented, at least in this country. It has carried mourning to almost every home, until it can almost be said that the "heavens are hung in black."

—Abraham Lincoln, speech at the Great Central Sanitary Fair, Philadelphia, June 16, 1864

On Good Friday, April 14, 1865, Abraham Lincoln attended the play *Our American Cousin* at Ford's Theater on Tenth Street in Washington, D.C. Just after 10 P.M. John Wilkes Booth quietly entered the president's box and shot him in the back of the head. Hopeless men, desperate for a miracle, carried the president across the street to William Peterson's boardinghouse. He never regained consciousness. The next morning, at 7:22 A.M., Abraham Lincoln was pronounced dead. He was fifty-six years, sixty-two days old.

Mary Lincoln chose to bury her husband and son Willie together in their beloved Springfield, Illinois. Administration officials decided to mourn Lincoln in a very public and a very national way. Secretary of War Edwin M. Stanton, who had wept openly at Lincoln's deathbed, appointed a committee of prominent railroad men to choose the route back to Springfield and to make other necessary arrangements. This funeral procession by rail from Washington, D.C., to Springfield, Illinois, became known as the Lincoln Funeral Train. Its route approximated, but was not identical to, Lincoln's Inaugural Train. Stops were scheduled for Baltimore, Harrisburg, Philadelphia, New York City, Albany, Buffalo, Cleveland, Columbus, Indianapolis, and Chicago. There would be twelve funeral services in seventeen hundred miles.

After Lincoln died on that Saturday morning, his body was placed in a coffin draped with an American flag. A lieutenant and ten privates gently put the coffin into a hearse

This photograph by Alexander Gardner, "Abraham Lincoln: Last Sitting Four Days Before His Assassination at Ford's Theater on April 14, 1865," was taken April 10, 1865, in Washington, D.C., and shows a significantly aged, fifty-six-year-old Lincoln. Courtesy of the Library of Congress.

outside the Peterson House and escorted it to the White House. At eleven o'clock an autopsy began in a second-floor guest room. A while later the body was embalmed and dressed in the suit Lincoln had worn at his second inauguration. Embalming was still new and relatively mysterious to the general public. For thousands of people who would view Lincoln's body during his Funeral Train, this was their first experience with an embalmed body. Newspapers across the nation carried not only a description of the dead president, but also a detailed explanation of how he had been preserved.

The government sought a suitable coffin for the assassinated president and finally selected one made of mahogany and lined with lead. Black cloth edged in silver braid draped its sides. Silver tacks and stars attached the black cloth to the coffin. Each side of the coffin had five black tassels and four handles, and silver stars decorated the coffin's head and footboards. On the lid, a row of silver tacks ran the entire length of each side, about two inches from the edge. A silver plate bearing the name of Abraham Lincoln along with his birth and death dates was on the top center. A shield of silver tacks surrounded the plate. The face lid was attached to the top by five silver stars. The inside of the faceplate was white silk, but the remainder of the interior was covered in box-plaited satin. The pillow was white silk, edged with a white satin fringe. The coffin cost fifteen hundred dollars.

Commissioner of public buildings Benjamin French was in charge of funeral arrangements in Washington, D.C. French designed a grand catafalque for the East Room of the White House, and carpenters worked feverishly to complete it. The constant hammering frightened Mrs. Lincoln. Monday evening Lincoln's body was taken to the East Room of the White House and placed on the catafalque to lie in state. On Tuesday, April 18, public viewing began at 9:30 A.M. and lasted until 5:30 P.M. From then until 7:30 P.M. there was a private viewing. The official Washington funeral began Wednesday, April 19, at 12:10 P.M. in the East Room. At its close the dead president traveled down Pennsylvania Avenue in a grand procession to the Capitol Building. At 3:30 P.M. his coffin was carried up the east steps to lie in state in the rotunda. On Thursday, April 20, public viewing began at 8 A.M. and continued all day.

On Friday morning the Reverend Dr. Phineas D. Gurley, pastor of the New York Avenue Presbyterian Church, conducted a short private service in the rotunda. Lincoln's body was taken to the Baltimore and Ohio train depot at New Jersey and C Streets, where at least ten thousand people gathered. Secretary of War Edwin Stanton, Secretary of the Interior John Usher, Secretary of the Navy Gideon Welles, Postmaster General William Dennison, and Lieutenant General Ulysses S. Grant looked on as Lincoln's body was placed on the car that would transport it back to Springfield.

Lincoln's Funeral Car, as it came to be known, was built in the United States military railroad yard in Alexandria, Virginia, between November 1863 and February 1865. Its exterior length was forty-eight feet, and its roof was raised in the center with sixteen windows on the raised portion. There were twelve windows and a painted oval panel with the coat of arms of the United States on each side of the car. At one time the car probably contained a parlor and a sitting room furnished with sofas and chairs, as well as a sleeping apartment.

After the president's death, the military railroad yard in Alexandria was ordered to convert the car into a hearse. A simple platform for Lincoln's coffin was draped in black and secured to the floor at the southern or rear portion of the car. A railing with a removable section surrounded the platform. Rollers were built into the end of the car to simplify the coffin's removal at each stop. Black drapes replaced the window curtains, interior furniture was wrapped in black, and black velvet was hung on each window panel.

At the opposite end of the car, a similar platform was built to hold the coffin of Lincoln's son (although the train conductor from Baltimore to Harrisburg later wrote that that coffin was transported in the baggage car). William Lincoln, who died in Washington, D.C., in 1862, had been buried in a Georgetown cemetery vault awaiting eventual interment in Springfield. Now in death he was going home with his father. A black walnut coffin with silver mounting replaced the original metal casket. A silver plate on the top of the coffin read, "William Wallace Lincoln, Born December 21st, 1850, Died February 20th, 1862."

The Funeral Car was joined with an engine and its tender car, a baggage car, and passenger cars for the journey. Stanton classified the Funeral Train as military. As such it com-

Inside President Lincoln's Funeral Car, Lincoln's coffin was placed on a small platform at the rear. His son's coffin was at the opposite end. Drawing. From the Philadelphia Inquirer, *April 25, 1865.*

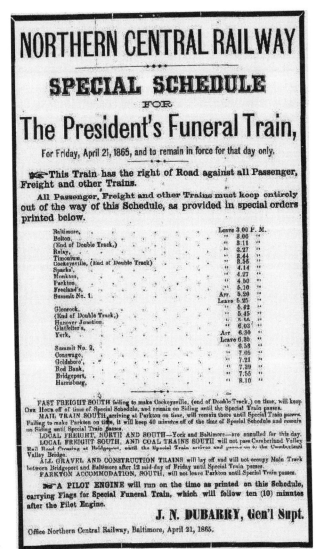

This Northern Central Railway special schedule for the president's Funeral Train was in effect between Baltimore, Maryland, and Harrisburg, Pennsylvania. Courtesy of the Historical Society of York County.

manded the right of way over all other trains, and the secretary of war had final authority as to who would ride on it. He appointed Assistant Adjutant General Edward D. Townsend as officer in charge. Neither Mary Lincoln nor Robert Todd Lincoln chose to ride the train. Four individuals who traveled on the Funeral Train had also ridden on the Inaugural Train: Supreme Court Justice David Davis, Major General David Hunter, Ward Hill Lamon, and *Philadelphia Inquirer* correspondent U. H. Painter. Family on board included Mrs. Lincoln's cousin General John Todd and her brothers-in-law Ninian Edwards and C. M. Smith. The congressional delegation included Lincoln's friend Elihu Washburne, who had welcomed him to Washington in February 1861; Ohio representative Robert C. Schenck, who traveled with Lincoln to Gettysburg; Lyman Trumball of Illinois; and Pennsylvania Senator Edgar Cowan. Governors Oglesby of Illinois, Stone of Iowa, Morton of Indiana, and John

Brough of Ohio—who had been on the speakers' platform at Gettysburg—came to Washington to ride the Funeral Train. Several military officers and a military honor guard of four commissioned officers and twenty-five sergeants were on board. Practical minds decided to include undertaker T. C. Sands and embalmer C. P. Brown.

For the first leg of its journey, from Washington, D.C., to Baltimore, the Funeral Train consisted of B & O engine no. 238, a tender car, six new passenger cars provided by the Baltimore and Ohio Railroad, and a baggage car. The Funeral Car containing Lincoln's body came next; and behind it, and last, was a director's car provided by the Philadelphia, Wilmington, and Baltimore Railroad. It contained a parlor, a chamber, a dining room, and a kitchen; and it transported, at various times, the sergeant's honor guard, Generals Hunter and Townsend, other military officers, and civilian officials. There were nine cars in all.

The plan called for a small pilot engine, no. 239, to precede the Funeral Train by ten minutes to announce the arrival of the train and to prevent accidents. It, along with a tender and one passenger car, left the Washington depot at 7:50 A.M. Military orders limited the train's speed to twenty miles per hour through the countryside and five miles an hour through stations. Reverend Gurley said a final prayer, and the Funeral Train left at 8 A.M.

It arrived at the Camden Street Station in Baltimore in the rain at 10 A.M. Minute guns fired from Federal Hill. Lincoln's coffin was taken to the Merchant's Exchange where he lay in state from noon until 2 P.M. The mourners filed through the Exchange and past the coffin, encircled by four large United States flags—one at each compass point. At 2:30 P.M. the president's coffin left the Exchange for the Calvert Street Station of the Northern Central Railroad.

At 3 P.M. the train left Baltimore to travel to Harrisburg, Pennsylvania. Northern Central train conductor William Gould described the trip:

The coffin in which President Lincoln's body lay rested on three trestles securely fastened to the floor of the car. Over these was crepe. Straps were fastened to the trestles and buckled around the coffin to hold it secure. The coffin was very large and appeared to be about seven feet long and fully three feet wide. It was covered with black cloth, and, besides the four silver handles on either side, there was considerable silver decoration in the form of wreaths. On the lid of the coffin was an engraved silver plate, which read:

ABRAHAM LINCOLN,
16th President of the United States.
Born Feb. 12, 1809.
Died April 15, 1865.

I was in the funeral car at various times in my line of duty. A part of the time the face lid was removed from the coffin, and I had several opportunities of seeing the face of the martyred President. His face was calmed and peaceful. He looked as if he was asleep in pleasant dreams. The body was dressed in black, with white shirt and black tie. . . .

None of the train crew was in uniform—in fact, in those days no uniform was worn by passenger train crews. I wore a black suit of clothes and black hat. On the front of my hat I wore a plate marked "Conductor."

There were about 75 people on the train beside the train crew. There were no women on the train. During the trip the men moved back and forth through the train. They were a distinguished looking group of men, but sad and solemn. Practically all their talk was of the greatness and goodness of Lincoln, and his untimely death. There were many men on the train who were soldiers, but none was in uniform.

Each member of the train crew, and all those who were entitled to ride on the train, wore a special badge. This badge was their ticket of transportation. Of course, I was very careful to see that every person riding on the train was entitled to do so.

Ten minutes before the special train pulled out of Baltimore, a pilot engine and one passenger car, in charge of Capt. George B. Kaufman and brakeman, with a crew started ahead of the special train for Harrisburg. Just at 3 o'clock on the afternoon of April 21, 1865, I gave the engineer the signal to start for Harrisburg. The engine gave a shrill whistle and the train slowly passed the depot. There was an immense crowd around the station at Baltimore to see the train leave, but they were very quiet. As we left Baltimore the weather was cloudy and warm.

At 5:30 P.M. Pennsylvania Governor Andrew Curtin, Major General George Cadwallader, and their respective staffs boarded the train near the Pennsylvania-Maryland state line. Curtin had been ill and confined to bed for several days. He joined Governor Augustus W. Bradford of Maryland in the front car. Governor Curtin decided to ride the Funeral Train for the entire time that it was in Pennsylvania and in doing so set a precedent: all other state governors rode with the train as it passed through their states.

At dusk it was raining as the train pulled into York, Pennsylvania, for a scheduled five-minute stop for water. City bells tolled, minute guns boomed, and the United States Hospital brass band played a funeral dirge. Although infantry tried to keep the crowd back, it seemed to some as if the train "plowed" its way through the crowd. Elderly men and women and wounded veterans crowded the tracks. Women held children aloft to see, and an aged black man said, "He was crucified for us."

Six York women dressed in black mourning clothes received permission from General Townsend to board the Funeral Car to place a special wreath by the coffin. The wreath's outer circle was three feet in circumference and was composed of white roses and camellias. Inside was a national shield with a blue background made of violets, stars made of white myrtle, and bars made alternately of red and white verbena.

The train left York at 6:50 P.M. Conductor Gould remembered: "At every cross road there were crowds of people, and as the funeral train passed them the men took off their hats, and I noticed many, both men and women, who shed tears as the train passed. It was the most solemn trip I ever took on a train. Everybody on the train was solemn and everybody the train passed was solemn. Just at 8 o'clock the train pulled into Harrisburg. The sky was cloudy, and there was a fine drizzle of rain. It seemed to me that nature was weeping because of Lincoln's death."

Near 8:15 P.M. a member of the Signal Corps posted on the west shore of the Susquehanna River across from the state capital signaled the train's approach. A cannon fired from the capitol grounds, and the bells of Harrisburg tolled. Citizens who

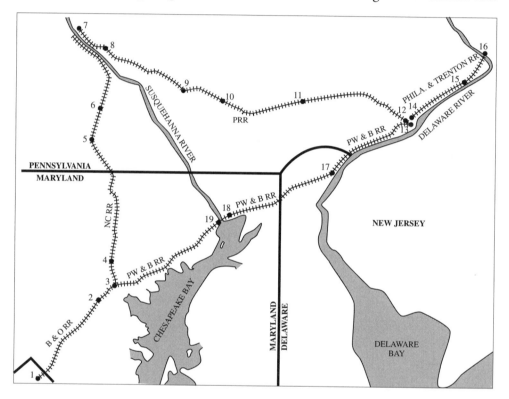

WASHINGTON, D.C., TO PHILADELPHIA, 1865. *Lincoln's Funeral Train, April 21, 1865–April 24, 1865* (1) *Washington, D.C.—Station at New Jersey and C Streets* (2) *Washington Junction/Relay House (B & O)* (3) *Baltimore, Maryland—Camden Street Station and Calvert Street Station* (4) *Relay (Northern Central)* (5) *Hanover Junction* (6) *York* (7) *Harrisburg* (8) *Middletown* (9) *Lancaster* (10) *Leaman Place* (11) *Downingtown* (12) *Philadelphia— West Philadelphia Station* (13) *Philadelphia—Broad and Prime Station* (14) *Philadelphia— Kensington Station* (15) *Bristol* (16) *Trenton, New Jersey* (17) *Wilmington, Delaware* (18) *Perryville, Maryland.* (19) *Havre de Grace, Maryland. The Train traveled northeast on the Baltimore and Ohio Railroad from Washington, D.C., to Baltimore; north on the Northern Central Railroad from Baltimore to Harrisburg; and east on the Pennsylvania Railroad from Harrisburg to Philadelphia. From the West Philadelphia Station it traveled the Junction Railroad to the Philadelphia, Wilmington, and Baltimore line and the Broad and Prime Street Station. From Kensington Station it traveled northeast on the Philadelphia and Trenton Railroad to Trenton, New Jersey.*

wished to join the procession gathered at the courthouse, while a multitude of others crowded the depot. As soon as the train arrived at the Pennsylvania Railroad Depot near Fifth and Market Streets, the military honor guard traveling with the train placed Lincoln's coffin on the waiting hearse. Sergeants were assigned to lead each of the four white horses that pulled the hearse through the city streets.

The procession from the depot to the Pennsylvania Capitol included the Sixteenth Regiment Veteran Reserve Corps, cavalry, artillery, veterans of the War of 1812, city and state officials, local citizens, and the hearse bearing Lincoln. Chemical lights placed especially for the evening provided illumination along the entire route. Soon after the procession started—even before it could reach Market Street—a tremendous thunderstorm began. Thunder rolled, lightning flashed, rain came down, muffled bells moaned, and mournful guns boomed. "Here the rain was terrific. Horses pranced in the lightning's glare, and men staggered under the watery elements. The portion of the military now filed around the hearse, which stood in the street for the space of about ten minutes. The watery elements were pouring down upon the remains of him we revere, and all the drapery of black was soaked in water. Heaven wept even more than the people. Red lights shine upon the street at every corner, lighting up the insignias of mourning:—'A Nation Mourns its Martyred Father.' 'A Great Man has Fallen.' 'We Mourn a Slaughtered Leader.'"

The marchers continued on Market Street to Second Street, and then turned north on Second to State Street and the Capitol Building (see chapter 1, page 18). When the cavalry and artillery units arrived at the capitol, they formed in open order, allowing infantry and civilian units to march through them as they approached the main capitol entrance from the west. The pallbearers placed the coffin on a catafalque in the House of Representatives, just in front of the clerk's desk. Philadelphia policemen stood guard.

Inside the House of Representatives, window frames, doors, speaker's stand and chair, and chandelier were draped in black. The windows were decorated with crossed battle flags of Pennsylvania regiments. Names of the battles in which the flags had been carried were attached. Black cloth trimmed with silver stars draped the catafalque. Evergreens edged the dais, with white roses and orange blossoms running inside the evergreens. Wreathes of white roses and orange blossoms decorated the speaker's area, and a portrait of the dead president and an emblem of an eagle were above the speaker's chair.

As the body of Lincoln arrived inside the House of Representatives, an immense crowd outside the capitol overwhelmed the military guard. In the crush and confusion, mourners were able to make their way to the rotunda doors before a semblance of order was restored. Public viewing began at 9:30 P.M. and continued until midnight. Entrance to the house chamber was through the capitol doors. "The countenance still preserved the expression it bore in life, though changed in hue, the lips firmly set but half smiling, and the whole face still indicating the energy and humor which characterized the living man. The beard was shaven close save a tuft on the chin." After viewing the president's body, the mourners had to exit through windows. Workmen had built steps up to and down from several windows to accommodate large numbers of people.

That evening, Friday, April 21, 1865, the *Harrisburg Pennsylvania Daily Telegraph* reported that all Episcopal churches in Richmond, Virginia, were closed by order of

Lincoln's bier in the Pennsylvania House of Representatives, Harrisburg, awaits the coffin. The room is draped, ready for public viewing. Photographs, MG-218, General Photograph Collection, Pennsylvania State Archives.

the government. The churches had omitted the usual prayers for the president of the United States from their service.

Saturday morning was wet and rainy. Minute guns began firing at dawn. In the light of day the flag flying above the capitol building could be seen, bordered in black, flying at half-mast. Trains continued to bring mourners from outlying towns and villages. The longest Cumberland Valley Railroad train yet seen brought twenty carloads of passengers to Harrisburg. Long before the capitol doors opened, the line of waiting people stretched west from the portico of the capitol building, down the hill, through the Third Street gates, and down Third Street. When the doors opened at 7 A.M., soldiers had to prevent people from overwhelming the entrance, as they had done the night before. People walked past the dead Lincoln, some quiet, some sobbing. One individual laid a beautiful flowered cross wreath near the coffin. At 9 A.M. public viewing ended, and city bells began to toll once again.

From 9 to 10 A.M. members of the civic procession that would escort the coffin back to the train viewed Lincoln's body. Governor Curtin, city and state officials, veterans of the War of 1812, veterans of the Civil War, delegations from other states, clergy, fire departments, civic associations, and invited citizens took part. The procession had formed earlier in the vicinity of Market Street; and at 8 A.M. it moved from Market to Second Street, Walnut Street, and Third Street. The mourners entered the capitol grounds through the gate at Third and State Streets, marched into the house chamber, viewed the body of Lincoln, and then exited to Fourth Street. From there they circled north around the capitol by way of Fourth, North, and Third Streets. At Third and State Streets, now facing south, they awaited the military portion of the funeral procession. One Harrisburg newspaper estimated that twenty-five thousand people filed through the house chamber in five and one-half hours, leaving a thick covering of dust inside. Lincoln's body was dusted and his face rechalked.

At 10 A.M. the honor guard placed the coffin in the waiting hearse. The procession began making its way back to the railroad depot. The hearse left Capitol Park through main gates overhung by a white arch bound in black. The procession itself was almost as long as the parade route. It moved past the mourners as they lined State Street, Front Street, and Market Street to the depot. Forty thousand people filled the streets, and each one wore a sign of mourning.

The original schedule called for departure at 12 noon, but on short notice the departure time was changed to 11 A.M. Those traveling with the Funeral Train were asked to be on board and ready to depart before the hearse arrived. Former Secretary of War Simon Cameron boarded to accompany the train to Philadelphia. The wreath from York, Pennsylvania, had been left in the Funeral Car in Harrisburg, and it too was transported on to Philadelphia. When Lincoln's coffin was in place at 11:15 A.M., the train left immediately. Mourners still arriving in Harrisburg were too late.

People lined the tracks leaving the state capital and waited for the train to pass. When it arrived at Middletown at 11:38 A.M., there was a crowd of people. Flags flew, and an evergreen arch stood over the tracks. When the train reached Elizabethtown at 12:15 P.M., there was another large crowd and a banner "We Mourn a Nation's Loss."

At 1 P.M. the Funeral Train arrived at the Pennsylvania Railroad depot in Lancaster. Estimates of the crowd ranged from five thousand to forty thousand people. They overran the tracks, occupied windows, and filled balconies. The depot was decorated in American flags and black drapes. A large sign edged in black crepe near the window of the Western Union Telegraph office read, "Abraham Lincoln the Illustrious Martyr of Liberty. The Nation Mourns His Loss: But Though Dead He Yet Lives!" The train paused only four or five minutes. A seven-woman committee of the Patriot Daughters entered the Funeral Car to place a bouquet of camellias and white roses by the coffin. Reportedly Thaddeus Stevens watched as the train entered Lancaster, and James Buchanan saw it from a carriage outside the depot.

The Funeral Train moved eastward, always preceded by the pilot engine with a single passenger car. On the eastern outskirts of Lancaster there were five to six hundred

David C. Burnite photographed Lincoln's Funeral Car at the Pennsylvania Railroad Station, near Fifth and Market Streets, Harrisburg on Saturday morning, April 22, 1865. This was the view from Market Street, looking eastward. Photographs, Lincoln's Funeral Train, MG-218, General Photograph Collection, Pennsylvania State Archives.

people, including the men of the Lancaster Iron Works who were along the tracks holding their hats uplifted in a salute of honor. At Strasburg Junction there was a large crowd, and at 2:15 P.M. the train passed Parkesburg and the one thousand people gathered there. The *Philadelphia Inquirer* reporter on board described the trip:

> At Parkesburg we found the whole country at the railroad station, but the train ran so swiftly by that there was barely time for them to catch a glimpse of the funeral car, toward which all eyes were strained. At Coatesville, that bee-hive in the great Chester Valley, the forges were silent, the town was closed, the artisan, the farmer, every one was at the station. On we ran rapidly to Downingtown, where we waited five minutes for wood and water. Here was gathered another large crowd. All was quiet; there was no swaying to and fro of an unruly mob, but they quietly gathered around the rear of the train, and stood with uncovered heads until we left. At Oakland, at Walkertown, and at Steamboat, hundreds of people were grouped; flags, draped in mourning, was the sole expression of their feelings. At West Chester Intersection about a thousand persons were gathered around the station; at Green Tree about a hundred men were ranged along the bank, with uncovered heads; the mournful flag was guarded by men in locks of grey; at Paoli, and all the stations to Philadelphia, we found the same demonstrations, the same tokens of grief, the same quiet groups, the uncovered heads, the dead silence speaking an eloquence that could not be misinterpreted. From our entrance into Hestonville and West Philadelphia, we found an unbroken column of people for miles along the road, until we reached the Pennsylvania Railroad depot, where there were acres. A small brass howitzer, firing minute guns, heralded our arrival as we passed down the Junction Railroad towards the Philadelphia, Wilmington and Baltimore depot.

A mass of humanity surrounded the depot in South Philadelphia. The military portion of the procession had formed on Broad Street facing west at 3:30 P.M. to await the train's arrival. The center of the military rested at the depot while various civilian groups formed in the surrounding streets. On Broad Street the depot was draped in black cloth. A wreath of white flowers hung under each window, and a United States flag edged in black flew above. Policemen were stationed at each entrance and allowed no one to enter without a special pass from the police chief. Outside the depot a hearse and more than thirty carriages designated for the train's funeral party waited.

The Funeral Train arrived at the Broad and Prime Street Station of the Philadelphia, Wilmington, and Baltimore Railroad at 4:50 P.M. It was twenty minutes late. When the train first appeared at the station, a signal cannon boomed. Minute guns began firing from a battery placed on Broad Street just south of Market Street. The firing would continue each minute from the time the train arrived at the depot until Lincoln's body was placed in Independence Hall at 8 P.M. The sound of muffled bells accompanied the guns.

After the train arrived, the Philadelphia honor guard assigned to escort Lincoln's coffin formed a double line from the depot to Broad Street. Military pallbearers removed the coffin from the train, walked between the lines formed by the honor guard, and placed the coffin onto the waiting hearse. The hearse and honor guard were ready to move by 5:15 P.M., but because of the difficulty of forming the large procession, the hearse had to wait.

The Philadelphia funeral procession consisted of eleven divisions. Participants included white and black military units. Military and civilian bands played funeral dirges. The governors of Pennsylvania, Ohio, Illinois, Indiana, and Iowa joined the procession. Elected city, state, and federal officials, including all of Philadelphia's United States congressmen marched. There were patriotic groups, such as the National Union League Club, and other civic groups. There were clergy, fire companies, employees of the Mint,

"The Catafalque Which Bore Abraham Lincoln's Body Through Philadelphia" was sixteen feet high, fifteen feet long, eight feet wide, and was pulled by eight black horses (Philadelphia Inquirer, *April 22, 1865). It was photographed outside the undertaking establishment of Edward S. Early, near Tenth and Green Streets, Philadelphia. Courtesy of the Print and Picture Collection, the Free Library of Philadelphia.*

and veterans of the War of 1812. Members of the Young Men's Christian Association marched, as did the Arsenal Guard.

Many groups had specially prepared banners. An African-American Masonic lodge displayed a banner of black cloth with white muslin on the top and sides. In the banner's center was a large print of Abraham Lincoln signing the Emancipation Proclamation. The top of the staff that supported the banner was capped with a gold eagle, and below this was a white flowered wreath.

A few minutes past 6 P.M. the procession began moving north on Broad Street. Bands played their dirges while the minute guns fired. Muffled bells sounded, and people mourned.

> Half a million of sorrow-stricken people were upon the streets to do honor to all that was left of the man whom they respected, revered and loved with an affection never before bestowed upon any other, save the Father of his Country. Universal grief was depicted on the faces of all. Hearts beat quick and fast with the throb of a sorrow which they had never experienced. Young and old alike bowed in solemn reverence before the draped chariot which bore the body of our deceased, assassinated president. The feeling was too deep for expression. The wet cheeks of the strong man, the tearful eyes of the maiden and the matron, the hush which pervaded the atmosphere and made it oppressive, the steady measured tread of the military and the civic procession, the mournful dirges of the bands, the dismal tolling of the bells and the boom of the minute guns, told more than it is possible for language to express. Slowly and sadly the funeral cortege moved over the designated route.

The previous day the funeral route had been lengthened in order to allow more space for people on the sidewalks. From Broad Street, the procession marched west on Walnut Street, north on Twenty-first Street, east on Arch Street, south on Third Street, and west on Walnut Street. It stopped at the Walnut Street gate of Independence Square (see chapter 1, page 12).

The square was illuminated with sixty calcium lights, some red, some white, and some blue. A band in the steeple of Independence Hall played funeral dirges before and during the procession. Members of the Union League of Philadelphia, dressed in black mourning suits and white gloves, formed a double line along both sides of the pathway leading from the Walnut Street gate of the square to the south door of Independence Hall. When the hearse arrived at the Walnut Street gate of Independence Square at 8 P.M., the pallbearers removed the coffin from the hearse and carried it between the lines of bareheaded Union League members.

Inside Independence Hall, Lincoln's coffin was placed in the center of the Assembly Room on a small platform draped in black. This was the same Assembly Room in which the Declaration of Independence was signed, and in which Lincoln spoke on February 22, 1861. Philadelphia newspapers reprinted a portion of that 1861 speech.

I have often inquired of myself, what great principle or idea it was that kept this Confederacy so long together. It was not the mere matter of the separation of the colonies from the mother land; but something in that Declaration giving liberty, not alone to the people of this country, but hope to the world for all future time. It was that which gave promise that in due time the weights should be lifted from the shoulders of all men, and that all should have an equal chance. This is the sentiment embodied in that Declaration of Independence.

Now, my friends, can this country be saved upon that basis? If it can, I will consider myself one of the happiest men in the world if I can help to save it. If it can't be saved upon that principle, it will be truly awful. But, if this country cannot be saved without giving up that principle—I was about to say I would rather be assassinated on this spot than to surrender it.

The coffin was aligned north-south with Abraham Lincoln's head at the south. The faceplate of the coffin was removed and the head and chest of the dead president exposed. The American flag, which draped the entire coffin during the procession, was pulled away from the area of the faceplate. The wreath that traveled on the train, and whose card read, "Presented by the ladies of York, Pennsylvania, to be laid on the body of our lamented President if possible," rested on the coffin. A beautiful floral cross was suspended at the coffin's head. Its card read, "To the memory of our beloved President, from a few ladies of the United States Sanitary Commission." An unknown elderly African-American woman donated a wreath whose card read: "The nation mourns his loss. He still lives in the hearts of the people." Eighteen candelabras with 108 lighted candles provided light. Twenty-five vases of japonicas, heliotropes, and other flowers gave a magnificent floral scent. The room itself was draped in black cloth, and wreaths were hung around the walls. Symbolically, the Liberty Bell was placed on a stand near Lincoln's head. The bell's inscription was visible to all who passed, "Proclaim LIBERTY throughout all the Land unto all the Inhabitants thereof" (Leviticus 25:10).

Another card on a wreath that lay near the head of the coffin read: "Before any great national event I have always had the same dream. I had it the other night. It is of a ship sailing rapidly." This card referred to a statement Lincoln made at a cabinet meeting on April 14, 1865, the day of his assassination. Secretary of the Navy Gideon Welles recorded it in his diary on April 17, 1865, and it was later corroborated by Frederick Seward who had also attended the meeting. Welles wrote that Lincoln said, "that he seemed to be in some singular, indescribable vessel, and that he was moving with great rapidity. That he had this dream preceding Sumter, Bull Run, Antietam, Gettysburg, Stone[s] River, Vicksburg, Wilmington, etc. After some discussion, he continued: I had this strange dream again last night, and we shall, judging from the past, have great news very soon."

From 10 P.M. to midnight on Saturday, April 22, 1865, there was a private viewing. Admission was by card sent on behalf of the mayor and city councils. Cardholders entered the Court of Quarter Sessions on Sixth Street below Chestnut, walked through the court building into the square, and entered Independence Hall's southern door. Once inside the hall they moved through a double line formed by Philadelphia police from the doorway to the wooden railings around the coffin. Standing at the coffin were members of the honor guard and Mayor Alexander Henry. A band seated inside the hall played funeral dirges. The *Philadelphia Inquirer* reported that Lincoln looked almost alive: "The eyes are very nearly closed; the lips slightly parted, and but for a faint discolorization, mainly of the lower part of the face, one would think the great departed had just sunk into a deep and tranquil slumber. The beard, which commences at the lower part of the chin, is about two inches in length, and presents a natural appearance, and the hair is brushed back from the forehead. The body is clothed in a full suit of black; a black silk cravat encircles the neck, over which turns a white linen collar."

The mourners exited the Assembly Room using the two eastern windows that fronted Independence Square. As in Harrisburg, carpenters had constructed steps up and down on either side of the windows specifically for the viewing. To accommodate the people expected at the public viewing the next day, workmen also built two entrances through windows that overlooked Chestnut Street. Two lines of mourners could file up the steps, walk through the open windows, and be directed to either side of the coffin by wooden railings. Exit would be onto Independence Square through the same two windows that private viewers had used the previous night.

Hundreds of people spent the night on Chestnut Street in order to be assured a place in line. When the windows opened for public viewing at 6 A.M. on Sunday, April 23, 1865, the line to the west extended as far as Eighth Street. The line to the east extended as far as Third Street. People poured into Philadelphia from all directions. By 11 A.M. the line westward on Chestnut Street extended to the Schuylkill River; and the line eastward extended to the Delaware River—a total of three miles. The distance between Independence Hall and the Delaware River was not large enough to accommodate the huge crowd, and the line to the east had to curve several blocks north on Second Street.

The crowd immediately in front of Independence Hall on Chestnut Street between Fifth and Sixth Streets was so dense that small boys were seen climbing over the heads of individuals until, every so often, one would fall to the ground. People held infants and children above their heads. Women fainted from the crush of the crowd. The pushing and shoving injured hundreds. In the midst of the disorder Governor Curtin appeared from the windows of Independence Hall and appealed to the crowd. Around 3 P.M. military and police reinforcements cleared Chestnut Street between Fourth and Sixth Streets of everyone who was not in an orderly line. People tried to circumvent police lines by going through public buildings on the north side of Chestnut Street so as to exit in front of Independence Hall. The police stopped those attempts by posting guards and making arrests. By dinnertime the wait in line had decreased to two hours. After dark a transparency portrait of Abraham Lincoln illuminated the crowd in front of Independence Hall. Gas jets above the transparency lit the words "Rest in

Peace." By 10 P.M. the line had shrunk to a length of one mile. Late that evening 75 Union veterans with leg amputations and using crutches were put in line in front of the hall. Shortly thereafter 150 Union soldiers brought from local military hospitals in ambulances were placed in line also.

At 1:17 A.M. on Monday morning, April 24, 1865, the entrance windows to Independence Hall closed. Newspapers attempted to estimate the number of persons who viewed Lincoln's body in Philadelphia. Two lines of viewers passed by the coffin uninterrupted for twenty hours. If one person passed per second, the maximum number of viewers was 144,000. An actual count of persons who passed through one of the entrance windows in five minutes was 268 persons. Two entrances were used. Generalizing this count over twenty hours gave the number of viewers as 128,640.

As soon as the entrances closed and the public was out of the Assembly Room, the task of cleaning the immense amount of dust and dirt caused by more than 100,000 people began. Embalmer Brown cleaned Lincoln's face of the dust that had accumulated during thirty-three hours in Philadelphia. At 2:30 A.M., little more than one hour after public viewing ended, the honor guard took Lincoln's coffin outside onto Chestnut Street and placed it into the waiting hearse. Torchbearers, pallbearers, and the honor guard surrounded the hearse. Cavalry and infantry led the march, while carriages containing the funeral party (which left the Continental Hotel at 2 A.M.), civic groups, and bands playing funeral marches followed behind. The procession moved east on Chestnut Street, north on Fifth Street, east on Oxford Street, and north on Front Street to the Kensington Railroad Station.

Thousands of people at Kensington Station watched as the hearse arrived at 3:45 A.M., was loaded onto the train, and left at 4 A.M. A few minutes out of Philadelphia the Funeral Train passed several hundred persons gathered at Bristol, Pennsylvania. The sun was just rising. At 5:30 A.M. the train crossed the Delaware River and entered New Jersey. Governor Curtin greeted New Jersey Governor Joel Parker when he boarded the train at Morrisville. Lincoln's sojourn in southeastern Pennsylvania was over.

In looking back, it could be seen that Philadelphia's public funeral for Lincoln was similar to her welcome of visiting dignitaries. An official escort met the remains upon arrival at the railroad depot and joined a grand procession through city streets. There were city officials, military, police, flags, cannon, and a crowd. However, in addition to the obvious, there were important differences between the two occasions. In the public funeral, a team of matched, black horses drew the hearse (compared to the public welcome where white horses drew the barouche). Flags were at half-staff (instead of being draped or waving). Cannon boomed once each minute (instead of volleys of salutes). Watchful mourners along the parade route were bareheaded and silent (instead of cheering), and the procession ended at Independence Hall (instead of the hotel), where the dignitary lay in state. These rituals developed over many decades, and Philadelphia's observances of the 1841 death of President William Henry Harrison and of the 1861 funeral of Colonel Elmer Ellsworth, a member of Lincoln's Inaugural Train, were comparable. In one rare break with tradition, Philadelphia appropriated

$14,000 for the 1865 presidential funeral expenses. In previous years, private groups or individuals had funded the homecomings of Philadelphia's many war dead.

During the days that followed the Funeral Train moved on to other cities, other funerals, and other mourners. The train visited Trenton, Jersey City, New York City, and Albany. On the morning of Wednesday, April 26, 1865, John Wilkes Booth was shot and killed in a tobacco barn on the Richard Garrett farm in Virginia. Later that same day Confederate General Joseph E. Johnston surrendered his command to Union General William T. Sherman. The war was really over!

The Funeral Train's schedule called for travel through Erie, Pennsylvania, during the early morning hours of Friday, April 28, 1865. A superintendent of the Cleveland and Erie Railroad contacted city officials and asked them not to have any ceremonies at that time of the morning because the people on the Funeral Train were exhausted. Erie canceled her plans, and city officials traveled to Buffalo, New York, to attend the funeral services. The train left Buffalo at 10:10 on Thursday evening. Major Scott of Erie was onboard to escort the train as it traveled through Erie County, and around midnight he telegraphed waiting mourners that the train would indeed stop briefly in Erie. At 1:32 A.M. the train crossed the Pennsylvania–New York state line. Erie Mayor F. F. Farrar came on board, and twelve-year-old Leonora Crawford presented a cross and wreath with a card that read, "Rest in Peace." The Funeral Train arrived in Erie at 2:50 A.M. Bells tolled, and there was a military salute. The faceplate of the coffin was removed, and a few local women along with their escorts were allowed to enter the Funeral Car to view the body. Both the *New York Tribune* and the *New York Times* reported that "there was no particular demonstration at this place." After a short stop the train continued on and reached the outskirts of Cleveland, Ohio, by 6:30 A.M.

On May 2, 1865, Mayor Farrar telegraphed a letter of explanation to major newspapers. "While acknowledging with profound humiliation the absence of a proper demonstration of respect on the part of this city to greet the remains of President Lincoln on their arrival here last Friday morning, justice to our citizens who have ever delighted to honor the lamented patriot while living, and who are second to none in heartfelt devotion to the memory of the distinguished dead, requires publicity of the fact, that in the midst of preparations for the mournful occasion they were informed by a Superintendent of the Cleveland & Erie railroad that the funeral escort had made a special request that no public demonstration be made at this place, in order that their committee might have rest and repose."

The Funeral Train traveled on to Cleveland, Columbus, and Indianapolis. On Monday, May 1, 1865, it reached Chicago. On Wednesday it reached Springfield, Illinois. On Thursday, May 4, 1865, Springfield held Lincoln's last funeral and buried him that same day in a vault in Oak Ridge Cemetery.

Whether intended or unintended, Abraham Lincoln's Funeral Train became a national event of immense proportions. During this great national funeral, hundreds of thousands of mourners filed past Lincoln's open coffin. It was a time of great sadness, a time of intense mourning. Poet Walt Whitman gave voice to the nation's despair in his poem "When Lilacs Last in the Dooryard Bloom'd":

> Coffin that passes through lanes and streets,
> Through day and night with the great cloud darkening the land,
> With the pomp of the inloop'd flags, with the cities draped in black,
> With the show of the States themselves as of crape-veil'd women standing,
> With processions long and winding and the flambeaus of the night,
> With the countless torches lit, with the silent sea of faces and the unbared heads,
> With the waiting depot, the arriving coffin, and the sombre faces,
> With dirges through the night, with the thousand voices rising strong and solemn,
> With the mournful voices of the dirges pour'd around the coffin,
> The dim-lit churches and the shuddering organs—where amid these you journey,
> With the tolling tolling bells' perpetual clang,
> Here, coffin that slowly passes,
> I give you my sprig of lilac.

After his death, people remembered many things about Abraham Lincoln's life. Personal secretaries John Hay and John Nicolay reminisced that Lincoln loved to read Shakespeare and that he often read it to them aloud. At Philadelphia's Great Central Sanitary Fair in June 1864, the president paraphrased the opening line to Shakespeare's play *King Henry the Sixth:* Lincoln said, "the heavens are hung in black." Surely Lincoln read beyond the opening line. When he did, perhaps he thought about King Henry's fate. Perhaps he wondered what fate awaited him.

> Hung be the heavens with black, yield day to night!
> Comets, importing change of times and states,
> Brandish your crystal tresses in the sky,
> And with them scourge the bad revolting stars
> That have consented unto Henry's death!
> King Henry the Fifth, too famous to live long!
> England ne'er lost a king of so much worth.

10

Postscript

The Literal Trail—Sites to Visit

Abraham Lincoln last visited Pennsylvania more than one hundred thirty years ago. Seasons pass and times change. It is no longer possible to experience Pennsylvania as Lincoln did so many years ago. The people, the sights, the sounds that he knew are gone. It is possible, however, to walk where Lincoln once walked, to measure the distances that he measured, and to see some of what he saw. This is the literal Lincoln Trail in Pennsylvania.

The trail as outlined in this chapter moves through the state from east to west. It could just as easily be traveled from west to east, or in segments. The descriptions and photographs that follow are aids to guide the traveler. A good road map of Pennsylvania would also be helpful, as well as street maps of Philadelphia and Pittsburgh. Not every site listed is of equal importance, nor is every site of equal interest. The asterisks indicate each location's degree of interest according to the following key:

*	location only
**	modern structure only
***	historical site of interest
****	historical site of significant interest
*****	historical site of outstanding interest

Bristol: From the Pennsylvania Turnpike (here designated as Interstate 276) exit at Route 13, the extreme eastern exit near the Delaware River. Take Route 13 south into Bristol. Turn left (east) onto Bath Street. Turn left at Buckley Street. Turn right onto Pond Street and proceed to 305 Pond Street, near the police station.

***1. **Site of an Inaugural Train whistle-stop and other passages by rail.** Bristol, northeast of Philadelphia, is on the rail line between Philadelphia and Trenton, New Jersey. Lincoln traveled through this community by rail in September 1848, February 1860, February 1861, June 1862, and April 1865 (Funeral Train). There is a historical marker and a section of rail line opposite 305 Pond Street. They commemorate Lincoln's whistle-stop speech on February 21, 1861, to a crowd of more than one thousand people.

PHILADELPHIA: From Bristol travel south on Route 13. Turn north onto Route 413 to the entrance of Interstate 95 south. Take Interstate 95 south into Philadelphia. Get off the expressway at the Central Philadelphia/Center City exit. Go south several blocks until you are able to turn left (east). Travel east to Sixth Street. Turn right (south) onto Sixth Street. Independence Hall is at Sixth and Chestnut Streets.

Independence Hall, Independence Square, Congress Hall, Old City Hall, Carpenter's Hall, and surrounding park areas are known as Independence National Historical Park. *****2. Independence Hall, Sixth and Chestnut Streets, is also known as the Old State House. In this Georgian design, knowledgeable colonists saw the influence of Italian Renaissance architect Andrea Palladio. Construction began in 1732 on the three-part structure that employed piazzas to connect the main central building to two smaller outbuildings. Members of the Continental Congress signed the Declaration of Independence here in 1776. The Constitutional Convention met in Independence Hall in 1787.

Lincoln visited Independence Hall on February 22, 1861, when the Inaugural Train was in Philadelphia. He gave a brief speech inside the Assembly Room. Outside on Chestnut Street he gave another brief speech and raised a thirty-four-star United States flag. Today a sidewalk plaque between Independence Hall and Chestnut Street marks the site where Lincoln stood on a wooden platform during the ceremony. Lincoln lay in state in the Assembly Room on April 22–24, 1865. More than 100,000 people filed past his open coffin.

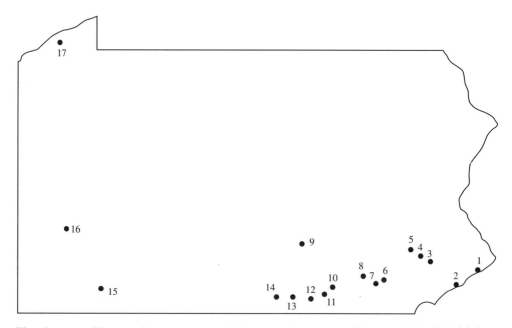

THE LINCOLN TRAIL IN PENNSYLVANIA: A GENERAL OVERVIEW. (1) *Bristol* (2) *Philadelphia* (3) *Coventryville* (4) *Hopewell Furnace* (5) *Lincoln and Boone sites* (6) *Leaman Place* (7) *Strasburg* (8) *Lancaster* (9) *Harrisburg* (10) *York* (11) *Hanover Junction* (12) *Hanover* (13) *Gettysburg* (14) *Caledonia* (15) *National Road* (16) *Pittsburgh* (17) *Erie*

Bristol's train track and marker testify to Lincoln's rail travel and whistle-stops. Photograph by the author.

PHILADELPHIA. (1) *Independence Hall* (2) *Declaration House* (3) *Continental Hotel site and Chinese Museum Building site* (4) *Girard House Hotel site* (5) *Musical Fund Hall* (6) *Union League 1864 site* (7) *Cathedral of Saints Peter and Paul* (8) *Logan Square site* (9) *Pennsylvania Railroad Station 1861 site* (10) *Broad and Prime Street Station site.*

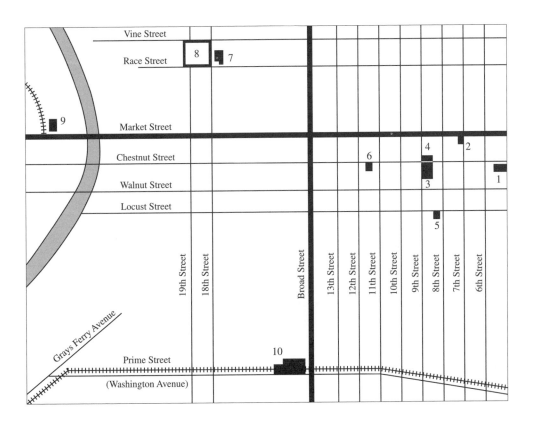

*****3. The Liberty Bell, north of Independence Hall, on Independence Mall. The Liberty Bell, inscribed, "Proclaim LIBERTY throughout all the Land unto all the Inhabitants thereof," was placed at the head of Abraham Lincoln's open coffin while he lay in state in the Assembly Room.

***4. Independence Square. The grassy area immediately south of Independence Hall is called Independence Square. Abraham Lincoln attended a "ratification meeting" in Independence Square on June 9, 1848, at the close of the Whig National Convention. The evening of April 22, 1865, an honor guard carried Lincoln's coffin through the square between two lines of Union League members. The lines stretched from the Walnut Street entrance of the square to the south entrance of Independence Hall.

****5. Declaration House replica, southwest corner of Seventh and Market Streets. Thomas Jefferson lived here when he was a delegate to the Second Continental Congress. In the second-floor rooms that Jefferson rented from the Graff family, he wrote the Declaration of Independence in 1776. The original house existed when Lincoln visited Philadelphia. The National Park Service maintains and interprets this reconstruction.

Independence Hall was the seat of Pennsylvania's government from 1736 to 1799. The Second Continental Congress met here beginning in 1775. Philadelphia's Select and Common Councils (city government) occupied this building when Lincoln visited in 1861. Photograph by the author.

Independence Square is diagonal to Washington Square and the tomb of the Unknown Soldier of the American Revolution. Photograph from the Walnut Street gate by the author.

The Declaration House replica on the southwest corner of Seventh and Market Streets exhibits two rooms that are furnished as they might have been in Thomas Jefferson's era. Photograph by the author.

**6. Site of the Continental Hotel, southeast corner of Ninth and Chestnut Streets.
Architect John McArthur Jr. designed the Continental Hotel (built 1857–60) with elements of the Italianate style that became popular in the 1840s. Generally felt to be
the finest hotel in the United States, it boasted one of the first vertical railways (an
elevator) and could accommodate up to 1,000 guests in its 700 rooms. The ground
floor held a lobby, public rooms, and shops. The first "self-sustaining" stairway (not
attached to a wall) in an American commercial building led from the main lobby to
the second floor. On the second floor a 165-foot promenade, flanked by public rooms
and dining rooms, opened onto an exterior balcony.

Abraham Lincoln was a guest at the hotel on the evenings of February 21, 1861, and
June 16, 1864. Here in 1861 Allan Pinkerton and Frederick Seward separately informed
Lincoln of the Baltimore plot to assassinate him.

The Benjamin Franklin Hotel occupies this site today. A plaque located on the hotel,
to the east of the main Chestnut Street entrance, commemorates Lincoln's February
21, 1861 speech, from the Continental Hotel's balcony. "May my right hand forget its

*Musical Fund Hall, 810 Locust
Street, was renovated, but the
original facade was retained.
Photograph by the author.*

cunning and my tongue cleave to the roof of my mouth if ever I prove false to those teachings [from Independence Hall]."

7. Site of the Chinese Museum Building. Located on the northeast corner of Ninth and Sansom Streets, the Chinese Museum Building was built circa 1836–38 from designs by Isaac Holden. It originally held a local merchant's extensive collection of Chinese artifacts on the first floor and a portion of Charles Wilson Peale's natural history collection on the second floor. Owners eventually sold both collections, and by 1844 the building became a public hall for exhibitions, concerts, and meetings. Philadelphia hosted the Whig National Convention here in June 1848. Abraham Lincoln attended as an observer and apparently enjoyed his role as the only Whig congressman from Illinois.

The museum building and much of the Chestnut Street block between Eighth and Ninth Streets burned on July 5, 1854. Workers demolished the ruins in 1857 in order to build the Continental Hotel. Visitors will note that this location is actually the southwest corner of the Benjamin Franklin Hotel.

8. Site of the Girard House Hotel, 825–27 Chestnut Street. Architects John McArthur Jr. and Edward Collins designed the Girard House. When the hotel opened in 1852, it was noted for its Italianate elements and the beautiful iron railing around its exterior balcony.

In February 1860, while en route to New York City to speak at the Cooper Institute, Lincoln attempted to visit Simon Cameron and David Wilmot at the Girard House. He had very little time and did not find them.

9. Site of the Union League, 1118 Chestnut Street. The Union League of Philadelphia was located at this site from February 23, 1863, to May 11, 1865. President Lincoln visited here on June 16, 1864, while in Philadelphia to attend the Great Central Sanitary Fair.

***10. Musical Fund Hall, 810 Locust Street.** Abraham Lincoln was an unsuccessful candidate for the Republican Party vice-presidential nomination here at the Republican Party's National Convention in June 1856. Lincoln did not attend. Compare the Italian Renaissance Revival facade in this photograph to the 1856 engraving in chapter 4. The artist obviously took liberties with his political illustration.

***11. Logan Circle, between Eighteenth and Twentieth Streets and Race and Vine Streets.** A slightly smaller Logan Square, limited on the west by the now removed Logan Street, was the site of the Great Central Sanitary Fair, which Lincoln visited on June 16, 1864.

The Cathedral of Saints Peter and Paul stands today on Logan Circle as it stood on Logan Square in the 1860s. Napoleon Labrun and John Notman designed this Italian Renaissance structure with Palladian facade. Constantino Brumidi, the artist who painted the interior of the United States Capitol dome, decorated the cathedral's interior.

*12. Train Stations.** No stations of Lincoln's era exist today. Those that he used were: *West Philadelphia Train Station,* northeast corner of Thirty-second and Market Streets. This was the passenger station of the Pennsylvania Railroad. Used by Lincoln 1861. *Broad and Prime Street Station,* northwest corner of Broad Street and Washington Avenue in South Philadelphia. It was also known as the Southern and Western Railroad Station. The 1852 architect used elements of Italian Renaissance Revival to fashion an untried form in an effort to address a new need, the grand railroad depot.

This was the station for the Philadelphia, Wilmington, and Baltimore Railroad. Used by Lincoln 1861, 1862, 1864, 1865.

Kensington Station, eastern side of Front Street between Berks and Montgomery Streets in the Kensington section of Philadelphia. This was the station for the Philadelphia and Trenton Railroad. Used by Lincoln in 1848, 1860, 1861, 1862, and 1865.
Eleventh and Market Street Station, southeast corner of Eleventh and Market Streets. This was the center city station of the Philadelphia, Wilmington, and Baltimore Railroad until operations were shifted to the new Broad and Prime Street Station in 1852. From 1854 to 1864 it was used by the Pennsylvania Railroad as a downtown passenger station. Used by Lincoln in 1848 and possibly in 1860.

No one knows exactly where Lincoln arrived in Philadelphia in 1860; however, rail service between Pittsburgh and Philadelphia did exist at that time. Lincoln could have arrived at the Eleventh and Market Street Station from Harrisburg; or he could have arrived at the Broad and Prime Street Station from Baltimore.
****13. Additional Places of Interest. The Civil War Library and Museum at 1805

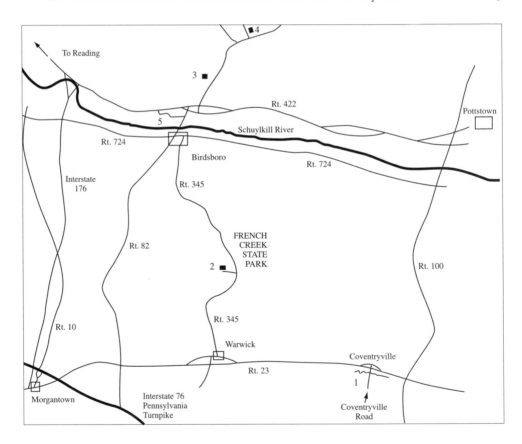

BERKS AND CHESTER COUNTIES. (1) *Coventry Forge site* (2) *Hopewell Furnace National Historical Site* (3) *Daniel Boone Homestead* (4) *Exeter Friends Meeting House* (5) *Mordecai Lincoln Homestead*

Pine Street maintains an excellent collection of Civil War memorabilia and has an outstanding Lincoln Room. The Historical Society of Pennsylvania at 1300 Locust Street is open to the public. The Union League of Philadelphia is at 140 South Broad Street. **Chester County:** From Central Philadelphia, get on the Schuylkill Expressway (Interstate 76). Travel northwest to the King of Prussia entrance of the Pennsylvania Turnpike (Interstate 76). Take the Turnpike west. Exit at Route 100 and travel north. Turn left (west) onto Route 23. Travel west. As you bypass Coventryville (Careful! It is easily missed!), turn left (south) onto Coventryville Road. Within 100 yards a bridge will cross French Creek. ***14. Site of Coventry Forge.** Abraham Lincoln's Pennsylvania great-great-grandfather Mordecai lived in this area and was a partner in the Coventry Iron Forge circa 1720 to 1725. If you visit this location, the meadow to the northwest of the intersection of Coventryville Road and French Creek is the site of Coventry Forge Number One, and the woods to the northeast of Coventryville Road and French Creek are the site of Forge Number Two. They no longer exist. **Berks County:** From the Coventryville area continue west on Route 23. At Warwick turn right onto Route 345. Follow it north into French Creek State Park (still on Route 345). Follow the signs to the Hopewell Furnace National Historical Site visitors' center.

Hopewell Furnace National Historical Site interprets the colonial iron industry at Mark Bird's Hopewell Furnace, built on French Creek circa 1770. Photograph by the author.

Leaving Hopewell Furnace, continue north on Route 345. Turn west onto Route 724. Follow it into Birdsboro. In Birdsboro turn right (north) onto Route 82. Travel north on Route 82. Cross over the Schuylkill River. At Lincoln Road turn left. Go 1.5 miles. The Mordecai Lincoln Homestead is on your left up a small hill. Retrace your steps to Route 82 and continue north. At Route 422, turn right (east). Go a short distance. Turn left, and follow the signs to the Daniel Boone Homestead. It is about one mile north of Route 422 near Baumstown. Leaving the Daniel Boone Homestead, turn left and follow the road to Meeting House Road. Turn left. Exeter Friends Meeting House will appear on your right.

*****15. Hopewell Furnace National Historical Site.** Hopewell Furnace was an active Pennsylvania iron plantation in the eighteenth and nineteenth centuries. Original buildings, history walks, films, and interpretive programs help the visitor understand the early iron industry and the lives of its workers.

***16. Mordecai Lincoln Homestead, Lincoln Road.** This stone home is dated 1733 and is on the National Historical Register. The two-story structure is similar in design

The stone foundation on the left and its spring cellar were part of the Boone family's original log cabin. The remainder of the Daniel Boone Homestead, as shown, did not exist when Squire and Daniel Boone lived on this land. Photographs. Daniel Boone Homestead, Buildings, MG-218, General Photograph Collection, Pennsylvania State Archives.

to the German bank barn in that it is built on the side of a hill, thus allowing ground level entrance on both stories. As Pennsylvanians migrated throughout the United States, they took this German design with them. This home is privately owned and is not open to the public.

*****17. The Daniel Boone Homestead, southeast of Reading near Baumstown. Daniel Boone, his father Squire, his mother, brothers, and sisters lived on this farm until 1750. The Mordecai Lincoln family and the Squire Boone family were neighbors and members of the Exeter (Oley) Friends Meeting. No doubt the Lincoln family visited the Boones at this location many times. There were four marriages between the extended Lincoln and Boone families during the mid-1700s. Lincolns and Boones migrated together to Virginia in 1765. Abraham Lincoln (grandfather of President Abraham Lincoln) went to Kentucky in the 1780s to land surveyed for him by Daniel Boone.

The house where Daniel Boone was born on November 2, 1734, and in which he lived for the first fifteen years of his life is gone. The 1750–70 two-story stone house with eaves on both the first and second stories incorporates the stone foundation and spring cellar of Squire Boone's log cabin. A flowing spring in the basement provided water and refrigeration and was an innovation sometimes found in other colonial farmhouses. Additional period outbuildings exist. State guides interpret the site.

***18. Exeter Friends Meeting House. This stone structure replaced a wooden building on the same land in 1759. The farmhouse appearance, simple in design and conspicuously lacking a tower or belfry, was typical of Quaker meetinghouses of this era. Mordecai Lincoln attended the Oley Meeting until his death in 1736. In 1742 the Oley Meeting was renamed the Exeter Meeting. Squire Boone and his family, including son

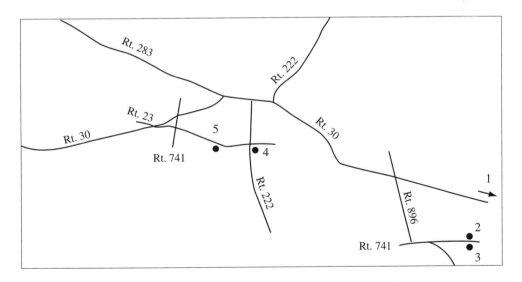

THE LANCASTER AREA. (1) *To Leaman Place* (2) *Strasburg Rail Road* (3) *Railroad Museum of Pennsylvania* (4) *Downtown Lancaster* (5) *Wheatland*

This carriage in the Railroad Museum of Pennsylvania has interior space for four occupants and might have carried Abraham Lincoln. In Pinkerton's book, History and Evidence . . . , *Pennsylvania Railroad General Agent G. C. Franciscus wrote, "I called at Coverly's [Jones House Hotel] with a carriage, at the hour agreed upon." Photograph by the author.*

CENTRAL LANCASTER. (1) *Lancaster Train Station site* (2) *Cadwell House Hotel site* (3) *Shreiner's Cemetery* (4) *Thaddeus Stevens's House site*

Daniel, attended until 1748 when the Meeting revoked Squire Boone's membership. They moved out of Pennsylvania in 1750. Mordecai Lincoln and George Boone Sr., Daniel Boone's grandfather, are buried in unmarked graves in the cemetery.

LANCASTER: From Exeter Friends Meeting House, retrace your route past the Daniel Boone Homestead and go to Route 422. Turn right (west). Travel west on Route 422 to Interstate 176. Travel south on Interstate 176 to the Pennsylvania Turnpike (Interstate 76). Go west. Exit the turnpike onto Route 222 south. Travel south until you meet Route 30. Go east. Just east of Paradise, Route 30 crosses over a rail line. This is the site of Leaman Place Train Station. Nothing of that era remains. Perhaps a more interesting itinerary would be to turn right (south) off of Route 30, before going as far as Paradise, onto Route 896. Travel Route 896 south to Strasburg. In Strasburg turn left onto Route 741. Travel one mile to the Railroad Museum of Pennsylvania and the Strasburg Rail Road. Take a ride on the Strasburg Rail Road at noon and enjoy the dining car as you travel through the countryside.

*19. **Site of the Leaman Place Train Station, on Route 30, east of Paradise**. At the point where Route 30 intersects the rail lines by bridge, the train station was on the southeastern corner of that intersection. No building remains. Lincoln spoke here briefly at a whistle-stop during his Inaugural Train on February 22, 1861.

*****20. **The Railroad Museum of Pennsylvania, near Strasburg.** Among its exhibits is an 1855 railroad passenger car and a replica of the engine "John Bull." Also in the

Thaddeus Stevens's grave, Shreiner's Cemetery, Lancaster. Stevens refused to be buried in any cemetery that did not permit the burial of African Americans. His epitaph, which he wrote, reads: "I repose in this quiet and secluded spot, / Not from any natural preference for solitude / But, finding other Cemeteries limited as to Race by Charter rules, / I have chosen this that I might illustrate in my death / The Principles which I advocated / Through a long life: / EQUALITY OF MAN BEFORE HIS CREATOR." *Photograph by the author.*

museum is a carriage that allegedly spirited Lincoln out of downtown Harrisburg to a waiting train on the evening of February 22, 1861, on the first leg of his secret trip back to Philadelphia and on to Washington, D.C.

****21. The Strasburg Rail Road. Just across the street from the Railroad Museum, the Strasburg Rail Road is the oldest, continuously operating rail line in the United States. It was chartered in 1832. The nine-mile, forty-five-minute ride reverses its direction a short distance from the site of the Leaman Place Train Station.

From the Strasburg Rail Road retrace your steps back to Route 30. Travel west on Route 30. Exit onto Route 222 south, and travel into downtown Lancaster.

*22. Site of the Lancaster Train Station, northeast corner of North Queen and East Chestnut Streets. Lincoln stopped here briefly during his Inaugural Train from Philadelphia to Harrisburg on February 22, 1861. He again passed through secretly that same evening on his way back to Philadelphia. His Funeral Train arrived April 22, 1865. There is now a parking lot here.

**23. Site of the Cadwell House, southeast corner of North Queen and East Chestnut Streets. On February 22, 1861, Lincoln got off his Inaugural Train at the Lancaster Train Station, crossed the street to the south, entered the Cadwell House Hotel, and spoke from the balcony of the hotel. A hotel occupies this site today. It is across the street from the site of the train station.

**24. Thaddeus Stevens's House. Thaddeus Stevens was the chairman of the House Ways and Means Committee and a radical Republican during the presidency of Lincoln. In Lancaster his home was at 45–47 South Queen Street.

***25. Grave of Thaddeus Stevens. Stevens is buried in Shreiner's Cemetery at the southeast corner of West Chestnut and North Mulberry Streets.

From downtown Lancaster, travel west on Route 23 (Walnut Street). Wheatland is on Route 23 at 1120 Marietta Avenue on the western side of town. It is on the left as you travel west.

*****26. Wheatland, the home of the fifteenth president of the United States James Buchanan. Lincoln asked someone to point out Wheatland to him as he left Lancaster on the Inaugural Train on February 22, 1861. He met President Buchanan in Washington, D.C., the following day but never visited the 1828 brick country great house. Guided tours of this Federal style mansion are available.

HARRISBURG: From Wheatland in Lancaster travel west on Route 23. In Rohrerstown turn right onto Route 741 west. Travel west to Route 30. Travel east on Route 30. Exit onto Route 283. Travel northwest to Harrisburg. Near Harrisburg, exit Route 283 onto Route 83 south. Get off at the Second Street exit. Traveling on Second Street in Harrisburg, turn right onto Chestnut Street.

**27. Harrisburg, Pennsylvania Railroad Station, Fourth and Chestnut Streets, Built 1887. The railroad station of 1857–87 was north of this site, closer to Fifth and Market Streets. Joseph C. Hoxie designed the station of Lincoln's era, with right and left sides separated by an Italianate tower at each end. Note the different second-floor window treatments in the chapter 9 photograph of the station. Allegedly two different rail companies shared the building.

Lincoln arrived at the depot on February 22, 1861. That evening, so as not to be seen, he departed Harrisburg by boarding a special train that was waiting some distance away from the station. His Funeral Train was at the station April 21–22, 1865. The existing building was built in 1887 and is on the National Historical Register.

28. Site of the Jones House Hotel, southeast corner of Second and Market Streets. A log building, the Union Hotel occupied this site in the 1790s. After Presi-

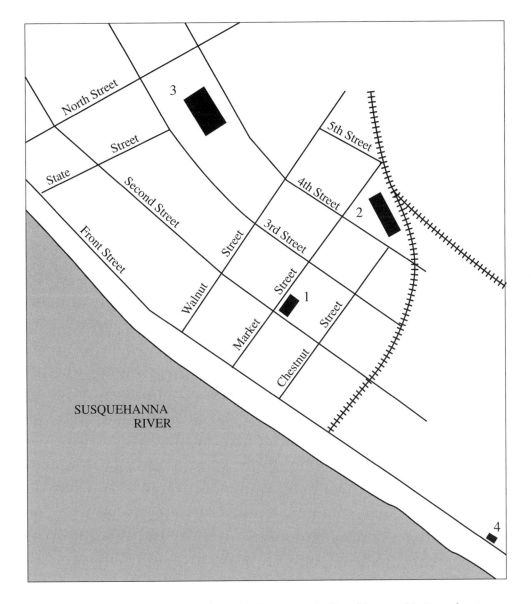

HARRISBURG. (1) *Jones House Hotel site* (2) *Harrisburg Railroad Station* (3) *Pennsylvania State Capitol* (4) *Simon Cameron House*

dent George Washington slept at the Union Hotel in October 1794 as he traveled from Philadelphia to Western Pennsylvania and the Whiskey Rebellion, the hotel's name changed to the Washington Hotel. The brick, Italianate Jones House Hotel was built 1857–58.

Lincoln was to have stayed at the Jones House Hotel on February 22, 1861. He entertained guests here in his rooms and attended a dinner in his honor. At dusk he secretly went back to Philadelphia and from there went on to Washington, D.C. Mrs. Lincoln and the Inaugural Train party stayed overnight.

The Market Street building adjacent to the Jones House in the chapter 1 engraving still exists. There is a historical marker on Second Street south of the corner of Market and Second Streets. (This area is also described as the intersection of Market Street and Market Square.)

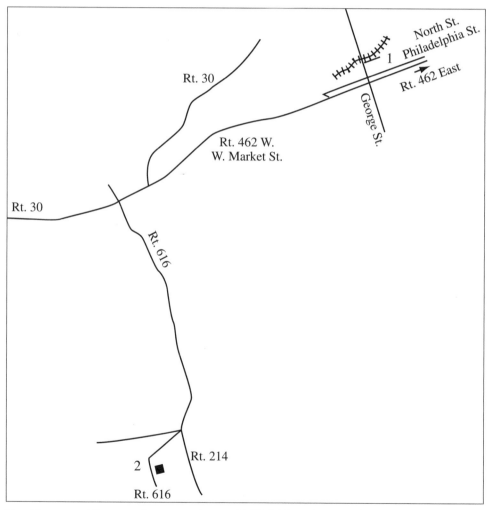

THE YORK AND HANOVER JUNCTION AREA. (1) *York Train Station* (2) *Hanover Junction*

In November 1863 Lincoln's special train changed from the Northern Central to the Hanover-Gettysburg Railroad at Hanover Junction. Tracks at the station's left lead to Gettysburg. Tracks at the right lead to York and Harrisburg. Top: Matthew Brady Studios. Photograph NWDNS 111 B 83 "Hanover Junction, Pa."; National Archives at College Park, College Park, Md. Bottom: Overgrowth of trees and shrubs in 1999 prevents duplication of the exact 1863 camera angle. Photograph by the author.

****29. The Pennsylvania Capitol Building, Third and State Streets. The old capitol building where Lincoln spoke on February 22, 1861, and where he lay in state April 21–22, 1865, burned in 1897. That brick building, designed by Stephen Hills and dedicated in 1822, combined a basic Federal design with Greek Revival columns and an Italian Renaissance dome.

President Theodore Roosevelt dedicated the present building on October 4, 1906. It is on the same site as the earlier building. Tours begin in the capitol rotunda. A stunningly beautiful mural *Lincoln at Gettysburg* by Violet Oakley is in the senate chamber.

***30. Simon Cameron/John Harris Mansion, 219 South Front Street. Cameron was a Pennsylvania political boss whose support at the convention and later during the campaign helped Lincoln win the presidency in 1860. Lincoln appointed Cameron to the cabinet post of secretary of war. He did not visit the Cameron home. Tours are available by advance reservation.

YORK: In Harrisburg travel Front Street back to the entrance of Route 83 south toward York. Go south on Route 83. Near York, exit Route 83 onto Route 30 west. Go west a short distance and turn left onto North George Street. Travel south on North George Street into central York. Just after crossing over the railroad tracks, turn left onto North Street. Go one-half block.

**31. Site of the Northern Central York Train Station. A disappointed crowd awaited Abraham Lincoln here in February 1861. The president-elect was already in Washington, D.C., when the Inaugural Train bearing Mary Lincoln passed through York, going from Harrisburg to Baltimore. When Lincoln's Funeral Train arrived on April 21, 1865, it stopped for a brief time. Local women placed a funeral wreath on the coffin. The Northern Central Railroad constructed the station at 53 East North Street circa 1900.

HANOVER JUNCTION: From the train station in York, get back onto George Street. Go south to Philadelphia Street (Route 462 west). Follow Route 462 west until it intersects with Route 30 west. At the traffic light on Route 30 west of York, turn left onto Route 616. Travel seven miles south on Route 616. Hanover Junction is on the left. (Careful! It is easy to make a wrong turn. At the intersection that seems to divide into three roads, Route 616 is the middle road.)

****32. Hanover Junction Station. Built in 1852–54 and located southwest of York, this was the junction of the Northern Central Railroad and the Hanover-Gettysburg Railroad. Ticket and telegraph office, waiting room for passengers, and dining room were on the ground floor. Rooms for overnight guests were on the second floor. The stationmaster and his family lived on the third floor.

On his way to Gettysburg on November 18, 1863, Lincoln was to meet Governor Andrew Curtin here, but Curtin's train was delayed. Returning on the evening of November 19, 1863, Lincoln waited at Hanover Junction for several hours for a connecting train to Baltimore and Washington, D.C. It was noted that he was uncharacteristically quiet. After Lincoln returned to the White House, his doctor diagnosed his illness as a mild form of smallpox.

During fall 1952 a controversy erupted. An enlargement of a National Archives photograph of Hanover Junction revealed an individual who resembled Abraham Lincoln. After much debate, expert consensus determined that Lincoln was not in the photograph. The individual seen may be 1863 railroad president A. W. Eichelberger.

York County owns the Hanover Junction Station and is restoring it to a circa 1930 appearance. The junction is part of the county parks system and is on the Rail Trail bicycle path.

Hanover: From Hanover Junction retrace your route to Route 30. Travel west on Route 30. North of Hanover turn left (south) onto Route 94. Go to the Hanover square.

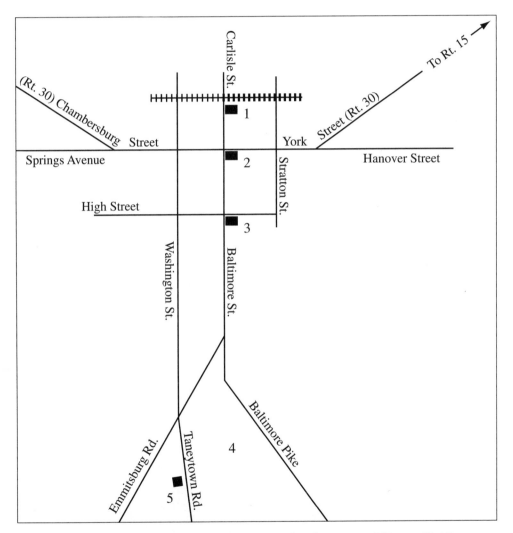

Gettysburg. (1) *Gettysburg Train Station* (2) *David Wills House and "Return Visit" statue* (3) *Gettysburg Presbyterian Church* (4) *Gettysburg Soldiers' National Cemetery* (5) *Gettysburg National Military Park Visitors' Center. Parade Route: From the Diamond by the Wills House, south on Baltimore Street, south on the Emmitsburg Road, south on the Taneytown Road, into the cemetery through a west gate from the Taneytown Road.*

Turn left. Go one block east and turn left again onto Railroad Street. A commemorative plaque is on the right of Railroad Street just north of Park Avenue.

**33. Hanover. Lincoln's train to Gettysburg was placed on a siding in Hanover for eight minutes on November 18, 1863. Official War Department telegrams attributed the delay to the passage of an eastbound freight train. Local lore said that railroad president Eichelberger directed the engineer to stop in Hanover to take on water, in preparation for the following day's return trip from Gettysburg to Hanover Junction. Whatever the reason for the delay, Lincoln spoke briefly to a crowd of people gathered to welcome him. One block northeast of the Hanover square, at Park Avenue and Railroad Street, a plaque commemorates his visit.

GETTYSBURG: From Hanover go back to Route 30. Travel west to Gettysburg. At the traffic circle, now named Lincoln Square, in Gettysburg travel one block north on Carlisle Street (Route 34). The Gettysburg Train Station is on the right.

***34. Gettysburg Train Station, 35 Carlisle Street. Wounded soldiers bound for hospitals in York, Harrisburg, Baltimore, Washington, and Philadelphia departed Gettysburg from this station. During his November 1863 visit, Lincoln arrived and departed from this 1858 structure; however there is no direct evidence that he actually entered the station. The 1858 depot is in the Italianate style.

The 1991 Lincoln statue "Return Visit" portrays the sixteenth president pointing to the second-floor bedroom in the Wills House where he finished the Gettysburg Address. Photograph by the author.

****35. Wills House, southeast corner of Lincoln Square (known as the Diamond in 1863). Abraham Lincoln was a guest here November 18–19, 1863. He probably finished writing the Gettysburg Address in his second-floor bedroom. The Lincoln Room Museum in the Wills House has preserved that room. The Wills House is built in the Federal style.

**36. Site of Robert G. Harper House. Secretary of State Seward was a guest of Robert Harper, editor of the pro-Republican newspaper the *Adams Sentinel,* on the evening of November 18, 1863. Lincoln visited briefly that evening, possibly to get Seward's opinion on a draft of the Gettysburg Address. No longer in existence, this house stood immediately south of the Wills House. The photograph in chapter 7 shows the Harper House to the right of the Wills House.

****37. "Return Visit" Statue, near the Wills House, Lincoln Square. Commissioned by the Lincoln Fellowship of Pennsylvania, J. Seward Johnson Jr. created this statue in 1991. Its importance lies in the sculptor's careful attention to detail. Lincoln's face and hands were modeled after casts taken during his life. The clothing was copied from clothing that Lincoln wore. The shoes were based on an outline of his feet made by a Pennsylvania bootmaker and signed by Lincoln himself. As a result, this statue may be the most accurate likeness of Abraham Lincoln in existence.

Go one block south of the traffic circle. At the intersection of Baltimore Street and Middle Street, turn right (west) onto Route 116. Travel west on Route 116 past the seminary on your right. Turn right onto Reynolds Avenue. The marker for John Reynolds's death is on the left near Route 30. His statue is on Route 30.

****38. First Day's Battle Site. Early on the morning of November 19 Secretary of State Seward, Canadian guest William McDougall, and Lincoln rode by carriage to see the Lutheran Theological Seminary and the site of General Reynolds's death.

***39. The Parade Route. The procession to the cemetery departed from the square near the Wills House just before 11 A.M. The marchers moved south on Baltimore Street, turned right onto Steinwehr Avenue, turned left onto the Taneytown Road, and entered the cemetery through a west gate off of the Taneytown Road.

*****40. The Gettysburg Soldiers' National Cemetery. Dedicated on November 19, 1863, and immortalized by Lincoln's Gettysburg Address, this cemetery contains the remains of known and unknown Civil War soldiers, as well as the remains of veterans of other wars. The site of the speakers' platform used by Lincoln in 1863 is actually a few yards to the east in Evergreen Cemetery.

*****41. The Visitors' Center and the Gettysburg National Military Park, Adjacent to the National Cemetery at the west gate on the Taneytown Road. Memorabilia from the dedication ceremonies, November 19, 1863, for example, Lincoln's saddle, speakers' platform chairs, and a drum used in the procession are in a basement display case. The visitors' center provides information about guided tours of the cemetery, the battlefield, and the Eisenhower National Historical Site. The display of Civil War artifacts is extensive. The national military park encompasses twenty-five square miles.

***42. Gettysburg Presbyterian Church, southeast corner of Baltimore and High Streets.** The First Division, Cavalry Corps, Army of the Potomac, used this church as a hospital during and after the battle. Abraham Lincoln and John Burns attended a patriotic program, hosted by the Ohio delegation, in the sanctuary on the afternoon of November 19, 1863. That church is gone. The newer structure retains the Lincoln and Burns pew. President and Mrs. Dwight D. Eisenhower were members of this church. Their pew, near the Lincoln pew, is also marked.

****43. Site of Thaddeus Stevens's House, 51 Chambersburg Street, Gettysburg.** Thaddeus Stevens lived at this location until 1842 when he moved to Lancaster.

CALEDONIA: Travel fifteen miles west on Route 30 to Route 233. The iron works ruins are on the northeast corner of the intersection of Route 30 and Route 233.

***44. Caledonia Iron Works.** Owned by Thaddeus Stevens, these iron works were looted and burned by Confederate General Jubal Early's cavalry on June 26, 1863. Stevens estimated his personal loss at $90,000; but for several years afterwards, he continued to support the workers who had lost their livelihoods as a result of the Confederate raid. The blacksmith shop and iron furnace ruins still exist. Charcoal Hearth hiking trail begins at the furnace ruins and takes the hiker past several clearings that formerly were charcoal hearths.

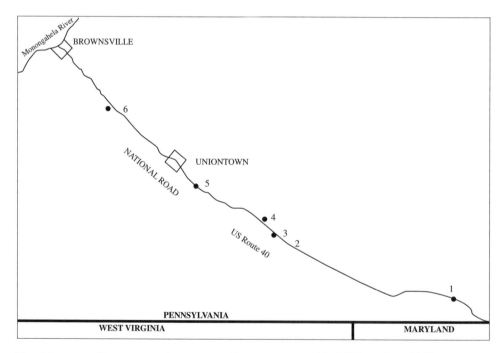

THE NATIONAL ROAD FROM ADDISON TO BROWNSVILLE. (1) *Old Petersburg Tollhouse* (2) *Entrance to Fort Necessity National Battlefield* (3) *Mount Washington Tavern* (4) *Braddock's grave and Braddock's Road trace* (5) *Hopwood Taverns* (6) *Searight's Tollhouse*

THE NATIONAL ROAD: Continue traveling west on Route 30. To get to the National Road by the fastest route, take Interstate 81 south to Interstate 70. Travel northwest on I-70 to Interstate 68. Travel west on Interstate 68 past Cumberland, Maryland. Exit Interstate 68 onto Route 40 near Addison, Pennsylvania. Travel west on Route 40.

****45. The National Road.** The route through southwest Pennsylvania is similar to Route 40. In 1806 Thomas Jefferson signed a bill that provided federal money to build a road from Cumberland, Maryland, to Wheeling, Virginia (now West Virginia). The goal of this first federal highway project was to improve access to the American West. Eventually the National Road extended from Washington, D.C., to Vandalia, Illinois. Controversial in its own day, Lincoln supported this federal project and traveled this route in 1847 and probably in 1848, at least from Brownsville, Pennsylvania, to Cumberland, Maryland. He may have traveled the National Road from Indianapolis to Washington, D.C., in 1849.

A traveler on the National Road in 1847–49 might have seen the following seven sites.

***46. Old Petersburg Tollhouse, in Addison.** Built in 1835, this was gate number one of the six Pennsylvania tollhouses on the National Road.

The Old Petersburg Tollhouse at Addison, Pennsylvania, was the southernmost tollhouse on Pennsylvania's section of the National Road. Photographs. Old Toll Gate, Old National Pike, Vacation and Travel Bureau, RG-31, Department of Commerce, Pennsylvania State Archives.

This National Road Stagecoach poster at Mount Washington Tavern advertises stagecoach service on the National Road during its heyday. Completion of the Baltimore and Ohio Railroad from Cumberland to Wheeling in 1852 ended much of the road's traffic. Photograph by the author.

****47. Mount Washington Tavern.** This restored nineteenth-century stagecoach inn is eleven miles east of Uniontown on Route 40. Visitors may examine period tavern rooms, National Road photographs, posters, mile markers, and other memorabilia. Tickets for Mount Washington Tavern are sold at the nearby Fort Necessity National Battlefield Visitors' Center.

***48. Braddock's Grave.** French and Indian forces ambushed and decimated British General Edward Braddock's army of 2,400 men as they attempted to advance on French Fort Duquesne. Braddock died on July 13, 1755, from wounds he received in the battle of Monongahela. To protect his body from desecration by the enemy, Braddock's men buried him in the middle of the road they had built through the forest. In 1804 workers discovered his body and reburied it. It now lies under a crest adjacent to Route 40, west of Mount Washington Tavern. The present monument was erected in 1913.

***49. Braddock's Road.** In the French and Indian War, British General Edward Braddock's army built this road through the Pennsylvania wilderness during their ill-fated attempt to capture Fort Duquesne. Daniel Boone and George Washington were members of the expedition and no doubt traveled the road. While here, Boone first learned of Kentucky from another soldier. Obsessed with Kentucky, Boone eventually convinced Abraham Lincoln's grandfather to settle there. Remnants of the road are visible from Braddock's grave, and also in Fort Necessity National Battlefield.

***50. Taverns in Hopwood, Pennsylvania.** Hopwood was a prudent place for the eastbound traveler to spend the night. Early the next morning, fresh horses were able to pull their stagecoach up the three-mile climb over Chestnut Ridge. Hopwood has the largest number of existing colonial stone buildings of any site on the National Road.

***51. Searight's Tollhouse.** Built in 1835, Searight's Tollhouse is five miles west of Uniontown on Route 40. It was gate number three on the Pennsylvania section of the National Road.

***52. Brownsville, Pennsylvania.** From 1844 to 1852, an estimated 200,000 people left Brownsville on their way to the American West via the Monongahela, Ohio, and Mississippi Rivers. Traveling the opposite direction, an eastbound steamboat traveler on the Ohio River had several choices. He could disembark at Wheeling and ride an eastbound stage over the National Road to Cumberland, Maryland. Alternatively he could continue up the Ohio River to Pittsburgh, travel south on the Monongahela River, and quickly reach Brownsville. At Brownsville he could get an eastbound stage to Cumberland. A rail line connected Cumberland, Maryland, and Washington, D.C. On his way to Congress, Lincoln traveled eastward, and he traveled through Brownsville if he traveled the National Road. Historic home Nemacolin Castle, begun in 1790, is open to visitors. The home was present during Lincoln's travels but not known to be associated with him.

PITTSBURGH: From Route 40 near Washington, enter Interstate 79 and travel north to Interstate 279. Take Interstate 279 into downtown Pittsburgh. It is best not to do this during morning rush hour.

53. Site of the Monongahela House Hotel, northwest corner of Smithfield Street and Water Street (Fort Pitt Boulevard). The hotel was built in 1847 after an earlier structure burned in April 1845. Its designer mixed Italian Renaissance Revival style with Italianate elements. The Monongahela House was a favorite of riverboat travelers and was in existence during Lincoln's 1847 trip to Congress. Abraham Lincoln stayed at this hotel the night of February 14, 1861. The next morning, he delivered his longest address of the Inaugural Train from the hotel's Smithfield Street balcony. After the hotel was torn down in 1935, the furniture from Lincoln's hotel room was kept on exhibit in a local museum for many years.

54. Site of the Allegheny City train station, southwest corner of Federal and South Commons Streets, Pittsburgh. Lincoln arrived in the Pittsburgh area at the Pittsburgh, Fort Wayne, and Chicago Railroad Station on February 14, 1861, and departed from the same station on February 15, 1861. The Allegheny City railroad station, 1851–1907, was also known as the Fort Wayne Station. Today the Allegheny Station post office occupies this site.

ERIE: From Pittsburgh take Interstate 279 north to Interstate 79. Travel Interstate 79 north to the Eighth Street exit in Erie. Travel northeast on Eighth Street. Go through the intersection of Eighth and Peach Streets; turn right onto State Street; and come back to Fourteenth and Peach Streets.

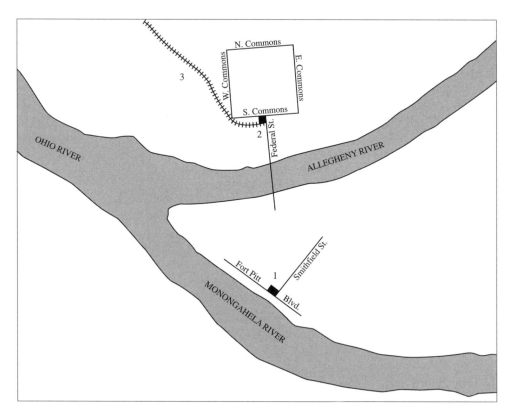

PITTSBURGH. (1) *Monongahela House Hotel site* (2) *Allegheny City "Fort Wayne" Railroad Station site* (3) *Pittsburgh, Fort Wayne, and Chicago Railroad, 1861*

**55. Union Station, Fourteenth and Peach Streets. Lincoln traveled through Girard, Erie, and North East, Pennsylvania, by train several times. In 1857 he and Mrs. Lincoln went to Niagara Falls and New York, passing through Erie. In 1860 he returned from the Cooper Institute speech by this route. Lincoln stopped here on February 16, 1861, with his Inaugural Train. He ate lunch in a frame structure that served as the Cleveland, Painesville, and Ashtabula train station. His Funeral Train arrived in Erie early on the morning of April 28, 1865. The 1861–65 station no longer exists but was located at the present site of Union Station.

In September 1848 Lincoln and his family were just off the Pennsylvania coast of Lake Erie during a lake steamer voyage from Buffalo to Chicago.

Miscellaneous

Historical markers identify additional Pennsylvania sites related to Abraham Lincoln's life but not visited by him.

• **28 West Market Street, West Chester.** The *Chester County Times* of February 11, 1860, printed Lincoln's first biography.

• **Eleventh Avenue at Thirteenth Street, Altoona.** The Conference of the Northern War Governors convened at the Logan House Hotel, September 24–26, 1862.

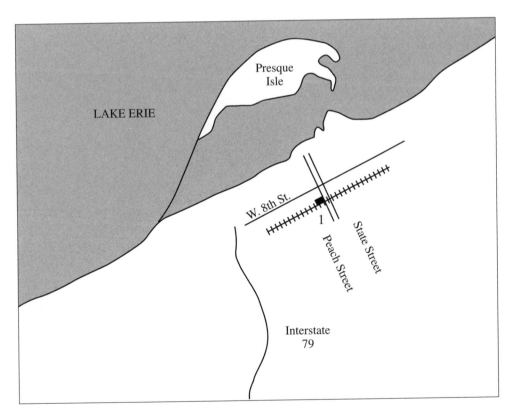

Erie. (1) *Cleveland, Painesville, and Ashtabula Train Station site*

Appendix A

Springfield to Washington, D.C., 1847

On August 3, 1846, Abraham Lincoln was elected to the Thirtieth Congress, which was scheduled to convene December 6, 1847. In fall 1847 he and his family set out for Washington. Which route they took has been a matter of minor debate for twentieth-century historians.

The Lincoln family's route from Springfield to Lexington, Kentucky, is reasonably documented and straightforward. On October 25, 1847, Lincoln, his twenty-eight-year-old wife Mary Lincoln, and their sons Robert and Edward left Springfield. They traveled by stagecoach to Alton, Illinois, and took the ferry down the Mississippi River to St. Louis, Missouri. At St. Louis they boarded a steamboat and traveled the short distance to Cairo, Illinois. From Cairo they traveled by steamboat up the Ohio River to Carrollton, Kentucky, at the mouth of the Kentucky River. A steamboat took them up the Kentucky River to Frankfort, and from there they traveled by train to Lexington, Kentucky. They arrived in Lexington to visit Mary Lincoln's parents and other relatives on or about November 2, 1847. The trip took about one week.

After visiting family and friends, they left Lexington on November 25, 1847, and arrived in Washington, D.C., on December 2, 1847. The second leg of their journey also lasted about one week, but the route the Lincolns followed from Lexington to Washington remains unknown. There is no known letter from Lincoln saying, "We went this way," and contemporary sources do not appear to exist either. On June 24, 1848, Lincoln repaid Allen Francis the $272 that he had borrowed to pay for his family's trip east to Washington, D.C. The government reimbursed Lincoln $1,300.08 for his round-trip.

In 1847, there were three possible routes between Lexington and Washington. Historians have debated from time to time the merits of each for the Lincolns. Circumstantial evidence, however, argues strongly for one of the routes.

One option was to take a stagecoach from Lexington, Kentucky, to Winchester, Virginia. From Winchester, a train line connected to Harpers Ferry and on to Washington. This route was the shortest in distance of the three but required the most time traveling in a stagecoach. It also required the longest total travel time.

The second possible route was by stagecoach from Lexington to Maysville, Kentucky, over the Maysville Road. From there a steamboat was available to transport the traveler up the Ohio River. One could disembark at Wheeling, Virginia, travel over the National Road by stagecoach to Cumberland, Maryland, and then continue on by train to Harpers Ferry and Washington, D.C.

In a variation of the second route, one could continue on the steamboat past Wheeling and travel on to Pittsburgh, Pennsylvania. From Pittsburgh a traveler could take a steamboat to

Brownsville, Pennsylvania, via the Monongahela River. From Brownsville a shorter stagecoach ride led to Cumberland, Maryland, and the train to Washington.

Congress paid each member eight dollars per twenty miles traveled from their home district to the opening of each congressional session, and also the same amount to get back home again after the session ended. According to the *New York Tribune,* the shortest postal route from Springfield to Washington in 1847 was 780 miles. However the law did not require a member of Congress to travel by the shortest route. Lincoln's trip, of course, detoured through Lexington, Kentucky, in order to visit Mary Lincoln's family. For purposes of reimbursement, Lincoln reported to Congress that he traveled a total of 1,626 miles from Springfield to Washington, D.C.

What about the miles that Lincoln claimed to have traveled? If "Honest Abe" said that he traveled 1,626 miles from Springfield, then he did. If surveyor Lincoln said that he traveled 1,626 miles, then as close as was humanly possible to calculate, he did travel 1,626 miles. The three routes must be calculated to determine which one best approximates the distance Lincoln said he traveled.

I have used several sources in calculating the distance involved in each of these routes. Mileage tables published by the United States Army Corps of Engineers provided modern-day distances on the Mississippi River, the Ohio River, and the Monongahela River. *Canals and Railroads of the Mid-Atlantic States, 1800–1860* by Christopher Baer includes train mileage from Cumberland, Winchester, and Harpers Ferry to Washington, D.C. And Mark Yarris's *Map of the National Road Pennsylvania* provides mileage on the National Road. All other distances were approximated by modern highways and calculated by computer using Rand McNally's *TripMaker 1999.* Obviously these distances only approximate the routes of 1847.

SPRINGFIELD TO LEXINGTON FOR ALL ROUTES

Springfield to St. Louis (stagecoach and ferry)	119
St. Louis to Cairo (steamboat)	183
Cairo to Carrollton (steamboat)	433
Carrollton to Frankfort (steamboat)	45
Frankfort to Lexington (train)	23
TOTAL	803 miles

ROUTE 1

Springfield to Lexington	803
Lexington to Winchester (stagecoach) via Mt. Sterling, Owingsville, and Catlettsburg, Kentucky	486
Winchester to Harpers Ferry (train)	32
Harpers Ferry to Washington (train) via Point of Rocks, Frederick, and Relay, Maryland	103
TOTAL	1,424 miles
Lexington to Washington, D.C.	
Total stagecoach miles	486
Total train miles	135

ROUTE 2

Springfield to Lexington	803
Lexington to Maysville (stagecoach)	64

Maysville to Wheeling (steamboat)	321
Wheeling to Cumberland (stagecoach)	131
Cumberland to Harpers Ferry (train)	97
Harpers Ferry to Washington (train)	103
TOTAL	1,519 miles
Lexington to Washington, D.C.	
Total stagecoach miles	195
Total steamboat miles	321
Total train miles	200

ROUTE 3

Springfield to Lexington	803
Lexington to Maysville (stagecoach)	64
Maysville to Pittsburgh (steamboat)	408
Pittsburgh to Brownsville (steamboat)	56
Brownsville to Cumberland (stagecoach)	75
Cumberland to Harpers Ferry (train)	97
Harpers Ferry to Washington (train)	103
TOTAL	1,606 miles
Lexington to Washington, D.C.	
Total stagecoach miles	139
Total steamboat miles	464
Total train miles	200

In comparing these calculations to Lincoln's mileage, route 1 appears to be a very unlikely fit. It is not possible to choose between route 2 and route 3, although route 3 mileage best approximates Lincoln's mileage.

An analysis of the time required to travel the various routes is illuminating. For purposes of analysis, assume the following. Stagecoach travel over relatively flat land between Lexington and Maysville could average eight miles per hour. Steamboat travel on the Ohio River in 1847 could average ten miles an hour against the current, including stops. Train travel could average ten to fifteen miles per hour. The Lincoln family completed their trip from Lexington to Washington, D.C., in seven and one-half days (November 25 to December 2).

Examining route 1, a stagecoach trip of 486 miles would have required sixty hours, or six ten-hour days of travel. The 135 train miles would have required one ten-hour day. It would have taken a superhuman effort to travel this route and arrive in Washington on time. But, are the assumptions valid? Rand McNally's *TripMaker 1999* computer program calculated the shortest possible route over modern highways, after being directed to follow the known 1847 stagecoach route from Lexington to Catlettsburg, Kentucky. The route taken by the computer from Catlettsburg then struck out through the Appalachian Mountains, via Charleston and Covington, to Winchester, Virginia. A stagecoach had little hope of averaging eight miles an hour through those mountains. In addition, the computer chose the shortest route available. Route 1 is 1,424 miles long. Lincoln sought reimbursement for 1,626. If Lincoln traveled the additional 200 miles overland that he claimed he traveled, there was no possible way he could have completed this journey in seven and one-half days.

Examining route 3, the stagecoach journeys from Lexington to Maysville and from Brownsville to Cumberland each required one day's travel. The steamboat route of 464 miles could have been traveled in forty-seven hours, or two days. Here the difference was, with the exception of changing steamboats in Pittsburgh, that the traveler did not get off of the steamboat to eat or to sleep at night, and the steamboat kept moving. Thus the time of travel was much shorter. The train distance of 200 miles could have been traveled in one day. Total time required for route 3 was five days. Thus a leeway of two and one-half additional days was available. It was not only possible for the Lincoln family to make the journey in the time allowed, it was relatively easy. Then too, there is the logic of the situation. In 1847 stagecoach journeys were difficult: they often began before dawn; the coaches were uncomfortable; breakdowns were frequent; and reckless drivers' attempts to meet tight schedules caused too many accidents. And stagecoaches were slow. For example, the sixty-four-mile trip from Lexington to Maysville usually took about eight and one-half hours. Stagecoach journeys were also subject to the whims of weather. At the end of November, cold weather and impassable, mud-choked or snow-filled roads through the mountains were distinct possibilities. Lincoln, traveling with a young wife and two small children would have tried to minimize his stagecoach travel.

When Henry Clay traveled from his home near Lexington, Kentucky, to Congress, his preferred route was the Ohio River–National Road. Undoubtedly, Mary Lincoln's father Robert Todd would have known or easily could have found out what route Clay traveled. It seems logical that Lincoln would have followed Clay's example and booked passage for his family on a steamboat that, in comparison to a stagecoach, was warm and comfortable. The travel was leisurely, and there was plenty of room on board for the children to play. From Lexington, Lincoln would have gone back to the Ohio River to continue his journey to Washington, D.C.

Finally, are there any independent sources that might give additional evidence that Lincoln was on the National Road in southwestern Pennsylvania? There is one intriguing published report. In 1913 James Hadden reported in *A History of Uniontown*, "Abraham Lincoln was elected to Congress in 1846, and in journeying to Washington City he had occasion to stop at Uniontown to transact some business with Daniel Downer, Esq., and nothing unusual was thought of the occurrence as Mr. Lincoln had not yet acquired national reputation." Uniontown, Pennsylvania, is on the National Road between Brownsville, Pennsylvania, and Cumberland, Maryland. If this visit occurred, it occurred in November or December of 1847 or 1848, during one of Lincoln's two trips from Springfield to Congress.

Route 3 minimizes stagecoach travel, maximizes steamboat travel, and most closely approximates the distance that Lincoln said he traveled. It was possible to travel route 3 in seven and one-half days. And, there might have been an eyewitness to Abraham Lincoln's presence on the National Road in southwestern Pennsylvania during that time period. Therefore it is highly probable that Abraham Lincoln and his family left Lexington and went back to the Ohio River at Maysville, Kentucky. From Maysville they took a steamboat up the Ohio River and possibly the Monongahela River, traveled a portion of the National Road in Pennsylvania, and boarded a train in Cumberland, Maryland, that was bound for Washington, D.C.

Appendix B

Lincoln and Pennsylvania's Railroads

In Pennsylvania, Lincoln's primary mode of travel was by railroad. A summary of his rail journeys through the Commonwealth follows.

September 1848—*Campaign Trip.* Washington, D.C., to New England. Lincoln went to New England to campaign for Zachary Taylor. He traveled with his wife Mary, five-year-old Robert, and two-year-old Eddie.

The Lincolns rode the Philadelphia, Wilmington, and Baltimore Railroad from Baltimore to the Eleventh and Market Street Station in Philadelphia [17 miles in Pennsylvania]. The ferry *Susquehanna* was required to cross the Susquehanna River at Havre de Grace, Maryland. Horses pulled their railroad passenger car on the city street rail system to the station in Philadelphia.

After a stay of an unknown length in Philadelphia, they traveled by city streets to Kensington Station. They left Philadelphia on the Philadelphia and Trenton Railroad traveling toward Trenton, New Jersey (26 miles in Pennsylvania).

NOTE: Lincoln might have traveled to the Whig National Convention in Philadelphia in June 1848 by rail or on horseback.

July 1857—*Vacation Trip.* Springfield, Illinois, to Niagara Falls, New York, and east and return. Lincoln traveled with his wife Mary.

They took the Cleveland, Painesville, and Ashtabula Railroad from Cleveland, Ohio, to Fourteenth and Peach Street Station in Erie (25 miles in Pennsylvania). In Erie they boarded the Erie and North East Railroad to travel to the New York state line and then on to Buffalo (18 miles in Pennsylvania). They returned by the same route.

February 1860—*Cooper Institute Speech.* Springfield to New York City.

Lincoln arrived in Philadelphia by an unknown route—either the Pennsylvania Railroad from Pittsburgh, or the Philadelphia, Wilmington, and Baltimore Railroad from Baltimore. He departed from Kensington Station of the Philadelphia and Trenton Railroad for New York City.

March 1860—*Return from Cooper Institute Speech.* New York City to Springfield.

Lincoln traveled on the Erie and North East Railroad from the New York state line to Erie. He left Erie from the Fourteenth and Peach Street Station on the Cleveland, Painesville, and Ashtabula Railroad bound for Cleveland.

February 1861—*Inaugural Train.* Springfield to Washington, D.C. The inaugural party took the Cleveland and Pittsburgh Railroad 22.5 miles from Wellsville, Ohio, to Rochester, Pennsylvania. From Rochester they traveled on the Pittsburgh, Fort Wayne, and Chicago Railroad to Allegheny City (now part of Pittsburgh) and the Old Fort Wayne Station. They traveled out of Pennsylvania toward Cleveland over the same route.

The party traveled from Cleveland to Buffalo using the Cleveland, Painesville, and Ashtabula Railroad and the Erie and North East Railroad through Erie, Pennsylvania. They traveled from Trenton, New Jersey, to Kensington Station in Philadelphia over the Philadelphia and Trenton Railroad.

Lincoln left Philadelphia on the Pennsylvania Railroad from the West Philadelphia Station and traveled to Harrisburg. He and Ward Hill Lamon returned to Philadelphia on the same route. Lincoln, Lamon, and Allan Pinkerton left Philadelphia on the Philadelphia, Wilmington, and Baltimore Railroad from the Broad and Prime Street Station. They traveled through Baltimore and on to Washington, D.C.

June 1862—West Point Trip. Washington, D.C., to West Point, New York, and return. The president traveled on the Philadelphia, Wilmington, and Baltimore Railroad from Baltimore. He arrived in Philadelphia at the Broad and Prime Street Station. He traveled over city streets to Kensington Station and left on the Philadelphia and Trenton Railroad for Trenton, New York City, and West Point. Lincoln returned on the same lines.

November 1863—Gettysburg Address. Washington, D.C., to Gettysburg, Pennsylvania, and return. The president traveled from Baltimore on the Northern Central Railroad to Hanover Junction, Pennsylvania. He transferred to the Hanover Railroad and traveled 12.9 miles to Hanover. On the Gettysburg Railroad he traveled 16.4 miles from Hanover to Gettysburg. The return trip was over the same lines.

June 1864—Great Central Sanitary Fair. Washington, D.C., to Philadelphia and return. From Baltimore President and Mrs. Lincoln traveled on the Philadelphia, Wilmington, and Baltimore Railroad to the Broad and Prime Street Station in Philadelphia. They returned on the same line.

April 1865—Funeral Train. Washington, D.C., to Springfield. From Baltimore Lincoln's body traveled to Harrisburg on the Northern Central Railroad and arrived at the Pennsylvania Railroad Station. The Funeral Train departed from the same station and traveled to Philadelphia on the Pennsylvania Railroad. It passed the West Philadelphia Station, entered the Junction Railroad (a branch that connected to the Philadelphia, Wilmington, and Baltimore Railroad), and arrived at the Broad and Prime Street Station.

The train left Philadelphia from the Kensington Station of the Philadelphia and Trenton Railroad and traveled to Trenton, New Jersey. It traveled from Buffalo to Cleveland using the Erie and North East Railroad and the Cleveland, Painesville, and Ashtabula Railroad and went through Erie, Pennsylvania.

Notes

Abbreviations

CW   *Collected Works of Abraham Lincoln,* ed. Roy P. Basler et al.
Day by Day *Lincoln Day by Day,* ed. Earl Schenk Miers et al.

Chapter 1. "An Omen of What Is to Come"

PAGE

2 *more than 212,000:* United States. Census Office, *Eighth Census of the United States, 1860,* 1:xxxi.

2 *in Baltimore:* Cuthbert, *Lincoln and the Baltimore Plot,* 3–9.

2 *individual capacity":* Ibid., 142.

3 *in Philadelphia:* Ibid., 3–9.

4 *Edwin V. Sumner:* Philadelphia Inquirer, February 22, 1861.

4 *the Continental Hotel:* Ibid.

4 *Judd said yes:* Cuthbert, *Lincoln and the Baltimore Plot,* 56–58.

4 *the crowd below:* Basler, ed., *CW,* 4:238–39.

4 *Lincoln was relieved:* Fehrenbacher and Fehrenbacher, *Recollected Words,* 329.

4 *but circumstances forbid":* CW, 4:239.

6 *where he stood:* Philadelphia Inquirer, February 22, 1861.

6 *was generally disdained:* Hemphill, *Bowing to Necessities,* 151, 152.

6 *were already there:* Cuthbert, *Lincoln and the Baltimore Plot,* 58–63.

6 *about 11 p.m.:* Ibid., 64–68.

6 *without previous notice":* Ibid., 131–32.

7 *a second time":* Ibid., 145–46.

7 *in the morning":* Fehrenbacher and Fehrenbacher, *Recollected Words,* 397.

7 *concert and fireworks:* Philadelphia Inquirer, February 22, 1861.

7 *back in Philadelphia:* Cuthbert, *Lincoln and the Baltimore Plot,* 68–69.

7 *arrive in Philadelphia:* Ibid., 12–13.

8 *at the station:* Ibid., 69–70.

8 *to Mexico City:* Philadelphia Inquirer, February 23, 1861.

9 *Taylor and Fillmore: Day by Day,* 1:312; *Philadelphia Cummings' Evening Telegraphic Bulletin,* June 10, 1848.

9 *to go inside: CW,* 4:244–45.

9 *at 5:30* A.M.: *Philadelphia Inquirer* February 23, 1861.

9 *barely audible voice:* Ibid.

9 *to surrender it: CW,* 4:240.

9 *God, die by": CW,* 4:240–41.

9 *an idle boast:* Cuthbert, *Lincoln and the Baltimore Plot,* 11–12.

9 *president-elect could participate:* Ibid., 124.

9 *and both sides: Philadelphia Inquirer,* February 23, 1861.

9 *to be again":* Penrose, Diary, entry for February 22, 1861.

11 *and precipitate action": CW,* 4:241.

11 *the program ended:* Sharf and Westcott, *History of Philadelpia,* 750–51; *Harrisburg Pennsylvania Daily Telegraph,* February 22, 1861; *Philadelphia Inquirer,* February 23, 1861.

11 *to take responsibility:* Cuthbert, *Lincoln and the Baltimore Plot,* 71.

11 *had been advised:* Ibid., 147.

11 *West Philadelphia Station:* Taylor, *Philadelphia in the Civil War,* 44.

11 *Street covered bridge:* Burgess and Kennedy, *Centennial History of the Pennsylvania Railroad Company,* 80.

11 *platform and bowed: Lancaster Daily Evening Express,* February 22, 1861; *Philadelphia Inquirer,* February 23, 1861.

12 *the organized parade:* Gallman, *Mastering Wartime,* 87, 88.

13 *all very straightforward:* Ibid., 88–105.

14 *her Washington's Birthday:* Ibid.

14 *and at Lancaster: Lancaster Daily Evening Express,* February 22, 1861.

14 *send a message:* Ibid.

14 *Sanford, and Franciscus:* Cuthbert, *Lincoln and the Baltimore Plot,* 112.

14 *get them together":* Fehrenbacher and Fehrenbacher, *Recollected Words,* 272.

14 SLAVERY—SECTIONAL": *Lancaster Evening Express,* February 22, 1861; *Philadelphia Inquirer,* February 23, 1861.

14 *train moved on: CW,* 4:242.

14 *out for days: Lancaster Evening Express,* February 22, 1861.

14 *the reception committee: Philadelphia Inquirer,* February 23, 1861.

14 *say as much": CW,* 4:242.

15 *in the distance: Lancaster Evening Express,* February 22, 1861.

15 *welcomed the train:* Ibid.

15 *of private residences": Harrisburg Pennsylvania Daily Telegraph,* February 22, 1861.

15 *await the president-elect: Philadelphia Inquirer,* February 23, 1861.

16 *'Honest Old Abe': Harrisburg Pennsylvania Daily Telegraph,* February 22, 1861.

16 *at thirty thousand: Lancaster Evening Express,* February 23, 1861.

16 *the Jones House": Harrisburg Pennsylvania Daily Telegraph,* February 22, 1861.

16 *to our Capitol' ":* Ibid.

16   *an outside balcony:* Pinkerton, *History and Evidence,* 37; *Harrisburg Pennsylvania Daily Telegraph,* February 22, 1861.

16   *applauded and cheered: Philadelphia Inquirer,* February 23, 1861.

17   *call you blessed": Harrisburg Pennsylvania Daily Telegraph,* February 22, 1861.

17   *will not fail": CW,* 4:243.

17   *Representatives at 2:30 P.M.: Harrisburg Pennsylvania Daily Telegraph,* February 22, 1861.

17   *Elisha W. Davis:* Ibid.

17   *had arranged it: CW,* 4:244–45.

17   *shortly after 4 p.m.: Harrisburg Pennsylvania Daily Telegraph,* February 22, 1861.

17   *At that point:* Pinkerton, *History and Evidence,* 37.

19   *in the night?' ":* McClure, *Abraham Lincoln and Men of War-Times,* 51–52.

19   *its momentous mission:* Ibid., 52–54.

19   *he was there":* Pinkerton, *History and Evidence,* 37–38. This quote is from a printed letter of Governor Curtin dated December 8, 1867.

20   *for the president-elect:* Ibid., 33.

20   *Central rail line:* Taylor, *Philadelphia in the Civil War,* 15.

20   *secured it in:* Pinkerton, *History and Evidence,* 39–40.

20   *would do nothing:* Cuthbert, *Lincoln and the Baltimore Plot,* 72–74.

20   *rested and waited:* Ibid., 75–76.

20   *Geo. H. Burns":* Ibid., 77.

21   *around the city:* Ibid.

21   *toward the station:* Taylor, *Philadelphia in the Civil War,* 16.

21   *Pinkerton was loyal:* Cuthbert, *Lincoln and the Baltimore Plot,* 77–78.

21   *through the rear:* Taylor, *Philadelphia in the Civil War,* 16.

21   *to help her:* Cuthbert, *Lincoln and the Baltimore Plot,* 80–81.

21   *also Pinkerton agents:* Taylor, *Philadelphia in the Civil War,* 16.

22   *of Carpenter Street:* Pinkerton, *History and Evidence,* 28.

22   *during the trip":* Cuthbert, *Lincoln and the Baltimore Plot,* 79.

22   *"all is right":* Pinkerton, *History and Evidence,* 26.

23   *to Willard's Hotel:* Cuthbert, *Lincoln and the Baltimore Plot,* 81–82.

23   *the Executive Mansion":* McClure, *Abraham Lincoln and Men of War-Times,* 54–55.

23   *at Hanover Junction: Philadelphia Inquirer,* February 25, 1861.

23   *and great" danger:* Donald, *Lincoln,* 278–79.

23   *not "bomb proof":* Neely, *Last Best Hope of Earth,* 185.

23   *Lincoln's crude speeches":* Cuthbert, *Lincoln and the Baltimore Plot,* xiv.

CHAPTER 2. "MYSTIC CHORDS OF MEMORY"

25   *imported from England:* Bining, *Pennsylvania Iron Manufacture,* 8.

25   *the new trade:* Lincoln, *History of the Lincoln Family,* 5–8.

26   *at 3,099 pounds:* Ibid., 15–19.

26   *and five daughters:* Ibid., 43.

26   *of fifty shillings:* Bining, *Pennsylvania Iron Manufacture,* 17.

26 *Nutt's bloomery furnace:* Ibid., 40.

27 *Branches of Brandywine":* Futhey and Cope, *History of Chester County, Pennsylvania,* 186.

27 *at French Creek":* Lincoln, *History of the Lincoln Family,* 45–46.

27 *for 500 pounds:* Lincoln, *History of the Lincoln Family,* 46.

27 *two rooms deep:* United States Department of Interior. National Park Service. National Register of Historic Places, "The Mordecai Lincoln House."

27 *appraiser Squire Boone:* Lincoln, *History of the Lincoln Family,* 48.

27 *farm in 1730:* Ibid., 974. The Squire Boone family moved to the land in 1731 (Faragher, *Daniel Boone*).

27 *November 2, 1734:* Faragher, *Daniel Boone,* 10. October 22 is the Julian calendar date. The Gregorian calendar date is November 2, 1734.

28 *sold in 1762:* Stevens, *Abraham Lincoln and Pennsylvania,* 2.

28 *the Cumberland Valley:* Faragher, *Daniel Boone,* 28.

29 *fifteen years earlier:* Ibid., 28.

29 *as "Virginia John":* Lincoln, *History of the Lincoln Family,* 93.

29 *January 6, 1778:* Ibid., 203.

29 *the new lands:* Faragher, *Daniel Boone,* 69–72.

29 *Boone family left:* Lincoln, *History of the Lincoln Family,* 93.

29 *for Abraham Lincoln:* Ibid., 193–94.

29 *for 5,000 pounds:* Ibid., 194.

29 *on 400 acres:* John G. Nicolay and John Hay, "Abraham Lincoln," *Century Magazine* 33, no. 1 (November 1886): 10–11.

29 *of Kentucky land:* Donald, *Lincoln,* 21.

29 *his father's body:* Ibid., 14.

31 *from Hodgenville, Kentucky:* Donald, *Lincoln,* 22; Nicolay and Hay, "Abraham Lincoln," *Century Magazine* 33, no. 1 (November 1886): 16.

31 *west each year:* Michael A. Morrison, *Slavery and the American West* (Chapel Hill: University of North Carolina Press, 1997), 4.

31 *"sifted the grain":* Bruce Catton and William B. Catton, *The Bold and Magnificent Dream: America's Founding Years, 1492–1815,* (Garden City, N.Y.: Doubleday, 1978), 158–80.

31 *President Thomas Jefferson's:* Nobles, *American Frontiers,* 115–20.

31 *twenty-nine-year age group:* Muller, *Concise Historical Atlas of Pennsylvania,* 87.

31 *lived near Pequea:* Baker, *Mary Todd Lincoln,* 5; *Lancaster Sunday News,* February 12, 1950.

31 *Lancaster County, Pennsylvania:* Seyfert, "Wallace Family," 23–24.

32 *Bloomington Daily Pantagraph:* Freeman, *Lincoln,* 180–81, 297.

32 *Berks County, Pennsylvania":* CW, 3:511.

Chapter 3. "Struck Blind"

33 *Beginning in 1834:* Day by Day, 1:41.

33 *Stuart in Springfield:* Ibid., 1:71.

33 *with Stephen T. Logan:* Ibid., 1:156.

33   *with William H. Herndon:* Ibid., 1:247.

33   *249 votes, respectively:* Ibid., 1:275.

36   *a convention delegate:* Ibid., 1:289.

36   *New York delegate:* Ibid., 1:291.

36   *October 25, 1847:* for detailed discussion and references see appendix A.

36   *any other slave-border":* CW, 2:320.

38   *along its path:* Dickens, *American Notes,* 73–74.

38   *died in accidents:* Hunter, *Steamboats on the Western Rivers,* 521.

38   *the hold exploded: Philadelphia Cummings' Evening Telegraphic Bulletin,* June 8, 1848.

38   *be safely made":* Dickens, *American Notes,* 74.

39   *do with pleasurers:* Ibid., 79–80.

39   *dams and locks:* Hunter, *Steamboats on the Western Rivers,* 41–42.

40   *neared Indianapolis, Indiana:* Hulbert, *Old National Road,* 42–44, 54.

40   *of each passenger:* Ibid., 93–94.

40   *in twenty-four hours:* Ibid., 81–84.

40   *agricultural goods east:* Ibid., 37.

41   *was buckwheat cakes:* Ibid., 112.

41   *eyes are, now":* Dickens, *American Notes,* 78.

41   *without further accident:* Mencken, *Railroad Passenger Car,* 119–21.

41   *in the South:* Ibid., 14, 15.

43   *miles per hour:* Ibid., 107.

43   *and family arrived: Day by Day,* 1:296.

43   *and John Pendleton:* Dyer, *Zachary Taylor,* 270.

44   *George (Sansom) Streets:* Hamilton, *Zachary Taylor,* 87.

44   *the Philadelphia Convention":* CW, 1:478.

44   *and Millard Fillmore:* Hamilton, *Zachary Taylor,* 87.

44   *votes of Arkansas":* CW, 1:495.

44   *the fourth ballot:* Information regarding the 1848 Whig National Convention may be found
      in *Philadelphia Cummings' Evening Telegraphic Bulletin,* June 8–10, 1848; Greeley and
      Cleveland, *Political Textbook for 1860,* 15–16; and Dyer, *Zachary Taylor,* 282–83.

44   *a dozen stumps": Day by Day,* 1:312.

44   *Alto, Buena Vista: Philadelphia Cummings' Evening Telegraphic Bulletin,* June 10, 1848.

44   *Party ratification meeting:* CW, 1:475–76.

44   *on Sunday morning:* CW, 1:477.

45   *truly, A Lincoln:* CW, 2:1.

46   *and Baltimore Railroad:* Baer, *Canals and Railroads; Day by Day,* 1:319.

46   *and Market Streets:* Mencken, *Railroad Passenger Car,* 109–10.

46   *Railroad's Kensington Station:* Harwood, *Royal Blue Line,* 15.

46   *Whig vice-presidential candidate: Day by Day,* 1:321.

47   *Buffalo by rail: 1848–1849 Commercial Advertiser Directory for the City of Buffalo,* 93.

47   *number of stops:* for distance, *1848–1849 Commercial Advertiser Directory for the City of
      Buffalo,* 94; for time, *Day by Day,* 1:321.

47 *the Great Lakes: 1848–1849 Commercial Advertiser Directory for the City of Buffalo,* 80–81.

47 *hand every morning:* Mansfield, *History of the Great Lakes,* 1:209–12.

47 *was in Chicago: Day by Day,* 1:322.

47 *received 1,220,544 votes:* Kane, *Facts About the Presidents,* 139.

48 *to be $676.80: New York Tribune,* December 22, 1848.

48 *change the law:* United States. Congress, *Congressional Globe,* December 27, 1848.

48 *in March 1849:* Findley, *Crucible of Congress,* 161.

48 *Niagara Falls, Canada: Day by Day,* 2:198–99.

CHAPTER 4. "DARE TO DO OUR DUTY"

49 *speech of it": CW,* 3:494.

49 *were club advisers:* Neely, *Abraham Lincoln Encyclopedia,* 72.

49 *rolled up 230,686:* Muller, *Concise Historical Atlas of Pennsylvania,* 112.

51 *Pennsylvania was 2,906,215:* United States. Census Office, *Eighth Census of the United States, 1860,* 1:439.

51 *with 40 percent:* Muller, *Concise Historical Atlas of Pennsylvania,* 87.

51 *than 30 percent:* Ibid., 108, graph.

51 *Of the 430,505:* United States. Census Office, *Eighth Census of the United States, 1860,* 1:xxix.

51 *born in Germany:* Ibid.

51 *56,849 African Americans:* Ibid., 1:xiii.

51 *was fifteenth in:* Muller, *Concise Historical Atlas of Pennsylvania,* 90, graph.

51 *Philadelphia's 585,529 inhabitants:* United States. Census Office, *Eighth Census of the United States, 1860,* 1:xxxi.

51 *Pittsburgh and Allegheny:* Ibid.

51 *151,145 farm workers:* Muller, *Concise Historical Atlas of Pennsylvania,* 93, table.

51 *almost 38 percent:* Ibid., 92.

51 *177 industrial sites:* Ibid., 102, table.

51 *ahead of Illinois's:* United States. Census Office, *Eighth Census of the United States, 1860,* 3:112, 113, 538, 539.

51 *years, to 1,711,951:* Ibid., 1:vi.

51 *7,628 African Americans:* Ibid., 1:xiii.

51 *Chicago, was home:* Ibid., 1:xxxi.

51 *50 percent of:* Ibid.

51 *significantly outpace Illinois:* Ibid., 2:vii.

51 *he reached Philadelphia:* Lincoln traveled from Springfield to Philadelphia in just two days. He therefore had to travel by train. However there were two probable routes that he could have used and therefore two possible train stations for his arrival in Philadelphia. The Pennsylvania Railroad established service from Pittsburgh to Philadelphia in 1857. Lincoln would have arrived at the Eleventh and Market Street Station. The Baltimore and Ohio Railroad established service from Wheeling, Virginia, to Baltimore several years earlier than that. Lincoln would have arrived from Baltimore on the Philadelphia, Wilmington, and Baltimore Railroad at the Broad and Prime Street Station. Lincoln's note to Cameron reads, "the card . . . was handed me yesterday

at Philadelphia, just as I was leaving for this city [New York]. I barely had time to step over to the Girard." Lincoln left on the train for New York City from Kensington Station, which was three miles from the Girard House Hotel. He surely was not at this station when he stepped over to the Girard. The Broad and Prime Street Station was more than one mile from the Girard House, not a "step over" distance either. The Pennsylvania Railroad's Eleventh and Market Street Station was, however, only three blocks from the Girard House. I believe that Lincoln arrived at this station and was waiting for the scheduled departure of an omnibus or carriage provided by the rail company to transport passengers the three miles to Kensington Station when he was given the cards of Cameron and Wilmot. He probably walked the three blocks to the Girard House, did not have much time, and walked back in time to catch his ride to Kensington Station and the train to New York.

51 *825–27 Chestnut Street:* The location of the Girard House Hotel has been problematic. City directories (*McElroy's Philadelphia City Directory*) before 1862 list the Girard House Hotel at 925–27 Chestnut Street. City directories beginning with 1862 list the address as "NE Chestnut and 9th." A city map of 1866 places it at that site also. Did it move? No it did not. *Gleason's Pictorial,* February 21, 1852, prints an engraving of the new Girard House Hotel. Beside the hotel in the engraving is the Presbyterian Board of Publications. In city directories, the Presbyterian Board of Publications is, during all the named years, located at 821 Chestnut Street. The 900-block address of the Girard Hotel before 1862 is simply a misprint that was subsequently corrected.

51 *Etiquette of the:* Hemphill, *Bowing to Necessities,* 152.

51 *truly A. Lincoln: CW,* 3:521.

52 *as campaign literature:* Neely, *Abraham Lincoln Encyclopedia,* 73; Lincoln, *Speech of Hon. Abraham Lincoln, of Illinois, at the Cooper Institute.*

53 *Pittsburgh and Philadelphia: Day by Day,* 2:274–75.

53 *the Erie Railroad:* Ibid., 2:276. Lincoln left New York for home on the Erie Railroad, whose destination is Lake Erie at Dunkirk, New York.

53 *Dunkirk, New York:* Baer, *Canals and Railroads,* 1860 map.

53 *March 14, 1860: Day by Day,* 2:276.

54 *of Independence Hall:* Palmer, and Ochoa, eds., *Selected Papers of Thaddeus Stevens,* 1:xxx; Brodie, *Thaddeus Stevens,* 117, 118.

54 *life in Gettysburg:* Palmer, and Ochoa, eds., *Selected Papers of Thaddeus Stevens,* 1:xxvii.

54 *as the savior:* Ibid., 60–61.

55 *In 1851 he:* Coleman, *Disruption of the Pennsylvania Democracy,* 30, 39, 40.

56 *prohibit slavery's introduction: Century Magazine* 33, no. 4 (February 1887): 528.

56 *be duly convicted":* Ibid.

56 *about forty times: CW,* 2:252.

56 *Hall in Pittsburgh:* Coleman, *Disruption of the Pennsylvania Democracy,* 85.

56 *the National Organization":* Ibid.

56 *became a member:* Ibid.

57 *valuable convention experience:* Greeley and Cleveland, *Political Textbook for 1860,* 22; (Washington, D.C.) *National Era,* June 26, 1856.

57 *by Southern leaders:* Republican Party, "James Buchanan, His Doctrines and Policy."

57 *and Fillmore 8:* Kane, *Facts About the Presidents,* 162–63.

58 *than the Constitution":* Buchanan, *Mr. Buchanan's Administration,* 9.

58 *for his property":* Ibid., 17.

59 *an honorable peace":* Ibid., 19.

59 *of the Commonwealth:* Coleman, *Disruption of the Pennsylvania Democracy,* 130.

59 *a large majority:* Ibid., 78.

59 *a transcontinental railroad:* Greeley and Cleveland, *Political Textbook for 1860,* 26–27.

61 *at the time:* Coleman, *Disruption of the Pennsylvania Democracy,* 133–35.

61 *ballot, nominated him:* Ibid., 134.

61 *by 32,000 votes:* Ibid., 140.

61 *away the case":* Fehrenbacher and Fehrenbacher, *Recollected Words,* 170.

CHAPTER 5. "TO SEE AND BE SEEN"

62 *an affectionate farewell:* CW, 4:190–91.

62 *arrived in Cincinnati:* Day by Day, 3:10–12.

63 *the same term: Chicago Tribune,* February 14, 1861.

63 *arrived in Columbus:* Day by Day, 3:12–13.

64 *and Pittsburgh Railroad:* Ibid., 3:13–14; Baer, *Canals and Railroads.*

64 *flag in Virginia):* Donald, *Lincoln,* 306.

64 *Western Union Telegraph: Philadelphia Inquirer,* February 22, 1861; *Pittsburgh Daily Post,* February 16, 1861.

64 *in the State: Beaver Weekly Argus,* February 20, 1861.

64 *of your head":* Dahlinger, "Abraham Lincoln in Pittsburgh," 162, 168.

65 *February 22, 1861: Pittsburgh Daily Post,* February 15, 16, 1861.

65 *a nearby hill:* Ibid.; Dahlinger, "Abraham Lincoln in Pittsburgh," 163.

66 *thirty-nine degrees Fahrenheit: Daily Pittsburgh Gazette,* February 16, 1861.

66 *its firing stopped: Pittsburgh Daily Post,* February 15, 1861.

67 *procession moved off: Daily Pittsburgh Gazette,* February 15, 1861; *Pittsburgh Post Gazette,* February 15, 1861.

67 *into the hotel: Pittsburgh Saturday Dollar Chronicle,* February 23, 1861; *Pittsburgh Post Gazette,* February 15, 1861.

68 *of the lobby:* Ibid.

68 *will be preserved":* CW, 4:208–09.

68 *all good night":* CW, 4:209–10.

68 *back, "Good night!": Daily Pittsburgh Gazette,* February 15, 1861.

68 *family and friends: Pittsburgh Daily Post,* February 15, 1861.

68 *number of weeks:* Day by Day, 3:14.

68 *him in engravings": Pittsburgh Evening Chronicle,* February 15, 1861 (as quoted by Dahlinger, "Abraham Lincoln in Pittsburgh").

68 *of the balcony: Pittsburgh Saturday Dollar Chronicle,* February 23, 1861; *Pittsburgh Daily Post,* February 16, 1861.

68 *prosper as heretofore: CW,* 4:210–13.

69 *squeezed very vigorously": Pittsburgh Saturday Dollar Chronicle,* February 23, 1861.

69 *cheered even more: Daily Pittsburgh Gazette,* February 16, 1861.

69 *being trampled on": Pittsburgh Saturday Dollar Chronicle,* February 23, 1861.

69 *Wayne Railroad Station: Pittsburgh Daily Post,* February 16, 1861.

69 *the excited multitude: Daily Pittsburgh Gazette,* February 16, 1861.

69 *newspapers, and thinking: Day by Day,* 3:15.

69 *in a snowstorm:* Ibid.

70 *three were empty: Pittsburgh Daily Post,* February 16, 1861.

70 *luxury railroad car: New York Tribune,* February 18, 1861.

70 *and blue blanket": New York Tribune,* February 18, 1861; *Erie Weekly Gazette,* February 21, 1861.

70 *to greet him: New York Tribune,* February 18, 1861.

71 *home-made mince pie": Erie Weekly Gazette,* February 21, 1861; *Erie Daily Times,* February 12, 1936.

71 *retired amidst applause": CW,* 4:219.

71 *he left Springfield: New York Tribune,* February 18, 1861.

71 *Philadelphia on board: Day by Day,* 3:16–19.

72 *and on roofs: Philadelphia Inquirer,* February 22, 1861.

72 *invited citizens followed:* Ibid.

73 *the Continental Hotel:* Ibid.

73 *bowed in acknowledgment:* Ibid.

73 *arrested three individuals:* Ibid.

73 *to the Union":* Ibid.

73 *maintain his place:* Ibid.

73 *in front of him:* Ibid.

73 *the United States: CW,* 4:238–39.

74 *oppose my administration?":* Fehrenbacher and Fehrenbacher, *Recollected Words,* 279–80.

74 *the Cameron appointment: Day by Day,* 3:20; Crippen, *Simon Cameron,* 241.

74 *consent to remain":* Fehrenbacher and Fehrenbacher, *Recollected Words,* 329.

74 *opposition is made":* Ibid., 108–09.

74 *was "an impossibility": CW,* 4:239.

74 *him his blessing!: Philadelphia Inquirer,* February 22, 1861.

75 *February twenty-first ended:* Ibid.

CHAPTER 6. "LOOKED AT THROUGH A FOG"

76 *for the North:* Neely, *Abraham Lincoln Encyclopedia,* 40–41.

76 *oath of office: Day by Day,* 3:24–25.

76 *happy man indeed":* Birkner, *James Buchanan and the Political Crisis of the 1850s,* 93.

77 *once in September: Day by Day,* 3:33, 35, 40, 65.

77 *Cameron's Senate seat:* Coleman, *Disruption of the Pennsylvania Democracy,* 144.

77 *several common goals:* Brodie, *Thaddeus Stevens,* 146.

77 *take that back*": McCall, *Thaddeus Stevens*, 311, 312. McCall says only that this is a story told to him by Stevens's associates in the House.

77 *for civil war:* Neely, *Abraham Lincoln Encyclopedia*, 46; McClure, *Abraham Lincoln and Men of War-Times*, 160.

77 *his old ties:* Ibid.

77 *the original report:* Ibid.; McClure, *Abraham Lincoln and Men of War-Times*, 162–63.

77 *minister to Russia: CW*, 5:96–97.

78 *to the public*": McClure, *Abraham Lincoln and Men of War-Times*, 165.

78 *at West Point: Philadelphia Inquirer,* June 25, 1862.

78 *what is afoot:* Ibid.

79 *with General Scott:* Ibid.

79 *a long day:* Ibid.; *Day by Day*, 3:123.

79 *rein on me*": *CW*, 5:284.

79 *and twenty minutes: Philadelphia Inquirer,* June 26, 1862.

79 *from Confederate attack: Day by Day*, 3:123; *CW*, 5:284.

79 *the Civil War:* Mencken, *Railroad Passenger Car*, 83–84.

80 *light at night:* Ibid., 12–13.

80 *and less fumes:* Ibid., 23.

80 *the ferry Susquehanna:* Burgess and Kennedy, *Centennial History of the Pennsylvania Railroad*, 391.

81 *Maryland had rails:* Ibid., 393.

81 *Cities prohibited locomotives:* Mencken, *Railroad Passenger Car*, 109–10.

81 *Philadelphia's passenger stations:* Baer, *Canals and Railroads*.

81 *the Kensington depot:* Harwood, *Royal Blue Line*, 15.

81 *The Baltimore rail:* Baer, *Canals and Railroads*.

82 *kitchen (The Funeral: Philadelphia Inquirer,* April 22, 1865.

83 *without being hungry*": Mencken, *Railroad Passenger Car*, 96.

83 *900 railroad accidents:* Wormser, *Iron Horse*, 16.

83 *was in mourning:* Kane, *Facts About the Presidents*, 154, 158.

83 *for many decades:* Mencken, *Railroad Passenger Car*, 89–91.

CHAPTER 7. "UNFINISHED WORK"

84 *the surrounding area:* Coco, *Vast Sea of Misery*, xii–xiii.

84 *July 10, 1863:* Klement, *Gettysburg Soldiers' Cemetery*, 7.

84 *and legs protruding:* Souder, *Leaves, from the Battle-field*, 17, 22, 23; Bartlett, *Soldiers' National Cemetery at Gettysburg*, 2.

84 *ate their fill:* Bartlett, *Soldiers' National Cemetery at Gettysburg*, Wills letter to Curtin, July 24, 1863, 2.

84 *filled the town:* Souder, *Leaves, from the Battle-field*, 17, 22, 23.

85 *July 24, 1863:* Pennsylvania, *Report of the Select Committee . . . 1864*, 62.

85 *lots for $2,475.87:* Ibid., 3, 6, 7.

85 *By August 17:* Ibid., 67–68.

85 *in Washington, D.C.: Day by Day,* 3:204.

85 *our early attention":* Pennsylvania, *Report of the Select Committee . . . 1864,* 68.

85 *On September 23:* Ibid., 68–69.

86 *accommodate his schedule:* Pennsylvania, *Report of the Select Committee . . . 1864,* 69–70.

86 *$1.59 per body:* Ibid., 7.

86 *bodies per day:* Klement, *Gettysburg Soldiers' Cemetery,* 10.

86 *the dry skeleton":* Pennsylvania, *Report of the Select Committee . . . 1864,* 40.

87 *on November 19:* Klement, *Gettysburg Soldiers' Cemetery,* 22, 248.

87 *of November 18:* Fortenbaugh, *Lincoln at Gettysburg,* 39.

87 *with "ultimate questions":* Neely, *Last Best Hope of Earth,* 154–58.

88 *in September 1862:* Neely, *Abraham Lincoln Encyclopedia,* 6–7.

88 *loss at $90,000:* Palmer and Ochoa, eds., *Selected Papers of Thaddeus Stevens,* 1:400.

89 *of the dead:* Wills, *Lincoln at Gettysburg,* 41, 55–62.

89 *and for all":* Ibid., 107.

89 *are created equal' ":* CW, 6:319.

90 *short, short, short":* Fehrenbacher and Fehrenbacher, *Recollected Words,* 46.

90 *than 2,500 people:* Fortenbaugh, *Lincoln and Gettysburg,* 8, uses 2,100. Gettysburg's 1863 population is not accurately known. The census of 1860 suggests that it was less than 2,500.

91 *fragments for sale: Washington Daily Morning Chronicle,* November 21, 1863.

91 *in ceaseless promenades": Philadelphia Inquirer,* November 21, 1863.

91 *knapsacks, were peeping:* Ibid.

91 *jasmine and evergreen:* Ibid.

92 *William H. Johnson: Day by Day,* 3:220; Klement, *Gettysburg Soldiers' Cemetery,* 11.

92 *around 1:10 p.m.: Day by Day,* 3:221; *Philadelphia Inquirer,* November 19, 1863.

92 *played several tunes:* Klement, *Gettysburg Soldiers' Cemetery,* 193.

92 *accompany the president: Day by Day,* 3:220.

92 *"hero" in Lincoln's:* Klement, *Gettysburg Soldiers' Cemetery,* 65.

92 *got on board:* Ibid., 193.

92 *the bands played:* Ibid.

93 *telegraph lines destroyed:* Gunnarsson, *Story of the Northern Central Railway,* 60–63.

93 *was not there: Philadelphia Inquirer,* November 21, 1863. Curtin's train arrived at 11 P.M.; Klement, *Gettysburg Soldiers' Cemetery,* 106.

93 *eastbound train passed: Day by Day,* 3:221.

93 *you should be": Day by Day,* 3:221; *Philadelphia Inquirer,* November 21, 1863; plaque in Hanover.

94 *around 5 p.m.: Day by Day,* 3:221.

94 *at the station:* Klement, *Gettysburg Soldiers' Cemetery,* 24, 44. Benjamin French arrived in Gettysburg on the seventeenth, and Ward Hill Lamon on the morning of the eighteenth to make last-minute preparations.

94 *carried Lincoln's carpetbag:* Ibid., 75.

94 *was feeling better: Day by Day,* 3:221.

94 *took turns playing:* Klement, *Gettysburg Soldiers' Cemetery,* 194.

95 *Wills House steps:* Gettysburg Presbyterian Church, "Presentation and Unveiling of the Memorial Tablets Commemorating the Lincoln and Burns Event," remarks by W. H. Tipton, 32. Also published in the *Gettysburg Compiler,* November 28, 1914.

95 *speech to make: CW,* 7:16–17.

95 *of the people":* Pennsylvania, *Report of the Select Committee . . . 1864,* 72–73.

96 *to Secretary Seward:* Klement, *Gettysburg Soldiers' Cemetery,* 77.

96 *Is Marching On":* Ibid., 194.

98 *the Wills House:* Ibid., 77.

98 *little historic town":* Philadelphia Inquirer, November 21, 1863.

98 *John Nicolay dropped: Day by Day,* 3:221.

98 *Reynolds of Pennsylvania:* Klement, *Gettysburg Soldiers' Cemetery,* 66, 78; *Washington Daily Morning Chronicle,* November 21, 1863.

98 *the square itself:* Pennsylvania, *Report of the Select Committee . . . 1864,* 76.

98 *mount his horse:* Klement, *Gettysburg Soldiers' Cemetery,* 26.

98 *personal secretary Nicolay:* Ibid., 26.

98 *the western gate:* Pennsylvania, *Report of the Select Committee . . . 1864,* 76.

98 *streets was occupied":* Gettysburg Compiler, November 23, 1863.

98 *confronting the stand":* Philadelphia Inquirer, November 21, 1863; *Gettysburg Compiler,* November 23, 1863; see photograph "Crowd of Citizens at Gettysburg, PA." The soldiers in the foreground are part of the cordon and are facing out.

98 *the military enclosure: Philadelphia Inquirer,* November 21, 1863.

99 *at 11:15 a.m.: Philadelphia Inquirer,* November 20, 1863.

99 *the front row:* Pennsylvania, *Report of the Select Committee . . . 1864,* 76; Klement, *Gettysburg Soldiers' Cemetery,* 26–29.

99 *to Seward's left:* Klement, *Gettysburg Soldiers' Cemetery,* 16.

99 *unknown) already interred:* Ibid., 135; *Adams Sentinel and General Advertiser,* November 24, 1863.

99 *from the sun:* Fortenbaugh, *Lincoln and Gettysburg,* 16–18; Klement, *Gettysburg Soldiers' Cemetery,* 134.

99 *Everett had ridden:* Souder, *Leaves, from the Battle-field,* 140.

99 *Band to begin:* Klement, *Gettysburg Soldiers' Cemetery,* 205.

99 *on Lincoln's right:* Ibid., 16.

99 Program: Pennsylvania, *Report of the Select Committee . . . 1864,* 76–77. Some newspapers erroneously reported that Dr. Stockton was chaplain of the Senate. He was chaplain of the House.

100 *from the earth: CW,* 7:19–21.

100 *Times, and Herald:* Ibid.

101 *eight-round salute:* Klement, *Gettysburg Soldiers' Cemetery,* 210.

101 *fifty Union veterans:* Pennsylvania, *Report of the Select Committee . . . 1864,* 66.

103 *bless Abraham Lincoln' ":* Klement, *Gettysburg Soldiers' Cemetery,* 67.

103 *louder than tongues":* Ibid., 210.

103 *pageant was over":* Souder, *Leaves, from the Battle-field,* 140–41.

103 *governors, and others:* Klement, *Gettysburg Soldiers' Cemetery,* 18.

103 *as they left:* Ibid., 18.

103 *seventy-year-old:* John Burns's tombstone, Evergreen Cemetery, Gettysburg, 1794–1872. Timothy H. Smith, author of *John Burns "The Hero of Gettysburg"* (Gettysburg: Thomas Publications, 2000), 6, says that the twentieth-century tombstone is wrong. The Burns family Bible gives the birth date as September 5, 1793.

103 *you, old man":* Adams Sentinel and General Advertiser, November 24, 1863.

103 *and assistant marshals:* Klement, *Gettysburg Soldiers' Cemetery,* 48, 68. David Wills attended the Presbyterian Church, arranged to use the church for the Ohio program, and encouraged Lincoln's attendance.

103 *Burns's left arm:* Ibid., 133.

104 *the aisle seat":* Gettysburg Presbyterian Church, "Presentation and Unveiling of the Memorial Tablets Commemorating the Lincoln and Burns Event," remarks by T. C. Billheimer, 4–6.

104 *Fort Sumter fame:* Klement, *Gettysburg Soldiers' Cemetery,* 61.

104 *beneath its sod":* Ibid., 68–69.

104 *left the church:* Gettysburg Presbyterian Church, "Presentation and Unveiling of the Memorial Tablets Commemorating the Lincoln and Burns Event," 6.

104 *of getting away":* Philadelphia Inquirer, November 21, 1863.

104 *7 and 8 p.m.:* Day by Day, 3:222.

105 *in their conversation":* Klement, *Gettysburg Soldiers' Cemetery,* 70.

105 *can be imagined":* Philadelphia Inquirer, November 21, 1863.

105 *than two weeks:* Day by Day, 3:222.

106 *give to everybody:* Fehrenbacher and Fehrenbacher, *Recollected Words,* 12–13.

106 *least disfigure me":* Ibid., 13.

106 *from the earth:* CW, 7:22–23.

106 *and cheering streets":* Burlingame and Ettlinger, *Inside Lincoln's White House,* 113.

CHAPTER 8. "COMFORT AND RELIEF"

107 *dollars in supplies:* Taylor, *Philadelphia in the Civil War* (from Lossing), 263.

107 *on wheels" program:* Livermore, *My Story of the War,* 129–33.

107 *one-half per cent":* Bellows, *Speech of the Rev. Dr. Bellows,* 19.

108 *million free meals:* Livermore, *My Story of the War,* 131.

108 *forty soldiers' homes:* Ibid., 131–32.

108 *at 244 F Street:* Bellows, *Speech of the Rev. Dr. Bellows,* 33–34; Taylor, *Philadelphia in the Civil War,* 262–63.

108 *it raised $135,000:* Stillé, *Memorial of the Great Central Fair,* 13.

108 *fair in Philadelphia:* Ibid., 14–15.

108 *Sanitary Commission agreed:* Ibid., 15–16.

108 *Chicago Sanitary Fair:* Ibid., 14.

108 *Holme in 1682:* Looney, *Old Philadelphia in Early Photographs,* 114.

108 *design additional buildings:* Sharf and Westcott, *History of Philadelpia,* 815–16.

109 *was 6,500 feet:* Jackson, *Encyclopedia of Philadelphia,* 1067.

109 *of the troops:* Stillé, *Memorial of the Great Central Fair,* 80; *CW,* 7:369.

109 *for opening ceremonies:* Stillé, *Memorial of the Great Central Fair,* 25–31.

110 *of the unknown":* Ibid., 30.

110 *and Boydell's Shakespeare:* Ibid., 34.

110 *of Indian life:* Ibid., 58.

111 *of donating money:* Jackson, *Encyclopedia of Philadelphia,* 1067.

111 *therefore raised $5,541:* Stillé, *Memorial of the Great Central Fair,* 42–43.

111 *election raised $10,457:* Ibid., 120.

111 *fair totaled $72,850:* Ibid., 96.

111 *Old Rye Whiskey:* Ibid., 99–100.

112 *and would visit:* Day by Day, 3:264.

112 *in his honor:* Philadelphia Inquirer, June 17, 1864.

112 *thirty-five-gun salute:* Ibid.

112 *It was 11:45 a.m.:* Ibid.

112 *into a barouche:* Ibid.

113 *the distinguished guest:* Ibid.

113 *clear and manly":* Whiteman, *Gentlemen in Crisis,* 74.

113 *Eighteenth Street gate:* Philadelphia Inquirer, June 17, 1864.

114 *areas was impossible:* Ibid.

114 *the United States":* Philadelphia Inquirer, June 17, 1864.

116 *thank you, gentlemen:* CW, 7:394–96.

116 *is not doubtful":* Philadelphia Inquirer, June 17, 1864.

116 *crossing a stream":* Ibid.

116 *as Whig congressmen:* New York Tribune, December 22, 1848; Engle, *History of the Commonwealth of Pennsylvania,* 256. Pollock was congressman from 1843 to 1849. Other sources state that they also roomed at the same Washington, D.C., boardinghouse. Pollock was Know-Nothing Party governor of Pennsylvania, 1855–1858. Coleman, *Disruption of the Pennsylvania Democracy,* 135, says that he was the presiding officer who appointed A. K. McClure, a Curtin ally, to the post of Pennsylvania State Republican Committee chairman in 1860, in the presence of a majority of committee members who were Cameron allies.

116 *United States Mint:* Engle, *History of the Commonwealth of Pennsylvania,* 256. Pollock was director of the Mint 1861–66. President Grant later appointed him director, also.

116 *of the ladies":* CW, 7:396.

116 *brought from Washington:* Philadelphia Inquirer, June 17, 1864.

117 *of our country":* CW, 7:397.

117 *in the field":* CW, 7:397.

118 *in my honor":* CW, 7:398.

118 *one million dollars!:* Gallman, *Mastering Wartime,* 151; Stillé, *Memorial of The Great Central Fair,* 150.

118 *"an incalculable blessing":* Woodward, *Speech of Hon. George W. Woodward,* 9; Lathrop, *History of the Union League of Philadelphia,* 11. George W. Woodward assumed office as a Pennsylvania Supreme Court justice on December 6, 1852. After his unsuccessful

campaign as Democratic candidate for governor in October 1863, he became chief justice of the Pennsylvania Supreme Court on December 7, 1863. He resigned that post on November 20, 1867, in order to take his seat in the U.S. House of Representatives. He was a member of the House during the impeachment of President Andrew Johnson.

118 *is in Philadelphia"*: Lathrop, *History of the Union League of Philadelphia,* 18.

118 *by 15,000 votes:* Ibid., 58.

118 *of Colored Troops:* Lathrop, *History of the Union League of Philadelphia,* 77, and Whiteman, *Gentlemen in Crisis,* 47, refer to the Supervisory Committee for the Enlistment of Colored Troops. The *Philadelphia Inquirer,* June 17, 1864, quoted earlier in this chapter, refers to the Supervisory Committee for Recruiting Colored Regiments. An 1863 broadside "The Battle Hymn of the Republic," published by the committee, also uses the latter name.

118 *the Union army:* Lathrop, *History of the Union League of Philadelphia,* 77–81.

118 *in 1864, 1,044,900:* Ibid., 67.

118 *New York and Boston:* Ibid., 36–42.

118 *Boston's organizing committee:* Ibid., 41.

118 *of the plans:* Ibid., 53.

118 *Sidney George Fisher:* Ibid., 82.

119 *of the Union:* Lathrop, *History of the Union League of Philadelphia,* 85; Whiteman, *Gentlemen in Crisis,* 78, 315.

119 *26 electoral votes:* Kane, *Facts About the Presidents,* 173.

120 *said the President":* Livermore, *My Story of the War,* 578–81.

CHAPTER 9. "THE HEAVENS ARE HUNG IN BLACK"

121 *after 10 p.m.:* Donald, *Lincoln,* 597.

123 *his second inauguration:* Kunhardt, *Twenty Days,* 93–95.

123 *had been preserved:* Harrisburg Pennsylvania Daily Telegraph, April 24, 1865.

123 *white satin fringe:* Ibid.

123 *fifteen hundred dollars:* Kunhardt, *Twenty Days,* 120.

123 *continued all day:* Ibid., 119–32.

123 *depot at New Jersey:* Ibid., 140; Baer, *Canals and Railroads.*

123 *back to Springfield:* Philadelphia Inquirer, April 22, 1865.

124 *a sleeping apartment:* Slusser, *Mr. Lincoln's Railroad Car,* 3–9.

124 *each window panel:* Ibid., 11–12.

124 *February 20th, 1862":* Harrisburg Pennsylvania Daily Telegraph, April 24, 1865; Slusser, *Mr. Lincoln's Railroad Car,* 13–14.

125 *General Edward D. Townsend:* Philadelphia Inquirer, April 22, 1865.

125 *Four individuals who:* Ibid.

126 *embalmer C. P. Brown:* Ibid.

126 *engine no. 238:* Ibid.

126 *and a kitchen:* New York Times, April 22, 1865; Slusser, *Mr. Lincoln's Railroad Car,* 13.

126 *cars in all:* Philadelphia Inquirer, April 22, 1865.

126 *hour through stations:* Slusser, *Mr. Lincoln's Railroad Car,* 13.

126 *a final prayer: New York Times,* April 22, 1865.

126 *Northern Central Railroad: Philadelphia Inquirer,* April 22, 1865.

127 *cloudy and warm:* Slusser, *Mr. Lincoln's Railroad Car,* 60–61, from Washington, D.C., *National Tribune,* May 27, 1915.

127 *in the front car: Harrisburg Pennsylvania Daily Telegraph,* April 24, 1865; *New York Tribune,* April 22, 1865; *Philadelphia Inquirer,* April 22, 1865.

127 *through their states:* Kunhardt, *Twenty Days,* 143.

127 *crucified for us": Philadelphia Inquirer,* April 22, 1865.

127 *and white verbena:* Gibson, *History of York County, Pennsylvania,* 179.

128 *of Lincoln's death":* Slusser, *Mr. Lincoln's Railroad Car,* 61.

129 *the city streets: Harrisburg Pennsylvania Daily Telegraph,* April 24, 1865; *Philadelphia Inquirer,* April 22, 1865.

129 *mournful guns boomed:* Ibid.

129 *a Slaughtered Leader' ": Philadelphia Inquirer,* April 22, 1865.

129 *policemen stood guard: Harrisburg Pennsylvania Daily Telegraph,* April 24, 1865.

129 *the speaker's chair:* Ibid.

129 *on the chin":* Ibid.

131 *toll once again:* Ibid.

131 *and one-half hours:* Ibid.

131 *his face rechalked:* Kunhardt, *Twenty Days,* 144.

131 *the railroad depot:* Ibid.

131 *Simon Cameron boarded: Harrisburg Pennsylvania Daily Telegraph,* April 24, 1865.

131 *were too late:* Ibid.

132 *a Nation's Loss": Philadelphia Inquirer,* April 24, 1865.

132 *He Yet Lives!": Lancaster Evening Express,* April 22, 1865.

132 *by the coffin: Lancaster Evening Express,* April 24, 1865.

132 *James Buchanan saw:* Kunhardt, *Twenty Days,* 144–45.

133 *salute of honor: New York Tribune,* April 24, 1865; *Philadelphia Inquirer,* April 24, 1865.

133 *and Baltimore depot: Philadelphia Inquirer,* April 24, 1865.

133 *funeral party waited:* Ibid.

133 *of Market Street: Philadelphia Inquirer,* April 22, 1865.

134 *had to wait:* Ibid.

135 *white flowered wreath:* Ibid.

135 *the designated route: Philadelphia Inquirer,* April 24, 1865.

135 *of Independence Square: Philadelphia Inquirer,* April 22, 1865.

135 *during the procession: Philadelphia Inquirer,* April 24, 1865.

136 *to surrender it: CW,* 4:240; paraphrased in *Philadelphia Inquirer,* April 22, 24, 1865.

136 *the Inhabitants thereof": Philadelphia Inquirer,* April 24, 1865.

136 *ship sailing rapidly":* Ibid.

136 *news very soon":* Fehrenbacher and Fehrenbacher, *Recollected Words,* 486.

137 *Mayor Alexander Henry: Philadelphia Inquirer,* April 24, 1865.

137 *white linen collar":* Ibid.

137 *for the viewing:* Ibid.

137 *on Second Street: New York Times,* April 24, 1865.

137 *to the ground: Philadelphia Inquirer,* April 24, 1865.

137 *to the crowd: Chicago Tribune,* April 24, 1865.

138 *"Rest in Peace": Philadelphia Inquirer,* April 24, 25, 1865.

138 *of the hall: Chicago Tribune,* April 25, 1865.

138 *in line also:* Ibid.

138 *viewers as 128,640: Philadelphia Inquirer,* April 25, 1865.

138 *Embalmer Brown cleaned: New York Times,* April 25, 1865; *Philadelphia Inquirer,* April 25, 1865.

138 *Kensington Railroad Station: Philadelphia Inquirer,* April 25, 1865.

138 *train at Morrisville: New York Times,* April 25, 1865.

139 *many war dead:* Gallman, *Mastering Wartime,* 106–13.

139 *At 1:32 a.m.: New York Tribune,* April 29, 1865.

139 *at 2:50 a.m.: New York Times,* April 29, 1865.

139 *at this place": New York Tribune,* April 29, 1865; *New York Times,* April 29, 1865.

139 *rest and repose": Erie Observer,* May 4, 1865.

140 *the Dooryard Bloom'd":* Marius, *Columbia Book of Civil War Poetry,* 337–38.

140 *to read Shakespeare:* Neely, *Abraham Lincoln Encyclopedia,* 275.

140 *so much worth:* Shakespeare, *King Henry the Sixth,* part 1, act 1, scene 1, in *Complete Works of William Shakespeare,* 495.

CHAPTER 10. POSTSCRIPT

141 *Bristol, northeast of:* existing section of rail and a historical marker.

142 *Independence Hall, Sixth:* existing building.

142 *two smaller outbuildings:* Richman, *Pennsylvania's Architecture,* 15.

144 *Liberty Bell, north:* existing bell on display.

144 *Independence Square. The:* existing square.

144 *Declaration House replica:* existing reconstructed building.

146 *the Continental Hotel:* map of Philadelphia, 1866; Sharf and Westcott, *History of Philadelpia,* 733.

146 *its 700 rooms:* White, *Philadelphia Architecture in the Nineteenth Century,* 29; Wolf, *Philadelphia: Portrait of an American City,* 188.

146 *an exterior balcony:* Tatum, *Penn's Great Town,* 98, 99.

147 *to those teachings":* plaque, east side of main Chestnut Street entrance of the Benjamin Franklin Hotel, Ninth and Chestnut Streets, Philadelphia. Erected February 21, 1961.

147 *Chinese Museum Building:* address on engraving of Chinese Museum Building printed in chapter 3.

147 *on the second floor:* Tatum, *Penn's Great Town,* 90, 184. See fig. 90 for an interior view of the Chinese Museum Building.

147 *concerts, and meetings:* Weigley, *Philadelphia, A 300-Year History,* 343, 348.

147   *demolished the ruins:* Ibid.

147   *Girard House Hotel:* map of Philadelphia 1866; *McElroy's Philadelphia City Directory 1862; Gleason's Pictoral,* February 21, 1852.

147   *designed the Girard:* Tatum, *Penn's Great Town,* 98.

147   *its exterior balcony:* Wolf, *Philadelphia: Portrait of an American City,* 188.

147   *the Union League:* Taylor, *Philadelphia in the Civil War,* 240.

147   *Musical Fund Hall:* Preserved façade on building; map of Philadelphia 1866.

147   *Logan Circle, between:* This existing circle includes the old Logan Square, whose west boundary stopped at Logan Street, now gone. Logan Street was west of Nineteenth Street. Also see Smedley, *Smedley's Atlas of the City of Philadelphia.*

147   *the cathedral's interior:* White, *Philadelphia Architecture in the Nineteenth Century,* 27.

147   *West Philadelphia Train:* map, Taylor, *Philadelphia in the Civil War,* end page.

147   *Broad and Prime:* Ibid.; map of Philadelphia 1866.

148   *Kensington Station, eastern:* Ibid.

148   *and Market:* Ibid.; Taylor, *Philadelphia in the Civil War,* 44.

149   *of Coventry Forge:* Chester County Historical Society, *History of Coventryville.*

150   *Hopewell Furnace National:* National Historical Site.

150   *Mordecai Lincoln Homestead:* existing building on the National Historical Register.

151   *design with them:* Richman, *Pennsylvania's Architecture,* 10.

151   *Daniel Boone Homestead:* existing building, although only a foundation section with its spring were present during Boone's life here.

151   *Exeter Friends Meeting:* existing building, built after Mordecai Lincoln died and Daniel Boone left the area.

151   *tower or belfry:* Richman, *Pennsylvania's Architecture,* 16.

153   *Leaman Place Train:* Everts and Stewart, *1875 Historical Atlas of Lancaster County Pennsylvania,* 32.

154   *carriage that allegedly:* One Harrisburg family's legend is that their ancestor, a chauffeur for Simon Cameron, was the driver of the carriage.

154   *Lancaster Train Station:* Everts and Stewart, *1875 Historical Atlas of Lancaster County Pennsylvania,* 4.

154   *The Cadwell House:* Ibid., 65.

154   *Thaddeus Stevens's House:* Moody and Brigens, *Map of the City of Lancaster 1850; Outline and Index Map of Lancaster 1875,* plate 12.

154   *Wheatland, the home:* existing building.

154   *Harrisburg, Pennsylvania Railroad:* Located from maps owned by the Historical Society of Dauphin County, e.g., Moody, *Harrisburg 1850;* and Brion, *Harrisburg 1875.*

154   *shared the building:* Meeks, *Railroad Station, An Architectural History,* 72.

155   *Jones House Hotel:* address noted on the engraving printed in chapter 1.

156   *the Whiskey Rebellion:* Steinmetz and Hoffsommer, *This Was Harrisburg,* 51.

158   *Pennsylvania Capitol Building:* existing building. See also Cummings, *Pennsylvania's State Houses and Capitols.*

158   *Italian Renaissance dome:* Richman, *Pennsylvania's Architecture,* 22, 23.

158   *Simon Cameron / John:* existing building.

158   *Northern Central York: 1876 Atlas of York County Pennsylvania, Illustrated, and 1903 City of York,* 68.

158   *Hanover Junction Station:* existing building.

158   *November 19, 1863:* Klement, *Gettysburg Soldiers' Cemetery,* 70.

158   *form of smallpox: Day by Day,* 3:222.

160   *Hanover. Lincoln's train:* existing plaque.

160   *Gettysburg Train Station:* existing building.

161   *Wills House, southeast:* existing building.

161   *Robert G. Harper:* Klement, *Gettysburg Soldiers' Cemetery,* 87, 96.

161   *First Day's Battle:* Conversation between Secretary Seward and Ohio delegation printed in *Washington Daily Morning Chronicle,* November 21, 1863.

161   *The Parade Route:* Pennsylvania, *Report to the Select Committee . . . 1864,* 76.

161   *Soldiers' National Cemetery:* existing cemetery.

162   *Gettysburg Presbyterian Church:* existing building, built/renovated on the same site as previous building.

162   *Thaddeus Stevens's House:* Beyer, *Guide to the State Historical Markers of Pennsylvania,* 77.

162   *Caledonia Iron Works:* existing blacksmith shop and iron furnace ruins.

163   *Old Petersburg Tollhouse:* existing building.

165   *Mount Washington Tavern:* existing building.

165   *Braddock's Grave. French:* historical monument.

165   *Braddock's Road. In:* Historical markers and traces are still visible in the forest. Maintained by the National Park Service.

165   *Taverns in Hopwood:* Vivian, *Driving Tour of the National Road in Pennsylvania,* 12, 13, 21.

165   *Searight's Tollhouse. Built:* existing building.

165   *Brownsville, Pennsylvania. From:* Vivian, *Driving Tour of the National Road in Pennsylvania,* 28–30.

165   *Monongahela House Hotel: Daily Pittsburgh Gazette,* February 15, 16, 1861; *Pittsburgh Press,* June 22, 1958; Dahlinger, "Abraham Lincoln in Pittsburgh," 165–68.

166   *in April 1845:* Baldwin, *Pittsburgh, the Story of a City,* 273.

166   *Allegheny City train:* Hopkins Co., *Atlas of the Cities of Pittsburgh and Allegheny.*

167   *Union Station, Fourteenth: Erie Times,* February 12, 1936. This article interviewed people who saw Lincoln at the Erie train station in February 1861. The wooden frame building that served as the train station was located at the same site as the New York Central station in 1936, the date of the article. That station was at Fourteenth and Peach Streets. (An erroneous location, Bay and State Streets, was given by another article. That train station was at the end of a rail spur that ran to the lakeshore. It was used for lake/rail connections.)

167   *Chester County Times:* Beyer, *Guide to the State Historical Markers,* 18.

167   *Logan House Hotel:* Ibid., 99.

APPENDIX A

169   *December 6, 1847: Day by Day,* 1:295–96.

169 *east to Washington:* Ibid., 1:313.

169 *three possible routes:* Riddle, *Congressman Abraham Lincoln,* 12–13. Riddle discusses two routes. To these two, add the variation of travel on the Monongahela River.

169 *to Winchester, Virginia:* Ibid.

169 *and Washington, D.C.:* Remini, *Henry Clay,* 412.

170 *the Monongahela River:* Hunter, *Steamboats on the Western Rivers,* 41–42.

170 *1,626 miles from Springfield.: New York Tribune,* December 22, 1848.

170 *Springfield to St. Louis (stagecoach:* Rand McNally *TripMaker 1999* (Skokie, Ill.: Rand McNally, 1998).

170 *St. Louis to Cairo (steamboat):* United States. Army. Corps of Engineers. Rock Island District, *Upper Mississippi River Navigation Charts.* St. Louis to confluence of the Mississippi and Ohio Rivers = 180 miles. Confluence of Mississippi and Ohio Rivers to Cairo docks on the Ohio River = 3 miles.

170 *Cairo to Carrollton (steamboat):* United States. Army. Corps of Engineers. Pittsburgh District, *Ohio River Navigation Charts.*

170 *Carrollton to Frankfort (steamboat):* Rand McNally *TripMaker 1999.*

170 *Frankfort to Lexington (train):* Rand McNally *TripMaker 1999.*

170 *Lexington to Winchester (stagecoach):* Rand McNally *TripMaker 1999.*

170 *Winchester to Harpers Ferry (train):* Baer, *Canals and Railroads.*

170 *Harpers Ferry to Washington (train):* Ibid. This figure is calculated. The distance from Relay to Baltimore is approximately 7 miles. From the tables, Harpers Ferry to Baltimore = 80 miles. 80 - 7 = 73 miles from Harpers Ferry to Relay. From the tables, Relay to Washington, D.C. = 30 miles. Therefore Harpers Ferry to Washington, D.C., in 1847 = 73 + 30 = 103 miles.

171 *Maysville to Wheeling (steamboat):* United States. Army. Corps of Engineers. Pittsburgh District, *Ohio River Navigation Charts.*

171 *Wheeling to Cumberland (stagecoach):* Yarris, *Map of the National Road in Pennsylvania.*

171 *Cumberland to Harpers Ferry (train):* Baer, *Canals and Railroads.*

171 *Maysville to Pittsburgh (steamboat):* United States. Army. Corps of Engineers. Pittsburgh District, *Ohio River Navigation Charts.*

171 *Pittsburgh to Brownsville (steamboat):* United States. Army. Corps of Engineers. Pittsburgh District, *Monongahela River Navigation Charts.*

171 *Brownsville to Cumberland (stagecoach):* Yarris, *Map of the National Road in Pennsylvania.*

171 *eight miles per:* Coleman, *Stage-Coach Days in the Bluegrass,* 113.

171 *current, including stops:* Lyell, *Second Visit to the United States,* 223.

171 *ten to fifteen miles:* Mencken, *Railroad Passenger Car,* 107.

172 *Lexington to Maysville usually:* Coleman, *Stage-Coach Days in the Bluegrass,* 80.

172 *Ohio River–National Road:* Remini, *Henry Clay,* 412.

172 *acquired national reputation":* Hadden, *History of Uniontown, the County Seat of Fayette County, Pennsylvania,* 773. If Lincoln stopped in Uniontown on his way to Congress, the time period would have been late November to early December 1847 or 1848. Of course there are many legal issues that Lincoln and Daniel Downer conceivably might have discussed that would

never have been recorded in the courthouse. In the hope that something was recorded, I searched every record in the Fayette County Courthouse for the two, six-month periods beginning November 1, 1847, and November 1, 1848. The only case that came close to satisfying the report was a replevin filed on November 28, 1848, by Daniel Downer on behalf of James Tibbs. Lincoln had represented and had known Tibbs families in Menard County, Illinois. I was not able to make a connection between James Tibbs of Fayette County, Pennsylvania, and John Tibbs of Lincoln's *Tibbs v. Miller* case in 1843–44 in Menard County, Illinois. Also, Tibbs family descendants report that Samuel Tibbs was a member of Lincoln's Black Hawk War militia company. I was not able to connect him with James Tibbs of Pennsylvania either.

APPENDIX B

173 *was by railroad:* Information in this table is either known information, or it is deduced, based on known locations of Abraham Lincoln as found in *Day by Day* and possible routes as found in Baer's *Canals and Railroads.* For example, on July 20, 1857, Lincoln was in Springfield, Illinois (and probably on July 21, 1857, also). On July 24, 1857, he registered at the Cataract House, Niagara Falls, with Mrs. Lincoln. He could not have made that trip in that short time by stagecoach (nor would he have wanted to do so) or by lake steamer. He must have traveled by railroad. The only railroad line along the shore of the Great Lakes went through Erie, Pennsylvania.

173 *traveling toward Trenton:* It is known that the Lincoln family traveled by railroad. The only rail line from Baltimore to Philadelphia at that time was the Philadelphia, Wilmington, and Baltimore. From Philadelphia to New York City, there was a choice of the Philadelphia and Trenton Railroad or the Camden and Amboy Railroad. In all of the known travels of Lincoln, he chose the Philadelphia and Trenton Railroad. It was more direct and required only a short ferry ride across the Hudson River from Jersey City to New York City. The Camden and Amboy Railroad required a ferry ride over the Delaware River to Camden, and then a longer ferry ride from New Jersey into New York City.

173 *to Niagara Falls:* See discussion at endnote *173, was by railroad* for information regarding this 1857 trip.

173 *Station in Erie:* This location was given in the *Erie Times,* February 12, 1936, by Erie residents who heard Lincoln speak in 1861, "The president-elect delivered a short address from the balcony of the old Cleveland & Erie railroad depot, a frame structure, which stood on the site of the present New York Central station." In 1936 the New York Central station was at Fourteenth and Peach Streets, the same site as the present Union Station in Erie.

173 *on to Buffalo:* Distances in Pennsylvania are from Baer.

173 *New York City:* Deduced as at endnote 173, *traveling toward Trenton.*

173 *bound for Cleveland: Day by Day,* 2:276, "March 12, *New York* and *en route.* In morning Lincoln leaves for home on Erie Railroad." This would take him to Dunkirk and Lake Erie. From there he must have taken the train. It was March, hardly lake steamer weather, and he arrived home "March 14. *Springfield.* Early in morning Lincoln arrives on Great Western [railroad]." The only route he could have taken was through Erie, Pennsylvania.

173 *the same route:* Documented in *Pittsburgh Daily Post,* February 15, 16, 1861; *Daily Pittsburgh Gazette,* February 15, 16, 1861; *Pittsburgh Saturday Dollar Chronicle,* February 23, 1861.

174 *through Erie, Pennsylvania: Erie Weekly Gazette,* February 21, 1861; The route is also documented in *New York Tribune,* February 18, 1861.

174 *and Trenton Railroad: Philadelphia Inquirer,* February 22, 1861.

174 *the same route: Philadelphia Inquirer,* February 23, 1861.

174 *to Washington, D.C.:* Cuthbert, *Lincoln and the Baltimore Plot,* 79–82.

174 *Railroad from Baltimore:* same and only route available, as before.

174 *and Trenton Railroad:* Ibid.; *Philadelphia Inquirer,* June 26, 1862.

174 *Hanover Junction, Pennsylvania: Day by Day,* 3:220–21.

174 *16.4 miles from Hanover:* Baer, *Canals and Railroads.*

174 *Station in Philadelphia: Philadelphia Inquirer,* June 17, 1864.

174 *Pennsylvania Railroad Station: Harrisburg Pennsylvania Daily Telegraph,* April 24, 1865.

174 *Prime Street Station: Philadelphia Inquirer,* April 22, 1865.

174 *Trenton, New Jersey: Philadelphia Inquirer,* April 25, 1865.

174 *through Erie, Pennsylvania: Erie Observer,* April 27, 1865.

Bibliography

Baer, Christopher T. *Canals and Railroads of the Mid-Atlantic States 1800–1860.* Wilmington, Del.: Eleutherian Mills-Hagley Foundation, 1981.

Baker, Jean H. *Mary Todd Lincoln.* New York: W. W. Norton, 1987.

Baldwin, Leland. *Pittsburgh, the Story of a City.* Pittsburgh: University of Pittsburgh Press, 1937.

Bartlett, John Russell. *The Soldiers' National Cemetery at Gettysburg.* Providence, R.I.: Providence Press, 1874.

Basler, Roy P., ed., Marion Dolores Pratt and Lloyd A. Dunlap, asst. eds. *The Collected Works of Abraham Lincoln.* 9 vols. New Brunswick: Rutgers University Press, 1953–55.

Bellows, Henry. *Speech of the Rev. Dr. Bellows, President of the United States Sanitary Commission, Made at the Academy of Music, Philadelphia, Feb. 24, 1863.* Philadelphia: Philadelphia Agency of the United States Sanitary Commission, 1863.

Beyer, George R. *Guide to the State Historical Markers of Pennsylvania.* Harrisburg: Pennsylvania Historical and Museum Commission, 1991.

Bining, Arthur C. *Pennsylvania Iron Manufacture in the Eighteenth Century.* Harrisburg: Pennsylvania Historical and Museum Commission, 1987.

Birkner, Michael J., ed. *James Buchanan and the Political Crisis of the 1850s.* Selinsgrove, Pa.: Susquehanna University Press, 1996.

Boker, George H. *First Annual Report of the Board of Directors of the Union League of Philadelphia, December 14th, 1863.* Philadelphia: King & Baird, Printers, 1863.

———. *Second Annual Report of the Board of Directors of the Union League of Philadelphia, December 12th, 1864.* Philadelphia: Henry B. Ashmead, Book and Job Printer, 1864.

Boritt, Gabor S. *Lincoln and the Economics of the American Dream.* Urbana: University of Illinois Press, 1994 ed.

Bradley, Erwin S. *Simon Cameron, Lincoln's Secretary of War.* Philadelphia: University of Pennsylvania Press, 1966.

Brodie, Fawn. *Thaddeus Stevens, Scourge of the South.* New York: W. W. Norton, 1959.

Brooks, Noah. *The Life of Lincoln,* published in *The Constitutional Edition of The Writings of Abraham Lincoln,* ed. A. B. Lapsley. 8 vols. New York: G. P. Putnam's Sons, 1923.

Buchanan, James. *Mr. Buchanan's Administration on the Eve of the Rebellion.* North Stratford, N.H.: Ayer, 1997.

Burgess, George H., and Miles C. Kennedy. *The Centennial History of the Pennsylvania Railroad Company 1846–1946.* Philadelphia: Pennsylvania Railroad, 1949.

Burlingame, Michael, and John R. T. Ettlinger, eds. *Inside Lincoln's White House: The Complete Civil War Diary of John Hay.* Carbondale: Southern Illinois University Press, 1997.

Cahalan, Sally Smith. *James Buchanan and His Family at Wheatland.* Lancaster, Pa.: James Buchanan Foundation, 1988.

Chester County Historical Society. "History of Coventryville, An Early Iron Making Community." Unpub. ms.

Clinton, George W. "Commercial Advertiser Directory for the City of Buffalo: Containing in Addition to the Usual Matter, a Sketch of the Early History of Buffalo." Buffalo, N.Y.: Jewitt, Thomas & Co., 1848.

Cole, James M., and Roy E. Frampton. *Lincoln and the Human Interest Stories of the Gettysburg National Cemetery.* Hanover, Pa.: Sheridan Press, 1995.

Coleman, J. Winston, Jr. *Stage-Coach Days in the Bluegrass.* Louisville, Ky.: Standard Press, 1936.

Coleman, John F. *The Disruption of the Pennsylvania Democracy 1848–1860.* Harrisburg: Pennsylvania Historical and Museum Commission, 1975.

Crippen, Lee F. *Simon Cameron: Ante-Bellum Years.* Oxford, Ohio: Mississippi Valley Press, 1942.

Cummings, Hubertis. "Pennsylvania's State Houses and Capitols." Harrisburg: Pennsylvania Historical and Museum Commission, 1969.

———. "Stephen Hills and the Building of Pennsylvania's First Capitol." *Pennsylvania History* 20, no. 4. (October 1953): 417–37.

Cuthbert, Norma B. *Lincoln and the Baltimore Plot 1861.* San Marino, Calif.: Huntington Library, 1949.

Dahlinger, Charles W. "Abraham Lincoln in Pittsburgh and the Birth of the Republican Party." *Western Pennsylvania Historical Magazine* 3, no. 4 (October 1920): 160–68.

Dickens, Charles. *American Notes,* 2d ed. 2 vols. London: Chapman and Hall, 1842.

Diffenderfer, F. R. "Report of the Committee on the W. U. Hensel Tablet Unveiling." *Lancaster County Historical Society Journal* 19, no. 4 (April 1915): 100–107.

Donald, David Herbert. *Lincoln.* New York: Simon and Schuster, 1995.

Dyer, Brainerd. *Zachary Taylor.* Baton Rouge: Louisiana State University Press, 1946.

1876 Atlas of York County and 1903 City of York. Reprint, Philadelphia: Hunter Printers, 1976.

Engle, William H. *History of the Commonwealth of Pennsylvania.* Philadelphia: E. M. Gardner, 1883.

Everett, Edward. *Address of Hon. Edward Everett, At the Consecration of the National Cemetery at Gettysburg 19th November, 1863, with the Dedicatory Speech of President Lincoln, and the Other Exercises of the Occasion; Accompanied by an Account of the Origin of the Undertaking and of the Arrangement of the Cemetery Grounds, and by a Map of the Battle-Field and a Plan of the Cemetery. Published For the Benefit of the Cemetery Monument Fund.* Boston: Little, Brown, 1864.

Everts and Stewart. *1875 Historical Atlas of Lancaster County Pennsylvania.* Reproduced for the Lancaster County Historical Society. Mt. Vernon, Ind.: Windmill Publications, 1994.

Faragher, John Mack. *Daniel Boone: The Life and Legend of an American Pioneer.* New York: Henry Holt, 1992.

Fehrenbacher, Don, and Virginia Fehrenbacher, eds. *Recollected Words of Abraham Lincoln.* Stanford: Stanford University Press, 1996.

Findley, Paul. *Lincoln: The Crucible of Congress.* New York: Crown Publishers, 1979.

Fortenbaugh, Robert. *Lincoln and Gettysburg.* Gettysburg: The Bookmart, 1949.

Foundation for Architecture. *Philadelphia Architecture.* Cambridge: MIT Press, 1984.

Frassanito, William A. *Gettysburg: A Journey in Time.* New York: Charles Scribner's Sons, 1975.

Freeman, Aileen S. *Lincoln: The Northeast Pennsylvania Connection.* Paupack, Pa.: FOSI, 2000.

Futhey, J. Smith, and Gilbert Cope. *The History of Chester County, Pennsylvania.* Philadelphia: J. B. Lippincott, 1881.

Gallman, J. Matthew. *Mastering Wartime: A Social History of Philadelphia During the Civil War.* New York: Cambridge University Press, 1990.

Georg, Kathleen R., and John W. Busey. *Nothing but Glory: Pickett's Division at Gettysburg.* Hightstown, N.J.: Longstreet House, 1987.

Gettysburg Presbyterian Church. "Presentation and Unveiling of the Memorial Tablets Commemorating the Lincoln and Burns Event." Rochester, N.Y.: Times-Union Press, 1920.

Gibson, Gail M. "James Buchanan." Harrisburg: Pennsylvania Historical and Museum Commission, 1992.

Gibson, John. *The History of York County, Pennsylvania.* Chicago: F. A. Battey, 1886.

G. M. Hopkins Company. *Atlas of the Cities of Pittsburgh and Allegheny.* Philadelphia, 1882.

Greeley, Horace, and John F. Cleveland. *A Political Text-Book For 1860.* New York: Tribune Association, 1860.

Gunnarsson, Robert L. *The Story of the Northern Central Railway: From Baltimore to Lake Ontario.* Sykesville, Md.: Greenberg Publishing Co., 1991.

Hadden, James. *History of Uniontown, the County Seat of Fayette County, Pennsylvania.* Evansville, Ind.: Whipporwill Publications, 1913.

Hamilton, Holman. *Zachary Taylor, Soldier in the White House.* New York: Bobbs-Merrill, 1951.

Harwood, Herbert, Jr. *The Royal Blue Line.* Sykesville, Md.: Greenberg Publications, 1990.

Hemphill, C. Dallett. *Bowing to Necessities, A History of Manners in America, 1620–1860.* New York: Oxford University Press, 1999.

Holtzer, Harold, ed. *The Lincoln-Douglas Debates.* New York: HarperCollins, 1993.

Horner, Harlan H. *Lincoln and Greeley.* Urbana: University of Illinois Press, 1953.

Hulbert, Archer B. *The Old National Road: A Chapter of American Expansion.* Columbus, Ohio: F. J. Heer, 1901.

Hunter, Louis C. *Steamboats on the Western Rivers.* New York: Dover Publications, 1993.

Jackson, Joseph. *Encyclopedia of Philadelphia.* Harrisburg: National Historical Association, 1933.

Jacobs, Michael. *Notes on the Rebel Invasion of Maryland and Pennsylvania, and the Battle of Gettysburg, July 1st, 2d, and 3d, 1863, Accompanied by an Explanatory Map.* Philadelphia: J. B. Lippincott, 1864.

Kane, Joseph N. *Facts About the Presidents*. New York: H. W. Wilson, 1960.

Kaplan, Justin, ed. *Bartlett's Familiar Quotations*. New York: Little, Brown, 1992.

Kent, Donald H. "The Fight For Free Schools in Pennsylvania." Harrisburg: Pennsylvania Historical and Museum Commission, 1976.

Klement, Frank L. *The Gettysburg Soldiers' Cemetery and Lincoln's Address: Aspects and Angles*. Shippensburg, Pa.: White Mane Publishing, 1993.

Kunhardt, Dorothy M., and Philip Kunhardt, Jr. *Twenty Days*. Secaucus, N.J.: Castle Books, 1965.

Kunhardt, Philip, Jr., Philip Kunhardt III, and Peter W. Kunhardt. *Lincoln*. New York: Alfred A. Knopf, 1992.

Lathrop, George P. *History of the Union League of Philadelphia*. Philadelphia: J. B. Lippincott, 1884.

Lea, Henry Charles, and George H. Boker. *No. 17. Abraham Lincoln*. Philadelphia: Union League of Philadelphia, 1864.

Lincoln, Abraham. *Speech of Hon. Abraham Lincoln, of Illinois, at the Cooper Institute, New York City, February 27, 1860*. Washington, D.C.: Republican Executive Congressional Committee, 1860.

Lincoln, Waldo. *History of the Lincoln Family: An Account of the Descendants of Samuel Lincoln of Hingham, Massachusetts, 1637–1920*. Worcester, Mass.: Commonwealth Press, 1923.

List of the Committees of the Great Central Fair for the U.S. Sanitary Commission Held in Philadelphia, June 1864. Philadelphia: Henry B. Ashmead, Book and Job Printer, 1864.

Livermore, Mary A. *My Story of the War: A Woman's Narrative of Four Years Personal Experience as Nurse in the Union Army, and in Relief Work at Home, in Hospitals, Camps, and at the Front, During the War of the Rebellion*. Hartford, Conn.: A. D. Worthington, 1890.

Lyell, Charles. *Second Visit to the United States of North America*. New York: Harper and Brothers, 1849.

MacKay, Carol A. "Simon Cameron." Harrisburg: Pennsylvania Historical and Museum Commission, 1974.

Mansfield, J. B., ed. and comp. *History of the Great Lakes*. 2 vols. Chicago: J. H. Beers, 1899.

Marius, Richard, ed. *The Columbia Book of Civil War Poetry*. New York: Columbia University Press, 1994.

McCall, Samuel W. *Thaddeus Stevens*. Boston: Houghton, Mifflin, 1899.

McClure, A. K. *Abraham Lincoln and Men of War-Times*, 4th ed. Lincoln: University of Nebraska, 1996.

McElroy's Philadelphia City Directory. Philadelphia: E. C. & J. Biddle & Co., 1859, 1862.

Meeks, Carroll L. V. *The Railroad Station, An Architectural History*. New Haven: Yale University Press, 1956.

Mencken, August. *The Railroad Passenger Car: An Illustrated History of the First Hundred Years*. Baltimore: Johns Hopkins University Press, 1957.

Miers, Earl Schenck, William E. Baringer, and C. Percy Powell, eds. *Lincoln Day by Day: A Chronology 1809–1865*. 3 vols. Washington, D.C.: Lincoln Sesquicentennial Commission, 1960.

Monaghan, Jay. *Lincoln Bibliography 1839–1939*, vol. 1. Springfield, Ill.: Illinois State Historical Library, 1943.

Muller, Edward K., ed. *Concise Historical Atlas of Pennsylvania*. Philadelphia: Temple University Press, 1989.

Neely, Mark E., Jr. *The Abraham Lincoln Encyclopedia*. New York: McGraw-Hill, 1982.

———. *The Last Best Hope of Earth*. Cambridge: Harvard University Press, 1993.

Nobles, Gregory H. *American Frontiers, Cultural Encounters and Continental Conquest*. New York: Hill and Wang, 1997.

Palmer, Beverly W., and Holly B. Ochoa, eds. *The Selected Papers of Thaddeus Stevens*. 2 vols. Pittsburgh: University of Pittsburgh Press, 1997.

Palmer, Robert M. *Washington and the Union: Oration Delivered by Hon. Robert M. Palmer, Speaker of the Senate of Pennsylvania, at the Reception of President Lincoln at Harrisburg, and the Raising of the National Flag on the Dome of the Capitol, on the 22d Day of February, 1861*. Harrisburg, 1861.

Pennsylvania. General Assembly. House of Representatives. Select Committee Relative to the Soldiers' National Cemetery. *Report of the Select Committee Relative to the Soldiers' National Cemetery, Together with the Accompanying Documents, as Reported to the House of Representatives of the Commonwealth of Pennsylvania*. Harrisburg: Singerly and Myers, State Printers, 1864.

———. *Revised Report of the Select Committee Relative to the Soldiers' National Cemetery, Together with the Accompanying Documents, as Reported to the House of Representatives of the Commonwealth of Pennsylvania*. Harrisburg: Singerly and Myers, State Printers, 1865.

———. *Revised Report Made to the Legislature of Pennsylvania, Relative to the Soldiers' National Cemetery, At Gettysburg, Embracing an Account of the Origin of the Undertaking; Address of Hon. Edward Everett, at its Consecration, with the Dedicatory Speech of President Lincoln . . . Together with the Address of Maj. Gen. O. O. Howard, Delivered July 4, 1866* [sic], *Upon the Dedication of the Soldiers' National Monument, and the Other Proceedings Upon That Occasion*. Harrisburg: Singerly and Myers, State Printers, 1867.

Penrose, Washington H. Diary, 1859–62. #492. E-54. Am. 912515. Collection of the Historical Society of Pennsylvania, Philadelphia.

Pinkerton, Allan. *History and Evidence of the Passage of Abraham Lincoln from Harrisburg, Pa., to Washington, D.C., on the 22nd and 23rd of February 1861*. New York: Rode & Brand, 1868.

Reilly, Bernard F., Jr. *American Political Prints 1766–1876*. Boston: G. K. Hall, 1991.

Remini, Robert V. *Henry Clay: Statesman for the Union*. New York: W. W. Norton, 1991.

Republican Party. "James Buchanan, His Doctrines and Policy, As Exhibited by Himself and Friends." New York: New York Tribune, 1856.

Richman, Irwin. *Pennsylvania's Architecture*. Pennsylvania Historical Studies, no. 10. University Park, Pa.: Pennsylvania Historical Association, 1969.

Riddle, Donald W. *Congressman Abraham Lincoln*. Urbana: University of Illinois Press, 1957.

Sandburg, Carl. *Abraham Lincoln: The Prairie Years*. New York: Harcourt, Brace, 1926.

Seyfert, A. G. "The Wallace Family and the Wallace Store of East Earl." *Lancaster County Historical Society Journal* 28, no. 2 (February 1924): 21–29.

Shakespeare, William. *King Henry the Sixth.* Text from First Folio of 1623 as reprinted in *The Complete Works of William Shakespeare.* London: Abbey Library, n.d.

Sharf, J. Thomas, and Thompson Westcott. *The History of Philadelphia 1609–1884.* 3 vols. Philadelphia: L. H. Everts, 1884.

Simpson, Brooks D. *The Reconstruction Presidents.* Lawrence: University Press of Kansas, 1998.

Slusser, H. Robert. *Mr. Lincoln's Railroad Car.* Alexandria, Va.: Alexandria Archaeology Publications, City of Alexandria, 1996.

Smedley, Samuel L. *Smedley's Atlas of the City of Philadelphia.* Philadelphia: J. B. Lippincott, 1862.

Souder, Mrs. Edmund A. (Emily Bliss Thacher). *Leaves From the Battle-field of Gettysburg. A Series of Letters From A Field Hospital. And National Poems.* Philadelphia: C. Sherman, Son & Co., 1864.

Steinmetz, Richard, Sr., and Robert D. Hoffsommer. *This Was Harrisburg, A Photographic History.* Harrisburg: Stackpole Books, 1976.

Stevens, S. K. "Abraham Lincoln and Pennsylvania." Harrisburg: Pennsylvania Historical and Museum Commission, 1977.

Stillé, Charles J. *How a Free People Conduct a Long War.* Philadelphia: Collins, Printer, 1862.
———. *Memorial of the Great Central Fair for the U.S. Sanitary Commission.* Philadelphia: Caxton Press of Sherman, 1864.

Storey, Walter J., Jr. *Stories of Uniontown and Fayette County.* Dunbar, Pa.: Stefano's Printing, 1993.

Tatum, George B. *Penn's Great Town.* Philadelphia: University of Pennsylvania Press, 1961.

Tax Lists of Chester County, Pennsylvania, 1720–25. Chester County Archives and Records Services. West Chester, Pa.

Taylor, Frank H. *Philadelphia in the Civil War.* Philadelphia: City of Philadelphia, 1913.

Union League of Philadelphia. *Address of the Union League of Philadelphia to the Citizens of Pennsylvania in Favor of the Re-Election of Abraham Lincoln.* Philadelphia: King & Baird Printers, 1864. UPA/PAM. E. 458.4.P54. 1864. Collection of the Historical Society of Pennsylvania, Philadelphia.

United States. Army. Corps of Engineers. Pittsburgh District. *Monongahela River Navigation Charts.* Pittsburgh: U.S. Army Engineer District, Pittsburgh, 1991.
———. *Ohio River Navigation Charts.* Pittsburgh: U.S. Army Engineer District, Pittsburgh, 1985.

United States. Army. Corps of Engineers. Rock Island District. *Upper Mississippi River Navigation Charts.* Rock Island, Ill.: U.S. Army Engineer District, Rock Island, 1989.

United States. Census Office. *Eighth Census of the United States, 1860.* 4 vols. Washington, D.C.: Government Printing Office, 1864.

United States Sanitary Commission. *List of the Committees of the Great Central Fair for the U.S. Sanitary Commission Held in Philadelphia June 1864.* Philadelphia: Henry B. Ashmead, Book and Job Printer, 1864.
———. *The Undersigned, Members of the Committee on Hats, Caps, and Furs, for the Great Central Fair for the Sanitary Commission . . . .* Philadelphia: 1864.

Vivian, Cassandra. *Driving Tour of the National Road in Pennsylvania*. Monessen, Pa.: Trade Routes Enterprises, 1994.

Weigley, Russell F., ed. *Philadelphia, a 300-Year History*. New York: W. W. Norton, 1982.

White, Theodore, ed. *Philadelphia Architecture in the Nineteenth Century*. Philadelphia: University of Pennsylvania Press, 1953.

Whiteman, Maxwell. *Gentlemen in Crisis: The First Century of the Union League of Philadelphia, 1862–1962*. Philadelphia: Winchell Company of Philadelphia, 1975.

———. *While Lincoln Lay Dying: A Facsimile Reproduction of the First Testimony Taken in Connection with the Assassination of Abraham Lincoln as Recorded by Corporal James Tanner*. Philadelphia: Union League of Philadelphia, 1968.

Wilkinson, Norman B. "Thaddeus Stevens: Champion of Freedom." Harrisburg: Pennsylvania Historical and Museum Commission, 1977.

Wilkinson, Norman B., and George R. Beyer. "The Conestoga Wagon." Harrisburg: Pennsylvania Historical and Museum Commission, 1997.

Wills, Garry. *Lincoln at Gettysburg*. New York: Simon and Schuster, 1992.

Wolf, Edwin, 2d. *Philadelphia: Portrait of an American City*. Philadelphia: Library Company of Philadelphia, 1990.

Woodward, George W. *Speech of Hon. George W. Woodward, Delivered at the Great Union Meeting in Independence Square, Philadelphia, December 13th, 1860*. Philadelphia: The Age Office, 1863.

Wormser, Richard. *The Iron Horse: How the Railroads Changed America*. New York: Walker, 1993.

Yarris, Mark. *Map of the National Road Pennsylvania*. Farmington, Pa.: National Road Heritage Park, 1996.

Index

political parties *(cont'd)*
   Free Soil Party, 56
   Know-Nothing Party, 56–57, 59, 61
Potomac River, 28, 41

Quaker, 14, 27–28, 32, 151

railroad, 14, 42, 49, 66, 76, 79, 104–5
   accidents and hazards, 11, 41, 81, 83
   companies, 81, 105, 173–74; Baltimore and
      Ohio, 41, 52, 91–92, 112, 126; Cleveland
      and Erie, 139; Cleveland and
      Pittsburgh, 64; Cleveland, Painesville,
      and Ashtabula, 70–71, 167;
      Cumberland Valley, 131; Erie (New York
      and Erie), 53; Erie and North East, 71;
      Great Western Railroad, 53, 62;
      Hanover-Gettysburg, 92–93, 158;
      Hanover Junction (*see* Hanover
      Junction, Pa.); Northern Central
      Railroad, 3, 20, 23, 125, 158;
      Pennsylvania, 11, 14, 20, 153–54;
      Philadelphia and Trenton, 46, 51, 71,
      148; Philadelphia, Wilmington, and
      Baltimore, 20–1, 46, 148; Pittsburgh,
      64; Pittsburgh, Fort Wayne, and
      Chicago, 64–65, 166; Strasburg, 153–54
   funeral train travels, 129, 132–33, 174
   speeds, 41, 49, 79, 126
   stations, 80–81, 84, 126, 147–48, 154, 173–
      74; Broad and Prime Street
      (Philadelphia), 20–1, 78, 118, 133, 148;
      Calvert Street (Baltimore), 3, 126;
      Camden Street (Baltimore), 3, 23, 92,
      112, 126; Eleventh and Market Street
      (Philadelphia), 11, 46, 148; Fort Wayne
      (Allegheny City), 65–66, 69, 166;
      Gettysburg, 94, 104–5, 160; Hanover
      Junction, 92–93, 105, 158, 174;
      Harrisburg, 154–55; Kensington
      (Philadelphia), 46, 51, 72; Lancaster, 14,
      154; Leaman Place, 153–54; President
      Street (Baltimore), 22, 112; Union(Erie),
      71, 167; West Philadelphia, 7, 11, 20
   transcontinental, 56, 59, 90
   transfer of railroad cars, 46, 81, 92, 112

Railroad Museum of Pennsylvania, 153–54
Republican, 106, 109, 111, 116, 119, 147
   Club, Young Men's, 49, 52
   convention. *See* political conventions
   party, 4, 51–53, 56–57, 61, 74, 161
   platform, 56, 59
Rochester, Pa., 64–65, 69, 173

Sanitary Commission, 107–9, 114, 118–19
Sanitary Fair, 107–8
   Chicago, 119
   Great Central (Philadelphia), 109–12, 118,
      140, 147, 174
   Union Avenue, 109, 114–15
Schuylkill, 26, 112
   River, 11, 27, 46, 112, 137, 150
Scott, Winfield, 6, 17, 44, 76, 78–79
secession, 2, 3, 61, 63–64, 78
Seward, Frederick, 1, 6–7, 11, 17, 21, 136, 146
Seward, William, 6, 46, 89
   1860 presidential election, 49, 59, 61
   at Gettysburg, 95–96, 98–99, 103–5, 161
   in Lincoln's cabinet, 74, 91
Shippensburg, Pa., 28
slavery, 27, 36, 41, 59, 77, 95, 118
   Founding Fathers' view, 52–53
   laws and judgments regarding: Dred Scott
      decision, 55, 59; Fugitive Slave Law, 54,
      58; Kansas Nebraska Act, 55; Missouri
      Compromise of 1820, 54; Wilmot
      Proviso, 55–56, 59; southern sympathy
      toward, 2, 14, 57–58, 118
smallpox, 105–6, 158
social customs of the era, 3, 6, 51, 99
Soldiers' National Cemetery. *See* Gettysburg
South Carolina, 3, 75
Springfield, Ill., 47, 49, 53, 173
   burial trip, 121, 123–24, 139, 174. *See also*
      funeral train
   Lincoln's early years in, 31, 33
   mileage to Washington, D.C., 48, 169–70
   travels to Washington, D.C., 3–4, 36, 62, 168
St. Louis, Mo., 36–37, 168–69
Stanton, Edwin, 79, 94, 121, 123–24
stars and stripes, 9, 11, 40, 44, 93, 113.
   See also flag